Lecture Notes in Computer Science 13570

More information about this series at https://link.springer.com/bookseries/558

Can Zhao · David Svoboda ·
Jelmer M. Wolterink · Maria Escobar (Eds.)

Simulation and Synthesis in Medical Imaging

7th International Workshop, SASHIMI 2022
Held in Conjunction with MICCAI 2022
Singapore, September 18, 2022
Proceedings

Springer

Editors
Can Zhao (iD)
NVIDIA
Santa Clara, CA, USA

Jelmer M. Wolterink (iD)
University of Twente
Enschede, The Netherlands

David Svoboda (iD)
Masaryk University
Brno, Czech Republic

Maria Escobar
Universidad de Los Andes
Bogotá, Colombia

ISSN 0302-9743   ISSN 1611-3349 (electronic)
Lecture Notes in Computer Science
ISBN 978-3-031-16979-3   ISBN 978-3-031-16980-9 (eBook)
https://doi.org/10.1007/978-3-031-16980-9

This Springer imprint is published by the registered company Springer Nature Switzerland AG
The registered company address is: Gewerbestrasse 11, 6330 Cham, Switzerland

Preface

The 7th SASHIMI workshop was successfully held in conjunction with the virtual 25th International Conference on Medical Image Computing and Computer Assisted Intervention (MICCAI 2022) as a satellite event via Singapore in September, 2022.

A total of 22 submissions were received after a call for papers. Each of the 22 submissions received underwent a triple-blind review by members of the Program Committee (PC), consisting of researchers actively contributing in the area. On average, each PC reviewer read four papers, and each paper was reviewed by at least three reviewers. At the conclusion of the review process, 15 papers were accepted.

The contributions span the following broad categories in alignment with the initial call for papers methods based on generative models or adversarial learning for MRI/CT/OCT/ microscopy image synthesis, evaluation of synthetic models, and several applications of image synthesis and simulation including data augmentation, image enhancement, anomaly detection, federated learning, or segmentation.

September 2022

Can Zhao
David Svoboda
Jelmer Wolterink
Maria Escobar

Organization

Program Committee Chairs

Escobar, Maria   Universidad de Los Andes, Colombia
Svoboda, David   Masaryk University, Czech Republic
Wolterink, Jelmer   University of Twente, The Netherlands
Zhao, Can   Nvidia, USA

Program Committee

Burgos, Ninon   CNRS, ARAMIS Lab, Paris Brain Institute, France
Carass, Aaron   John Hopkins University, USA
Dewey, Blake   Johns Hopkins University, USA
Dubost, Florian   Liminal Sciences/Hyperfine Inc., USA
Escobar, Maria   Universidad de Los Andes, Colombia
Maška, Martin   Masaryk University, Czech Republic
Mukhopadhyay, Anirban   Technische Universität Darmstadt, Germany
Nie, Dong   Alibaba, USA
Noble, Jack   Vanderbilt University, USA
Pham, Dzung   Uniformed Services University of the Health Sciences, USA
Svoboda, David   Masaryk University, Czech Republic
Varray, François   CREATIS, Université Lyon 1, France
Wolterink, Jelmer   University of Twente, The Netherlands
Yang, Heran   Xi'an Jiaotong University, China
Zhao, Can   Nvidia, USA

Additional Reviewers

Bottani, Simona   Helmholtz Zentrum München, Germany
Li, Bowen   John Hopkins University, USA

Contents

Subject-Specific Lesion Generation and Pseudo-Healthy Synthesis for Multiple Sclerosis Brain Images

Berke Doga Basaran[1,2(✉)] , Mengyun Qiao[2] , Paul M. Matthews[3,4] ,
and Wenjia Bai[1,2,3]

[1] Department of Computing, Imperial College London, London, UK
bdb19@imperial.ac.uk
[2] Data Science Institute, Imperial College London, London, UK
[3] Department of Brain Sciences, Imperial College London, London, UK
[4] UK Dementia Research Institute, Imperial College London, London, UK

Abstract. Understanding the intensity characteristics of brain lesions is key for defining image-based biomarkers in neurological studies and for predicting disease burden and outcome. In this work, we present a novel foreground-based generative method for modelling the local lesion characteristics that can both generate synthetic lesions on healthy images and synthesize subject-specific pseudo-healthy images from pathological images. Furthermore, the proposed method can be used as a data augmentation module to generate synthetic images for training brain image segmentation networks. Experiments on multiple sclerosis (MS) brain images acquired on magnetic resonance imaging (MRI) demonstrate that the proposed method can generate highly realistic pseudo-healthy and pseudo-pathological brain images. Data augmentation using the synthetic images improves the brain image segmentation performance compared to traditional data augmentation methods as well as a recent lesion-aware data augmentation technique, CarveMix. The code will be released at https://github.com/dogabasaran/lesion-synthesis.

Keywords: Lesion generation · Image synthesis · Generative modelling · Data augmentation · Attention mechanisms

1 Introduction

Multiple sclerosis (MS) is a demyelinating neurodegenerative disease of the nervous system [9]. On brain magnetic resonance (MR) images such as fluid-attenuated inversion recovery (FLAIR), MS is often manifested as hyperintense lesions distributed mostly in the white matter [1]. Identification and understanding the intensity patterns of these lesions thus plays a crucial role in diagnosing

Supplementary Information The online version contains supplementary material available at https://doi.org/10.1007/978-3-031-16980-9_1.

and tracking the progression of the disease. Being able to model the lesion intensity patterns also enables us to generate synthetic images for data augmentation purposes and to perform counter-factual inference to understand disease progression. Although many efforts have been dedicated in the past to the general image synthesis problem [11,14,18], little has been investigated for subject-specific MS lesion synthesis.

In this work, we propose a novel generative method to model the MS lesion characteristics. It is able to perform subject-specific lesion synthesis given a healthy image, as well as synthesise a pseudo-healthy image given a pathological one. An attention mechanism is designed so as to only modify the intensities in the lesion region while maintaining the structure in other brain regions. We demonstrate that the proposed method achieves high realism in both lesion generation and pseudo-healthy synthesis. In addition, using the synthetic images for training image segmentation networks, we can improve the lesion segmentation performance even in a low-data setting.

1.1 Related Works

Brain Lesion Synthesis. Learning-based brain lesion synthesis has received a lot of attention recently [3,22]. Salem et al. uses an encoder-decoder U-Net structure to fuse lesion masks acquired from MS patients to healthy subjects [20]. Bissoto et al., Jin et al., and Li et al. utilise generative adversarial networks (GANs) to synthesize new image samples [2,13,15]. Yet, [2] and [15] use semantic maps from pathological subjects to generate images, which lead to augmented images which have identical foreground shapes and labels to the samples that they are drawn from. [13] uses a user-specified tumour mask to generate synthetic tumours on healthy scans. These methods do not generate diverse data samples with high foreground variance (lesion/tumour masks) which differ from already present samples in the training dataset. Reinhold et al. employs a casual model using variational autoencoders to generate lesions with predefined lesion load [19]. As for subject-specific pathological to healthy image synthesis, known as pseudo-healthy synthesis, Xia et al. uses a framework that consists of a generator, a segmentor and a reconstructor, along with a mask discriminator which distinguishes segmented masks from pathology masks [24].

Data Augmentation. With the assistance of data augmentation methods, deep learning has defined the state-of-the-art for lesion segmentation [26]. Data augmentation has improved model generalisability by increasing dataset variance, and has alleviated some of the issues caused due to scarcity of labelled data. However, traditional data augmentation methods, which include flipping, rotating, scaling, intensity alterations, and elastic deformations, do not significantly alter the original image, e.g. the appearance of lesions. Zhang et al. proposed CarveMix, derived from CutMix [25], which utilises a lesion-aware mix-based method to combine carved lesion patches with non-lesion images [27]. Both of these methods directly employ foreground masks from other subjects to compose an augmented image with already present lesion shapes and characteristics.

Current data augmentation methods for brain lesions do not drastically change the local features of lesions, and a technique which can realistically generate new lesions from a learnt distribution will increase training sample diversity and segmentation performance.

1.2 Contributions

We present a novel brain lesion synthesis method for multiple sclerosis images. Our contributions are four-fold: (1) Differing from other techniques, our method is able to preserve subject identity and generate a new lesion foreground class without directly sampling a lesion mask from another subject. (2) An attention-based foreground discriminator is introduced to generate realistic images focusing at the lesion region. (3) The method is able to generate both synthetic lesions as well as pseudo-healthy images, achieved via a cyclic structure. This enables generating a diverse set of brain images for data augmentation purposes. (4) Our method is stochastic, and is able to generate multiple augmented images with different lesion appearances from a single input image.

2 Methods

The goal is to generate pathological images with lesions, given healthy images as input, while preserving the subject identity, and vice versa, create pseudo-healthy images without the lesions in the pathological subjects. Inspired by CycleGAN [28] and AttentionGAN [23], we adopt a two-branch architecture to learn both the lesion generation and pseudo-healthy synthesis tasks. We employ the attention and content decoders from [23], which provide maps on *where* and *what* the important features of the foreground and background classes of the image are, respectively. However, we encourage the foreground decoder to learn lesion specific features. In particular, we introduce a foreground-based discriminator to focus on the generation of the lesion region. We assume that two unpaired datasets are available for learning: a healthy dataset, $X_H = \{x_H\}$, and a pathological dataset with lesions or white matter hyperintensities (WMHs), $X_P = \{x_P\}$. Lower case x_H and x_P denote single image samples from these datasets. For the pathological dataset, a corresponding foreground dataset, $X_F = \{x_F\}$, is constructed using the lesion masks. Each foreground image is a masked lesion intensity image, generated by multiplying the original pathological image from X_P with its respective lesion mask.

Figure 1 illustrates the proposed framework, which consists of two branches, one generator, G_P, for synthetic lesion generation and the other generator, G_H, for pseudo-healthy synthesis. We represent the lesion generation branch as $H \rightarrow P$, and the pseudo-healthy synthesis branch as $P \rightarrow H$, where H denotes healthy images, and P denotes pathological images. The lesion generator, G_P, takes in a healthy brain image, x_H, and generates a pathological image with lesions, $\hat{x}_P$, while also aiming to preserve subject identity. It is composed of an encoder, Enc, which maps the input image into a latent code z, a content decoder, Dec_C, that decodes z into a foreground content map, C^{fore}, and an attention decoder, Dec_A, that decodes z into the two attention maps, namely A^{fore} for foreground and A^{back} for background. Subsequently, the foreground content, C^{fore}, in our case the lesion-related regions, and attention map, A^{fore}, are fused to generate a foreground output, O^{fore}. The input image, x_H, and background attention, A^{back}, is fused to generate a background output, O^{back}. The summation of O^{fore} and O^{back} produces the generated synthetic image, $\hat{x}_P$. The pseudo-healthy synthesis branch, G_H, takes an image with lesions, x_P, as input and produces an pseudo-healthy image, $\hat{x}_H$. This branch is constructed in a similar way as the lesion generation branch.

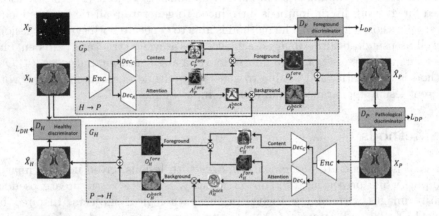

Fig. 1. Proposed framework for subject-specific lesion generation and pseudo-healthy synthesis of brain images, consisting of two generators, G_P and G_H. See text for detail.

2.1   Generators

The two generators, G_P and G_H, are both constructed using the ResNet architecture with nine blocks. Each generator features an encoder with three downsampling paths, and two decoders, one for generating content masks, and one for attention masks. For a given input image, our model generates n attention masks, 1 for background attention, A^{back}, and $n-1$ for foreground attention, A^{fore}, and also generates $n-1$ foreground content masks, C^{fore}. Here foreground broadly refers to regions relevant to lesions and background refers to the rest of the brain image. Producing multiple foreground attention masks allows lesions of varying shape and location characteristics to be decoded, thus producing synthetic images with different lesion distributions. Similar ideas have been explored in [5], where an input image is disentangled into multiple channels representing different anatomical structures. The synthetic image $G(x)$ is generated as,

$$G(x) = C^{fore} * A^{fore} + x * A^{back} \qquad (1)$$

which combines the foreground content, C^{fore}, multiplied with their respective attention masks, A^{fore}, and the original input image, x, multiplied with the background attention mask, A^{back}. The separation of foreground and background allows us to explicitly focus on the lesions in the generating process by developing a lesion-aware foreground discriminator.

2.2 Discriminators

To generate realistic brain images, three discriminators are introduced. The pathological discriminator, D_P, distinguishes synthetic images with lesions from real pathological images. The healthy discriminator, D_H, distinguishes pseudo-healthy images from real healthy subjects. The third discriminator, D_F, which is lesion-aware, encourages the foreground (synthetic lesions) to look realistic compared to real lesion masks in the pathological dataset.

2.3 Losses

The total generator loss, $\mathcal{L}_{G_{total}}$, consists of three loss terms: generation loss, $\mathcal{L}_G$, cycle-consistency loss, $\mathcal{L}_{CC}$, and identity loss, $\mathcal{L}_{idt}$. We employ the least squares GAN loss [17] for the generation loss, also known as $\mathcal{L}_2$ loss. For pseudo-healthy synthesis $(P \rightarrow H)$, the generation loss is formulated as,

$$\mathcal{L}_{G_H} = \mathbb{E}_{x \sim X_P} \left[(D_H(G_H(x)) - 1)^2 \right] \tag{2}$$

where D_H denotes the healthy discriminator for the pseudo-healthy image $G_H(x)$. For lesion generation $(H \rightarrow P)$, the generation loss is formulated as,

$$\mathcal{L}_{G_P} = \mathbb{E}_{x \sim X_H} \left[\left(\tfrac{1}{2}(D_P(G_P(x)) + D_F(O_P^{fore})) - 1 \right)^2 \right] \tag{3}$$

where D_P denotes the pathological discriminator for the lesion image $G_P(x)$ and D_F denotes the foreground discriminator for the foreground output O_P^{fore}, which penalises non-realistic lesion regions.

The cycle-consistency loss, $\mathcal{L}_{CC}$, evaluates a full cycle of an image through the network, $P \rightarrow H \rightarrow P$ or $H \rightarrow P \rightarrow H$. We encourage the output of these cycles to be equivalent to the input as we wish to preserve subject identity. This also ensures that the generated synthetic lesions do not appear at unrealistic locations. The cycle-consistency loss, $\mathcal{L}_{CC}$, is formulated as,

$$\mathcal{L}_{CC} = \mathbb{E}_{x \sim X_H} \left[\|G_H(G_P(x)) - x\|_1 \lambda_H \right] + \mathbb{E}_{x \sim X_P} \left[\|G_P(G_H(x)) - x\|_1 \lambda_P \right] \tag{4}$$

Finally, we incorporate the identity loss, $\mathcal{L}_{idt}$, with the objective of getting an identical image out of a generator if its healthiness is not changed, such that $G_H(x_H)$ would return an image identical to x_H. We use the $\mathcal{L}_1$ loss for this task.

$$\mathcal{L}_{idt} = \mathbb{E}_{x \sim X_H} \left[\|G_H(x) - x\|_1 \lambda_H \lambda_{idt} \right] + \mathbb{E}_{x \sim X_P} \left[\|G_P(x) - x\|_1 \lambda_P \lambda_{idt} \right] \tag{5}$$

We utilise hyperparameters λ_H, λ_P, and λ_{idt} for weighting these losses. The total loss for the generator is summarized as,

$$\mathcal{L}_{G_{total}} = \mathcal{L}_{G_H} + \mathcal{L}_{G_P} + \mathcal{L}_{CC} + \mathcal{L}_{idt} \tag{6}$$

The discriminators aim to minimize the sum of the squared difference between predicted and expected values for real and synthetic images. We use the least squares loss for the three discriminators, D_H, D_P, D_F, formulated as,

$$\mathcal{L}_{D_H} = \mathbb{E}\left[(D_H(x_H) - 1)^2 + (D_H(G_H(x_P)))^2\right] \tag{7}$$

$$\mathcal{L}_{D_P} = \mathbb{E}\left[(D_P(x_P) - 1)^2 + (D_P(G_P(x_H)))^2\right] \tag{8}$$

$$\mathcal{L}_{D_F} = \mathbb{E}\left[(D_F(x_F) - 1)^2 + (D_F(O_P^{fore}))^2\right] \tag{9}$$

3   Experiments

3.1   Evaluation

We evaluate the method performance in data augmentation using the synthetic data for downstream segmentation task as well as evaluate the image quality of synthetic data. To assess performance we conduct two experiments, employing our method as a data augmentation tool and comparing segmentation perfor-mance when trained on only synthetic data. To evaluate quality we ask three raters to assess healthiness and realism of generated images.

The proposed method is compared with traditional data augmentation (TDA) techniques which come default with nnU-Net [12], including rotation, scaling, mirroring, elastic deformation, intensity perturbation, and simulation of low resolution. We also compare to a state-of-the-art lesion-aware augmen-tation method, CarveMix [27]. We utilise offline versions of our method and CarveMix to double the training dataset for those experiments. When perform-ing data augmentation using the proposed method, lesion masks are required for the foreground discriminator. After lesion generation, we perform free-form deformation registration of the healthy subject image, x_H, to the corresponding synthesized pathological image, $\hat{x}_P$, threshold the difference of the two images and generate the lesion masks. We report the mean and variance of the Dice scores of the segmentation.

3.2   Implementation

GAN Network. We implement the generative model with a single channel input and single channel output. We set the generated mask number n to 10, as our experiments show more variety of realistic lesion characteristics and intensities are synthesised with a higher n. Our generative framework method also features data augmentation in the form of sagittal mirroring and elastic deformation.

Training. The proposed method is developed on PyTorch and trained on one NVIDIA GeForce RTX 3080. We use the Adam optimizer with an initial learning rate of 0.001 and 0.5 dropout. The network is trained for 400 epochs and with a linear decay of the learning rate after 200 epochs with a batch size of 1, due to GPU memory limit. We set the generator loss trade-off hyperparameters λ_H, λ_P, and λ_{idt} to 10, 10, and 0.5, respectively. For evaluating segmentation per-formance, nnU-Net is trained for 1,000 epochs using stochastic gradient descent.

3.3 Data

A private dataset is used for training the proposed method, which consists of FLAIR MRI scans of 120 subjects, including 60 healthy scans and 60 scans with MS lesions. For evaluation, we train the segmentation networks using the 2016 Multiple Sclerosis Lesion Segmentation dataset (MS2016) [6], and test on the 2008 MICCAI MS Lesion Segmentation dataset (MS2008) [21] and 2015 ISBI Longitudinal MS Lesion Segmentation dataset (ISBI2015) [4]. We resample all images into $1 \times 1 \times 1$ mm^3 voxel spacing and extract the centre axial slice of each image. These images are reshaped into 256×256 dimensions to pass through the network. The private, MS2008, ISBI2015, and MS2016 datasets provide 120, 20, 21, and 15 2D FLAIR images, respectively.

3.4 Results

Data Augmentation Performance. We train twelve separate segmentation models using different dataset sizes and data augmentation methods. We use nnU-Net in 3D full resolution, utilizing 100%, 53.3%, 26.6% and 12.3% of the training dataset, corresponding to 15, 8, 4, and 2 subjects.

Table 1. Mean and standard deviations of the Dice scores (%), at different sizes of training data. Best results are in bold. Asterisks indicate statistical significance (*: $p \leq 0.05$, **: $p \leq 0.001$) when using a paired Student's t-test compared to baselines.

Size	TDA		TDA+CarveMix [27]		TDA+Proposed	
	MS2008	ISBI2015	MS2008	ISBI2015	MS2008	ISBI2015
100%	$33.06^{**}_{17.37}$	$63.20_{16.70}$	$32.32^{**}_{15.23}$	$57.82_{16.56}$	$\mathbf{44.77_{15.87}}$	$\mathbf{63.90_{16.45}}$
53.3%	$34.03_{17.83}$	$58.84_{24.54}$	$35.39_{17.36}$	$61.25_{19.06}$	$\mathbf{39.70_{18.44}}$	$\mathbf{62.35_{13.21}}$
26.6%	$31.55_{18.62}$	$\mathbf{64.43_{12.64}}$	$\mathbf{39.21_{18.86}}$	$60.28_{21.22}$	$34.58_{15.47}$	$60.83_{10.03}$
13.3%	$28.96_{23.55}$	$37.34^{**}_{23.81}$	$23.57*_{23.18}$	$38.94^{**}_{21.81}$	$\mathbf{32.29_{16.16}}$	$\mathbf{56.64_{13.23}}$

Table 1 indicates that the average Dice score is increased using the proposed method in three of the four dataset sizes when compared to TDA and CarveMix, while also decreasing the standard deviation in most cases. Figure 2 demonstrates different stages of the proposed method and augmentation examples from CarveMix [27]. The generator of the method is stochastic, which employs dropout to generate multiple diverse augmented images for each given sample (Supple. Fig. 2). This increases the diversity of training image samples. We report the mean and variance of the Hausdorff distances in Supple. Table 1.

Synthetic Data Segmentation Performance. We compare segmentation performance when training a model using a fully synthetic dataset against a model trained on a real dataset. We generate 15 synthetic images from the

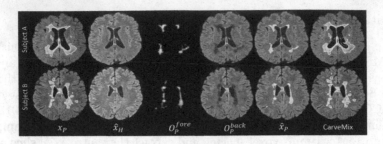

Fig. 2. Different stages of the proposed method. Lesions are contoured in red. **Left to right**: Real pathological image, x_P; pseudo-healthy image $\hat{x}_H$; foreground output for lesion synthesis on pseudo-healthy image O_P^{fore}; background output for lesion synthesis O_P^{back}; the synthetic pathological image generated from the pseudo-healthy image $\hat{x}_P$; augmented image using CarveMix, unrealistic lesions circled in yellow. (Color figure online)

MS2016 dataset and test on the MS2008 and ISBI2015 datasets. We compare our results to nnU-Net with TDA at 100% dataset size. Table 2 suggests a model trained on our generated data performs comparable to a model trained on a real dataset.

Table 2. Segmentation performance using fully synthetic data for model training, compared to using real data. Mean and standard deviations of the Dice scores (%) are reported with best results in bold.

Test data	Real training data	Synthetic training data
MS2008	$33.06_{17.37}$	$\mathbf{35.74_{19.85}}$
ISBI2015	$\mathbf{63.20_{16.70}}$	$52.72_{18.61}$

Expert Evaluation. In order to assess quality of generated images, we ask three human raters to evaluate images in healthiness and realism. We define "healthiness" as a brain MR image with no visible pathological features, and "realism" as an image which possesses the same quality and authentic look as one obtained by a scanner. We collate 50 real healthy, 50 real pathological, 50 pseudo-healthy, and 50 pseudo-pathological images. Raters are asked to classify each image as healthy (1) or pathological (0), and real (1) or fake (0). We produce the results for the real images as a benchmark to compare our generated images. Table 3 shows that the generated pseudo-healthy and pseudo-pathological images closely follow real images for the assessed metrics.

Correlation with Radiological Findings. The spatial heatmap of the synthetic lesions closely resemble those of the real lesions from clinical data, including the private dataset and the MS2016 dataset (Supple. Fig. 3). Furthermore,

Table 3. Rater classification of real and generated images on realism and healthiness. Asterisk (*) indicates that a lower score is better.

Realism			Healthiness		
	Real	Proposed		Real	Proposed
Healthy images	85%	82%	Healthy images	85%	83%
Pathological images	84%	82%	Pathological images*	5%	1%

generated pseudo-pathological images show an increase in the ventricular volume, while pseudo-healthy images tend to have a decreased ventricular volume (Supple. Fig. 4). The change in the ventricular volume is consistent with literature [7,8,10,16].

4   Conclusion

We have proposed a novel method for generating lesions and pseudo-healthy images while preserving subject-specific features, providing a useful tool for data augmentation in brain image analysis to complement real patient datasets. It is lesion-aware in the generating process. In quantitative evaluation, the method improves lesion segmentation performance in downstream tasks. In our human rater assessment, the generated images achieved a high realism score close to the real images, and generated lesions follow a spatial distribution consistent with real clinical datasets.

Acknowledgements. This work is supported by the UKRI CDT in AI for Healthcare http://ai4health.io (Grant No. EP/S023283/1). For the purpose of open access, the author has applied a 'Creative Commons Attribution (CC BY) licence to any Author Accepted Manuscript version arising.

References

1. Bakshi, R., Ariyaratana, S., Benedict, R.H.B., Jacobs, L.: Fluid-attenuated inversion recovery magnetic resonance imaging detects cortical and juxtacortical multiple sclerosis lesions. Arch. Neurol. **58**(5), 742–748 (2001). https://doi.org/10.1001/archneur.58.5.742

2. Bissoto, A., Perez, F., Valle, E., Avila, S.: Skin lesion synthesis with generative adversarial networks. In: Stoyanov, D., et al. (eds.) CARE/CLIP/OR 2.0/ISIC - 2018. LNCS, vol. 11041, pp. 294–302. Springer, Cham (2018). https://doi.org/10.1007/978-3-030-01201-4_32

3. Bowles, C., Qin, C., Guerrero, R., et al.: Brain lesion segmentation through image synthesis and outlier detection. NeuroImage Clin. **16**, 643–658 (2017). https://doi.org/10.1016/j.nicl.2017.09.003

4. Carass, A., Roy, S., Jog, A., et al.: Longitudinal multiple sclerosis lesion segmentation: resource and challenge. Neuroimage **148**, 77–102 (2017). https://doi.org/10.1016/j.neuroimage.2016.12.064

5. Chartsias, A., Joyce, T., Papanastasiou, G., et al.: Disentangled representation learning in cardiac image analysis. Med. Image Anal. **58**, 101535 (2019). https://doi.org/10.1016/j.media.2019.101535
6. Commowick, O., Istace, A., Kain, M., et al.: Objective evaluation of multiple sclerosis lesion segmentation using a data management and processing infrastructure. Sci. Rep. **8**(1), 13650 (2018). https://doi.org/10.1038/s41598-018-31911-7
7. Dalton, C.M., Brex, P.A., Jenkins, R., et al.: Progressive ventricular enlargement in patients with clinically isolated syndromes is associated with the early development of multiple sclerosis. J. Neurol. Neurosurg. Psychiatry **73**(2), 141–147 (2002). https://doi.org/10.1136/jnnp.73.2.141
8. Dalton, C.M., Miszkiel, K.A., O'Connor, P.W., et al.: Ventricular enlargement in MS. Neurology **66**(5), 693–698 (2006). https://doi.org/10.1212/01.wnl.0000201183.87175.9f
9. Ghasemi, N., Razavi, S., Nikzad, E.: Multiple sclerosis: pathogenesis, symptoms, diagnoses and cell-based therapy. Cell J. **19**(191), 1–10 (2017). https://doi.org/10.22074/cellj.2016.4867
10. Guptha, S.H., Holroyd, E., Campbell, G.: Progressive lateral ventricular enlargement as a clue to Alzheimer's disease. The Lancet **359**(9322), 2040 (2002). https://doi.org/10.1016/S0140-6736(02)08806-2
11. Huang, H., Yu, P.S., Wang, C.: An introduction to image synthesis with generative adversarial nets (2018). https://doi.org/10.48550/ARXIV.1803.04469
12. Isensee, F., Jaeger, P.F., Kohl, S.A.A., Petersen, J., Maier-Hein, K.H.: nnU-Net: a self-configuring method for deep learning-based biomedical image segmentation. Nat. Methods **18**(2), 203–211 (2021). https://doi.org/10.1038/s41592-020-01008-z
13. Jin, Q., Cui, H., Sun, C., Meng, Z., Su, R.: Free-form tumor synthesis in computed tomography images via richer generative adversarial network. Knowl.-Based Syst. **218**, 106753 (2021). https://doi.org/10.1016/j.knosys.2021.106753
14. Karras, T., Laine, S., Aila, T.: A style-based generator architecture for generative adversarial networks. In: 2019 IEEE/CVF Conference on Computer Vision and Pattern Recognition (CVPR), pp. 4396–4405 (2019). https://doi.org/10.1109/CVPR.2019.00453
15. Li, Q., Yu, Z., Wang, Y., Zheng, H.: TumorGAN: a multi-modal data augmentation framework for brain tumor segmentation. Sensors **20**(15), 4203 (2020). https://doi.org/10.3390/s20154203
16. Luxenberg, J.S., Haxby, J.V., Creasey, H., Sundaram, M., Rapoport, S.I.: Rate of ventricular enlargement in dementia of the Alzheimer type correlates with rate of neuropsychological deterioration. Neurology **37**(7), 1135 (1987). https://doi.org/10.1212/WNL.37.7.1135
17. Mao, X., Li, Q., Xie, H., et al.: Least squares generative adversarial networks. In: 2017 IEEE International Conference on Computer Vision (ICCV), pp. 2813–2821 (2017). https://doi.org/10.1109/ICCV.2017.304
18. Reed, S., Akata, Z., Yan, X., et al.: Generative adversarial text to image synthesis. In: Proceedings of the 33rd International Conference on Machine Learning. Proceedings of Machine Learning Research, New York, USA, 20–22 June 2016, vol. 48, pp. 1060–1069. PMLR, New York (2016)
19. Reinhold, J.C., Carass, A., Prince, J.L.: A structural causal model for MR images of multiple sclerosis. In: de Bruijne, M., et al. (eds.) MICCAI 2021. LNCS, vol. 12905, pp. 782–792. Springer, Cham (2021). https://doi.org/10.1007/978-3-030-87240-3_75

20. Salem, M., Valverde, S., Cabezas, M., et al.: Multiple sclerosis lesion synthesis in MRI using an encoder-decoder U-NET. IEEE Access **7**, 25171–25184 (2019). https://doi.org/10.1109/ACCESS.2019.2900198

21. Styner, M., Lee, J., Chin, B., et al.: 3D segmentation in the clinic: a grand challenge II: MS lesion segmentation (2008). https://doi.org/10.54294/lmkqvm

22. Sun, L., Wang, J., Huang, Y., et al.: An adversarial learning approach to medical image synthesis for lesion detection. IEEE J. Biomed. Health Inform. **24**(8), 2303–2314 (2020). https://doi.org/10.1109/JBHI.2020.2964016

23. Tang, H., Xu, D., Sebe, N., Yan, Y.: Attention-guided generative adversarial networks for unsupervised image-to-image translation. In: 2019 International Joint Conference on Neural Networks (IJCNN), pp. 1–8 (2019). https://doi.org/10.1109/IJCNN.2019.8851881

24. Xia, T., Chartsias, A., Tsaftaris, S.A.: Pseudo-healthy synthesis with pathology disentanglement and adversarial learning. Med. Image Anal. **64**, 101719 (2020). https://doi.org/10.1016/j.media.2020.101719

25. Yun, S., Han, D., Chun, S., et al.: Cutmix: regularization strategy to train strong classifiers with localizable features. In: 2019 IEEE/CVF International Conference on Computer Vision (ICCV), pp. 6022–6031 (2019). https://doi.org/10.1109/ICCV.2019.00612

26. Zeng, C., Gu, L., Liu, Z., Zhao, S.: Review of deep learning approaches for the segmentation of multiple sclerosis lesions on brain MRI. Front. Neuroinform. **14**, 610967 (2020). https://doi.org/10.3389/fninf.2020.610967

27. Zhang, X., et al.: CarveMix: a simple data augmentation method for brain lesion segmentation. In: de Bruijne, M., et al. (eds.) MICCAI 2021. LNCS, vol. 12901, pp. 196–205. Springer, Cham (2021). https://doi.org/10.1007/978-3-030-87193-2_19

28. Zhu, J.Y., Park, T., Isola, P., Efros, A.A.: Unpaired image-to-image translation using cycle-consistent adversarial networks. In: 2017 IEEE International Conference on Computer Vision (ICCV), pp. 2242–2251 (2017). https://doi.org/10.1109/ICCV.2017.244

Generating Artificial Artifacts for Motion Artifact Detection in Chest CT

Guus van der Ham[1,2], Rudolfs Latisenko[2], Michail Tsiaousis[2],
and Gijs van Tulder[1(✉)]

[1] Radboud University, Nijmegen, The Netherlands
g.vantulder@cs.ru.nl
[2] Thirona, Nijmegen, The Netherlands
http://www.thirona.eu

Abstract. Motion artifacts can have a detrimental effect on the analysis of chest CT scans, because the artifacts can mimic or obscure genuine pathological features. Localising motion artifacts in the lungs can improve diagnosis quality. The diverse appearance of artifacts requires large quantities of annotations to train a detection model, but manual annotations can be subjective, unreliable, and are labour intensive to obtain. We propose a novel method (Code is available at https://github.com/guusvanderham/artificial-motion-artifacts-for-ct) for generating artificial motion artifacts in chest CT images, based on simulated CT reconstruction. We use these artificial artifacts to train fully convolutional networks that can detect real motion artifacts in chest CT scans. We evaluate our method on scans from the public LIDC, RIDER and COVID19-CT datasets and find that it is possible to train detection models with artificially generated artifacts. Generated artifacts greatly improve performance when the availability of manually annotated scans is limited.

Keywords: Artifact generation · Motion artifact detection · Fully convolutional network · Chest CT · Thoracic CT · ASTRA toolbox

1 Introduction

Motion artifacts are a common problem in computed tomography (CT) imaging. They are caused by patient movement during scanning, and can complicate both manual and automated analysis of the images [2,4,10]. For example, in chest CT, breathing and heart motion can introduce artifacts such as intensity undershoots and deformations [2,15]. These artifacts can interfere with tasks such as gross tumor volume estimation [13], automated airway segmentation [4] and automated nodule detection [10].

In this paper, we focus on localizing motion artifacts in lung CT. Knowing the location and severity of artifacts could help to reduce misinterpretations and improve diagnosis quality [12]. Previously, convolutional neural networks (CNNs) have been used to detect artifacts in cardiac CT images [6,7,12]. Recently, Beri [3] applied a U-Net-based model to detect motion artifacts in chest CT images.

C. Zhao et al. (Eds.): SASHIMI 2022, LNCS 13570, pp. 12–23, 2022.
https://doi.org/10.1007/978-3-031-16980-9_2

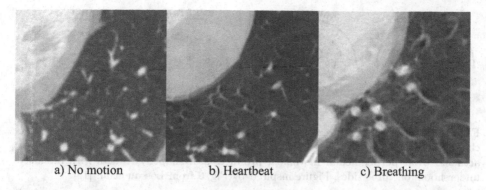

a) No motion   b) Heartbeat   c) Breathing

Fig. 1. Examples of motion artifacts in chest CT: Motion in the lungs can have multiple causes. In b) a heartbeat causes spiky artifacts near the heart. In c) the whole lung is affected with smeared-out features and intensity undershoots.

Training a detection model requires a large training set with annotated CT scans, especially because motion artifacts in the lungs have a very diverse appearance [2] and need a large number of examples to cover all variations. However, manually annotating motion artifacts is time-consuming, subjective, and error-prone. In this study, we observe a large inter-rater variability in the annotated artifacts, despite the strict annotation protocol and training of the annotators.

To address this data scarcity, we propose a novel method to generate artificial motion artifacts in chest CT. Starting from clean CT images, our method introduces motion in a simulated CT acquisition. By controlling the location, severity, and direction of the movement, we can generate a large variety of artifacts, which can then be used to train a detection model for real motion artifacts.

Our approach has several advantages. It increases the amount of training data and reduces the dependence on manual annotations. Since it is based on a simulated CT acquisition, it can use standard CT images and does not require raw projection data, which is often not available. Finally, the method provides detailed information about the motion causing the artifacts, which is not available for real artifacts and could be used to train a motion estimation model.

Related Work. Motion artifacts are common during CT acquisition [2] and are difficult to correct in post-processing. Most motion artifact removal methods require raw CT projection data (e.g., [10,22]), although some recent methods work directly on reconstructed images (e.g., using generative adversarial networks [9]). Methods for motion correction often have high computational requirements, produce imperfect results, and can even introduce new artifacts [7].

As an alternative to removing motion artifacts, detection models can be used to detect them, e.g., for quality assurance. Many detection methods rely on raw CT projection data, for example, by looking for discontinuities in the sinograms [14]. Other detection approaches use the final reconstructed image. For example, Sun et al. [20] developed a pre-processing method that enhances motion artifacts

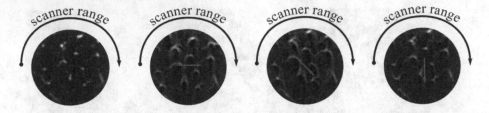

Fig. 2. Effects of motion direction: The motion direction relative to the scanner range changes how blood vessels are deformed. Parallel movement results in arc-shaped artifacts while perpendicular movement produces star-shaped artifacts with intensity undershoots on three sides. Figure inspired by Fig. 6 from Lossau et al. [12]

features for easier detection and trained CNNs that classify images containing artifacts. Beri [3] applied a U-Net to detect artifacts in lung CT images.

Detection models can be trained using artificial artifacts. One way to generate these artifacts is by using a generative adversarial network (GAN) [19,24], but these approaches provide little to no control over the resulting artifacts. Furthermore, GANs require a large amount of training data and can lead to unreliable results (e.g., [5]).

In this paper, we use a more principled approach to generate artifacts, by introducing motion in a simulated CT acquisition with a predefined motion model. This is somewhat similar to the work by Lossau et al. [6,7,12], who generate artifacts in blood vessels in the heart and use those to train an artifact detection CNN for coronary CT angiography. However, their method relies on perturbing projection data that is often not available in chest CT. Our approach uses simulated CT acquisition, which allows us to use reconstructed images directly and avoid this limitation.

2   Methods

We generate images with artificial artifacts by introducing motion during simulated CT acquisition. Figure 3 shows an overview of our method.

Motion Parameters. The appearance of motion artifacts depends on two key factors: the direction, and the severity of the motion. The direction of the motion, relative to the rotation of the detector, determines the shape of the artifact. For example, small blood vessels that appear as white dots can turn out as spiky arc or star-shaped artifacts (Fig. 2), depending on the direction of movement. The severity of the motion determines the size of the artifacts. This motion is often not equal throughout the lung: for example, heartbeats cause large movements and strong artifacts near the heart, but have weaker effects elsewhere (Fig. 1b). Further examples of generated artifacts are shown in Fig. 6.

Artifact Generation. The ASTRA Toolbox [21] for Python simulates CT acquisition based on previously acquired scans. It rotates a virtual detector around an

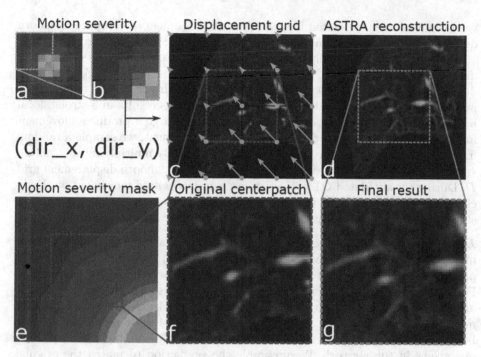

Fig. 3. Generating motion artifacts: a) $M \times M$ Gaussian matrix ($M = 9$, $\sigma = 0.4$) to simulate decreasing motion severity away from source, b) random $N \times N$ sub-matrix ($N = 5$) for varying source location, multiplying severity matrix with a vector $(-10, 10)$ results in c) $N \times N$ displacement vector grid over input image determining the movement at different locations, d) the CT simulation with motion produces the ASTRA reconstruction of the input image containing artifacts and e) an output from the elastic deformation algorithm: a mask of movement severity detailing the movement of every pixel in the input image, f) original center patch (for reference post-processed the same as final result), g) post-processed final center patch containing artifacts.

existing CT image, makes projections of the tissue density from different angles, and then computes a reconstruction of the original image using filtered back projection [16]. We adapt this process by introducing motion during the simulated acquisition process. For several projection angles, we replace the input image with an image that has been moved slightly. This mimics a fluid movement, resulting in realistic-looking motion artifacts in the final reconstruction.

Motion Simulation. To simulate realistic motion, we adapt an existing elastic deformation library [23] to create deformed images and compute a pixel-wise deformation mask showing the location, strength, and direction of movement.

The elastic deformation method defines a displacement grid D with $N \times N$ control points to cover the input image. For each control point i, j, a displacement vector $D_{i,j}$ defines the deformation in the x and y directions. The displacement vectors are then interpolated for each pixel in the image to compute a smooth deformation field, which is used to map the input image to the deformed output.

For our purpose, we define the displacement grid to describe the severity and direction of motion (Fig. 3). We generate a Gaussian matrix of size $M \times M$, with $M > N$ and random standard deviation σ, and crop this to $N \times N$ to define the motion severity at each control point. For small σ, this results in a strong, local motion concentrated at one control point, whereas a large σ produces movement in a larger area. To obtain the direction of the movement, we sample a random motion vector from a uniform distribution $U(-d, d)$. By multiplying this motion vector with the severity at each grid point, we obtain a smooth displacement grid D. During the simulated CT projection, we simulate a fluid movement by slowly changing the displacement grid: from zero displacement in the first projection step to the full displacement D at the end, with linear interpolation in between.

Detection Network. We evaluate our artificial artifacts by training detection models. We train fully convolutional networks (FCN) [11] that take a 64×64 patch as input and output a single probability. The architecture is shown in Fig. 5. The fully convolutional nature of the network allows for input images of arbitrary size. Inputs larger than the original input size produce a probability map in which each output pixel corresponds to a 64×64 input region. The boundaries of this region can be calculated based on the number of max pooling operations in the network. We upsample the prediction to match the original input resolution, averaging the probabilities in regions with overlapping receptive fields. This produces a coarse heatmap with high probabilities in the core areas containing artifacts and decreasing probabilities around the borders.

3 Experiments

For our evaluation, we generated motion artifacts to train the FCN detection model under varying conditions. In all settings, we used the Adam optimizer with binary cross-entropy loss, a minibatch size of 128, and a learning rate of 10^{-4} decaying by 2% each epoch to 10^{-5}. After training for 128 epochs, the model with best validation performance is selected. All components were implemented in Python using the Tensorflow framework.

Data. We used the public LIDC dataset [1] for most of our experiments. We created random subsets of 75, 32, 25 scans for training, validation, and testing. To measure generalizability, we used two additional test sets of 9 randomly selected scans each from the RIDER [17] and COVID19-CT [18] datasets.

Annotations. Each scan was annotated by one of three analysts following an annotation protocol. For the 75 training scans, the analysts were supervised by an analyst with more experience in annotating motion artifacts. We only used annotations located within the lungs.

To measure the inter-annotator agreement, 25 scans in the LIDC test set were annotated by all three analysts. The agreement was computed using Fleiss' κ [8], taking every voxel inside the lung masks as a sample (motion / no motion). This resulted in a κ of 0.35. This relatively low agreement illustrates the difficult and subjective nature of the manual annotation task.

To strengthen the reliability and consistency of the evaluation, each scan in the LIDC, RIDER and COVID19-CT test sets was also annotated by the more experienced analyst. By going through all scans, checking and combining the different annotations, the experienced analyst obtained a more consistent and complete ground truth. We used these final annotations in our evaluation.

Patch Sampling and Artifact Generation. Scans were normalized and masked using lung masks. We sampled 'real motion' (RM) patches of 64×64 pixels from areas with annotated motion artifacts, and 'clean' patches of the same size from slices with no annotated motion artifacts. To generate 'artificial artifact' (AA) patches, we sampled clean patches of 128×128 pixels and generated motion artifacts using our proposed method. For motion simulation we used $M = 9$, $N = 5$ and a random σ between 0.1 and 1.2. Finally, we extracted the 64×64 center patch to avoid border artifacts. We observed that the ASTRA reconstruction algorithm sometimes produced slightly pixelated outputs. We applied mild Gaussian filtering ($\sigma = 0.5$) to remove this effect. We also applied smoothing to all other training patches and test images, to prevent the model from learning to recognize AA patches by the amount of smoothing.

Evaluation. We evaluated the models by comparing their pixel-wise predictions for all CT slices in all test scans with the ground-truth annotations. Only the predictions inside the lung masks were evaluated. We computed the area under the ROC-curve as our main metric, as this shows the model's ability to separate positive from negative samples over a broad range of operating points. Based on a visual verification of the predictions, we found that an AUC over .80 represents excellent performance at localizing the core areas that are affected by motion, with most errors located near the (subjective) boundaries of the annotations.

Experiment Set-Up. We performed three experiments: training AA models using AA patches and clean patches, RM models using RM patches and the same sets of clean patches, and combined models using all three types of patches.

In the first experiment, we looked at how the artifacts generated by our method compare against real motion artifacts. Both models were trained on 100 000 clean patches and 100 000 AA or RM motion patches.

In the second experiment, we explored how the models perform with limited training data. One of the advantages of the proposed method is its ability to generate a large amount of AA patches from a small set of clean patches. In this experiment, we compared the performance of AA, RM and combined models trained on subsets of our full training set, by extracting patches from a random subset of 1 to 75 training scans. The RM models have to rely on the small amount of RM patches that they can sample from a set of scans. In contrast, using our method, the AA models have access to a wide variety of AA patches

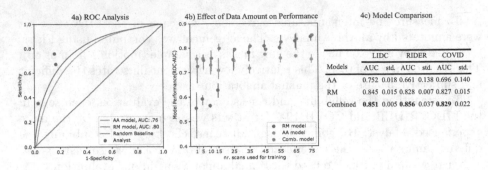

Fig. 4. Experiment results: a) An AA and RM model trained with 200 000 patches each show comparable performance, signifying that artificial artifacts are relatively good representations of real artifacts. Analyst performance relative to ground truth is shown. b) Generating artificial artifacts improves performance greatly when access to scans is limited. c) The RM models and the combined model show better generalizability than the AA models.

generated from a much larger set of clean patches. For comparison, we also trained 'combined' models' by sampling 50% of training patches from the pool of AA patches and the other 50% from the pool of RM patches that are available in each condition. We repeated this experiment three times for each condition, and report the mean and range of performances over all runs.

In the final experiment, we evaluated the generalizability of our models. We trained three AA, RM and combined models using the complete LIDC training set, and report their mean performance and standard deviation on the LIDC, RIDER and COVID19-CT test sets.

4   Results

Experiment 1: Training with Equal Amounts of Data. In the experiment with an equal amount of training data (Fig. 4a), the performance of the AA model (AUC of .765) trained with artificial motion patches comes close to that of the RM model (AUC of .800) trained with real motion patches. This indicates that the proposed method generates motion artifacts that look sufficiently convincing to train a model to detect real motion artifacts in unseen scans. The slightly lower performance of the AA model suggests that the artificial artifacts are not perfect imitations of real motion artifacts. We suspect this might be caused by pixelation introduced by the ASTRA-reconstruction algorithm, by a limitation of the relatively simple motion model used in our experiments, or because the automatic segmentations do not perfectly match the manual annotations of the test set (e.g., because of a consistent over- or undersegmentation).

Experiment 2: Advantage of Generating Data. When training data is scarce, generating and training with artificial artifacts improves performance (Fig. 4b). The RM models trained with real motion artifacts perform poorly when only 1 to 20 training scans are available. In contrast, the AA models trained with artificial artifacts perform much better. As expected, adding more scans improves the performance of the RM model, but this improvement levels off after about 45 scans. The AA models are less dependent on the amount of available training scans. Using our method we can train an effective model with very little training data. If enough data is available, training with real motion artifacts is slightly better. Combining both types of motion patches usually works best: it outperforms the RM model if the available RM data is limited, and does not perform worse than the RM model if the amount of RM data is large enough.

Experiment 3: Model Comparisons and Generalizability. As in the previous experiments, we find that given enough data a model trained using real artifacts outperforms a model trained using only artificial motion artifacts. We find that both the combined and RM models generalize well (Fig. 4c), while the AA model shows decreased performance on the RIDER and COVID test sets. In this experiment, where the number of real artifacts is sufficiently large, combining artificial and real artifacts does not strongly improve the performance.

5 Discussion

In this work we proposed a novel method to generate artificial motion artifacts by introducing motion in a simulated CT acquisition. The artificial artifacts can be used to train artifact detection networks without requiring manual annotations. We evaluated our method on three public datasets by training detection networks with real or artificial artifacts. We found that the artificial artifacts were realistic enough to train models that can detect real motion artifacts. Our method was especially effective when the availability of annotated CT scans was limited.

By using simulated CT acquisition, our method can be applied on CT images directly, without the need for projection data. By visual inspection we found that the generated artifacts look very convincing, although post-processing was needed to remove some pixelation introduced by the reconstruction algorithm. Our method allows precise control over the simulated motion. By varying the motion hyperparameters we can easily generate additional training data with a great diversity of artifacts, starting from a small set of CT images.

In addition to the reconstructed image, our method generates a 'motion mask' that specifies by how much and in which direction each pixel in the input image has moved during the simulation. This information can not be obtained from manual annotations, but would be very useful for training motion severity estimation models. These models can determine the severity of artifacts in real CT images [12]. Some lung analysis tasks are more sensitive to motion than others. For these applications, motion estimation models trained with artificial artifacts could be used to automate quality assurance decisions.

Our finding that models trained using only artificial artifacts performed slightly worse than models trained using only real motion artifacts suggests that, even though the proposed method generates realistic artifacts, the distribution of the generated artifacts does not perfectly match the distribution of real motion

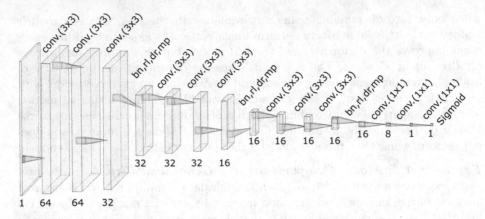

Fig. 5. Network architecture: The FCN takes a 64 × 64 patch and passes it through 3 convolutional blocks. Each block consists of 3 convolutional layers. Kernel sizes are indicated at the top and number of filters are indicated at the bottom. Each block ends with a Batch Normalization (bn), ReLU (rl), Dropout (dr) and MaxPooling (mp) layer. After the three blocks an additional three 1 by 1 convolutions and Sigmoid activation produce a single probability.

artifacts. This may be caused by pixelation introduced by the ASTRA-Toolbox, or by a mismatch between the artificial segmentations and the manual ground truth, but it might also be related to the diversity of the generated artifacts.

The diversity of artificial artifacts depends on the motion model. The proposed motion simulation can generate a wide range of artifacts but it is not exhaustive: the generated artifacts only represent a subset of all possibilities. Given a sufficient number of real artifacts, the method might observe a greater diversity in artifact appearances, which could explain why detection models trained with a large number of real motion artifacts outperform the models trained with artificial artifacts. This could be resolved with a more advanced motion model.

Motion artifact detection is a challenging task, and determining the boundaries of areas affected by motion can be subjective. This is also reflected in the low inter-annotator agreement of our manual annotations. In our experiments, we evaluated voxel-level predictions, which gives a good idea of the performance of the model but is sensitive to over- and undersegmentation. By visual inspection, we found that the models were often able to locate the affected areas, but had a tendency to overpredict. This might be solved by improving the detection model, e.g., using false-positive mining [3] or other forms of regularization.

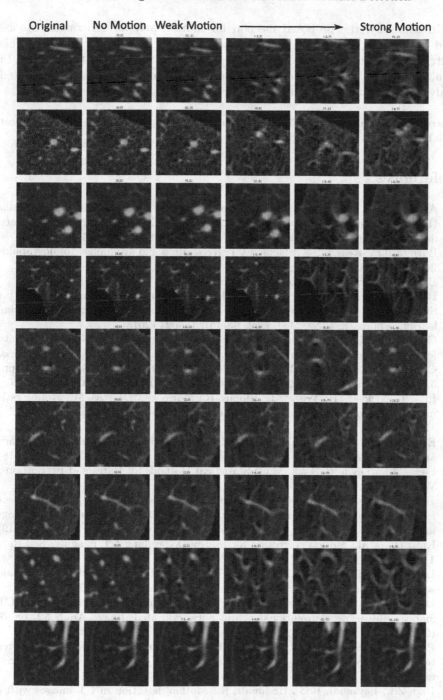

Fig. 6. Further examples of artificial motion artifacts generated with the proposed method: The first column shows the center patch of the original input image. The second column shows the ASTRA reconstruction without any motion. Columns 3 to 6 show ASTRA reconstructions with increasing motion severity. The motion vector is indicated above the patch. All patches received the same post-processing as described in the paper.

In summary, the proposed method for motion artifact generation can be used to obtain additional training data with a great diversity of artifacts. This contributes to better artifact detection and motion severity estimation models. In turn, these models could improve scan and diagnosis quality for both automated analysis pipelines and human analysts.

Acknowledgments. G. van Tulder was financially supported by EFRO/OP-Oost (PROJ-00887).

References

1. Armato, S.G., III., McLennan, G., et al.: The lung image database consortium (LIDC) and image database resource initiative (IDRI): a completed reference database of lung nodules on CT scans. Med. Phys. **38**(2), 915–931 (2011)
2. Barrett, J.F., Keat, N.: Artifacts in CT: recognition and avoidance. Radiographics **24**(6), 1679–1691 (2004)
3. Beri, P.: Detection of motion artifacts in thoracic CT scans (2020)
4. Bian, Z., Charbonnier, J.P., Liu, J., Zhao, D., Lynch, D.A., van Ginneken, B.: Small airway segmentation in thoracic computed tomography scans: a machine learning approach. Phys. Med. Biol. **63**(15), 155024 (2018)
5. Cohen, J.P., Luck, M., Honari, S.: Distribution matching losses can hallucinate features in medical image translation. In: Frangi, A.F., Schnabel, J.A., Davatzikos, C., Alberola-López, C., Fichtinger, G. (eds.) MICCAI 2018. LNCS, vol. 11070, pp. 529–536. Springer, Cham (2018). https://doi.org/10.1007/978-3-030-00928-1_60
6. Elss, T., Nickisch, H., Wissel, T., Bippus, R., Morlock, M., Grass, M.: Motion estimation in coronary CT angiography images using convolutional neural networks. MIDL (2018)
7. Elss, T., et al.: Deep-learning-based CT motion artifact recognition in coronary arteries. In: Medical Imaging 2018: Image Processing, vol. 10574, p. 1057416 (2018)
8. Fleiss, J.L., Levin, B., Paik, M.C.: Statistical Methods for Rates and Proportions. Wiley, Hoboken (2013)
9. Jiang, C., et al.: Wasserstein generative adversarial networks for motion artifact removal in dental CT imaging. In: Medical Imaging 2019: Physics of Medical Imaging, vol. 10948, p. 1094836. International Society for Optics and Photonics (2019)
10. Kim, D., et al.: Motion correction for routine X-ray lung CT imaging. Sci. Rep. **11**(1), 1–10 (2021)
11. Long, J., Shelhamer, E., Darrell, T.: Fully convolutional networks for semantic segmentation. IEEE Trans. Pattern Anal. Mach. Intell. **39**(4), 640651 (2014)
12. Lossau, T., et al.: Motion artifact recognition and quantification in coronary CT angiography using convolutional neural networks. Med. Image Anal. **52**, 68–79 (2019)
13. Persson, G.F., et al.: Artifacts in conventional computed tomography (CT) and free breathing four-dimensional CT induce uncertainty in gross tumor volume determination. Int. J. Radiat. Oncol. Biol. Phys. **80**(5), 1573–1580 (2011)
14. Rad, Z.I., Peyvandi, R.G., Heshmati, R.: Motion detection in CT images with a novel fast technique. Instrum. Exp. Tech. **56**(3), 276–282 (2013)
15. Rohkohl, C., Bruder, H., Stierstorfer, K., Flohr, T.: Improving best-phase image quality in cardiac CT by motion correction with mam optimization. Med. Phys. **40**(3), 031901 (2013)

16. Schofield, R., et al.: Image reconstruction: part 1-understanding filtered back projection, noise and image acquisition. J. Cardiovasc. Comput. Tomogr. **14**(3), 219–225 (2020)
17. Zhao, B., Schwartz, L.H., Kris, M.G.: Data From RIDER Lung CT. The Cancer Imaging Archive (2015). https://doi.org/10.7937/K9/TCIA.2015.U1X8A5NR
18. Shakouri, S., Bakhshali, M.A., Layegh, P., et al.: Covid19-CT-dataset: an open-access chest CT image repository of 1000+ patients with confirmed Covid-19 diagnosis. BMC Res. Notes **14**(1), 1–3 (2021)
19. Su, K., Zhou, E., Sun, X., Wang, C., Yu, D., Luo, X.: Pre-trained StyleGAN based data augmentation for small sample brain CT motion artifacts detection. In: Yang, X., Wang, C.-D., Islam, M.S., Zhang, Z. (eds.) ADMA 2020. LNCS (LNAI), vol. 12447, pp. 339–346. Springer, Cham (2020). https://doi.org/10.1007/978-3-030-65390-3_26
20. Sun, X., et al.: Motion artifacts detection from computed tomography images. In: Yang, X., Wang, C.-D., Islam, M.S., Zhang, Z. (eds.) ADMA 2020. LNCS (LNAI), vol. 12447, pp. 347–359. Springer, Cham (2020). https://doi.org/10.1007/978-3-030-65390-3_27
21. Van Aarle, W., et al.: The ASTRA toolbox: a platform for advanced algorithm development in electron tomography. Ultramicroscopy **157**, 35–47 (2015)
22. Van Stevendaal, U., Von Berg, J., Lorenz, C., Grass, M.: A motion-compensated scheme for helical cone-beam reconstruction in cardiac CT angiography. Med. Phys. **35**(7Part1), 3239–3251 (2008)
23. Van Tulder, G.: elasticdeform: elastic deformations for n-dimensional images (2021). https://doi.org/10.5281/zenodo.4569691. Accessed 01 Mar 2022
24. Wang, C., Sun, X., Zhang, B., Lai, G., Yu, D., Su, K.: Brain CT image with motion artifact augmentation based on PGGAN and FBP for artifact detection. In: Yang, X., Wang, C.-D., Islam, M.S., Zhang, Z. (eds.) ADMA 2020. LNCS (LNAI), vol. 12447, pp. 370–378. Springer, Cham (2020). https://doi.org/10.1007/978-3-030-65390-3_29

Probabilistic Image Diversification to Improve Segmentation in 3D Microscopy Image Data

Dennis Eschweiler$^{(\boxtimes)}$, Justus Schock, and Johannes Stegmaier

Institute of Imaging and Computer Vision, RWTH Aachen University,
Aachen, Germany
{dennis.eschweiler,johannes.stegmaier}@lfb.rwth-aachen.de

Abstract. The lack of fully-annotated data sets is one of the major limiting factors in the application of learning-based segmentation approaches for microscopy image data. Especially for 3D image data, generation of such annotations remains a challenge, increasing the demand for approaches making most out of existing annotations. We propose a probabilistic approach to increase image data diversity in small annotated data sets without further cost, to improve and evaluate segmentation approaches and ultimately contribute to an increased efficacy of available annotations. Different experiments show utilization for benchmarking, image data augmentation and test-time augmentation on the example of a deep learning-based 3D segmentation approach. Code is publicly available at https://github.com/stegmaierj/ImageDiversification.

Keywords: Augmentation · Segmentation · 3D microscopy

1 Introduction

In recent years, automated machine learning-based and deep learning-based approaches have become the state-of-the-art for segmentation in biomedical image data [3]. Since these approaches often require large amounts of annotated training data to become generalist, there is a high demand for fully-annotated image data sets. Due to the very costly, time-consuming and, especially for 3D image data, often infeasible creation of annotations, fully-annotated data sets are rarely available. To overcome this limitation and increase the efficacy of existing annotated data sets, different types of augmentations (such as, *e.g.*, rotation, translation, noise injection) can be applied to existing image data, increasing image diversity and, therefore, segmentation robustness without the need to acquire further annotations [6]. Cost-free specialization to specific image domains or data sets can be achieved by using augmentations in an autoencoder-based pretraining [10] and resilience towards data diversity during inference can be gained by using test-time augmentation [5].

This work was funded by the German Research Foundation DFG with the grant STE2802/2-1 (DE).

Image augmentation approaches, however, often enrich image data sets with overly artificial modifications that do not represent the real diversity found in image data sets. Incorporating real image data intensity statistics into the augmentation process has proven to be beneficial for segmentation approaches [4,9]. Consequently, we want to propose a simple approach that focuses on transforming image intensities using real microscopy image data statistics for increased segmentation robustness and efficacy of annotated image data sets, virtually without any cost. We envision that this approach encourages robustness to the diversity present in real image data, while being complementary to existing methods. Moreover, altered image data can be generated on-the-fly, once local intensity statistics have been determined in a preprocessing step. We test the usability of this approach on different experiments, including benchmarking, image data augmentation and test-time augmentation.

2   Probabilistic Image Diversification

In the proposed approach, each image voxel is represented as a distribution of possible image intensities, rather than a single fixed scalar, which allows to randomly create new samples from a range of appearances. In contrast to image simulation approaches, the distribution representation does not aim at modelling the image formation and degradation process, but it rather determines the range in which a specific image intensity can be realistically changed, given a predefined neighborhood region. By choosing a normal distribution to model these local changes, the proposed transformation generally does not change the underlying data set-dependent global intensity distribution. Therefore, a standard normal distribution is re-parametrized to represent intensities, following

$$\tilde{I}(\mathbf{x}) = \mathcal{N}(0,1) \cdot w_v \cdot \sigma_{\mathbf{x}} + w_i \cdot I_{\mathbf{x}}, \tag{1}$$

with $\mathcal{N}(0,1)$ being the standard normal distribution, $\mathbf{x} = (x,y,z)$ representing a given voxel position, and $I_{\mathbf{x}}$ and $\sigma_{\mathbf{x}}$ being the intensity value and determined variance statistics for position $\mathbf{x}$. Both, intensity and variance are weighted by global scalar values w_i and w_v, respectively, to be able to influence the determined intensity statistics. The variance is estimated from a small cubic neighborhood with size s_{σ} centered at position $\mathbf{x}$, while $I_{\mathbf{x}}$ represents the original voxel intensity at position $\mathbf{x}$. This serves two purposes, since it allows for the aforementioned realistic change of intensity values rather than modelling it, and it introduces a neutral element to this concept with $w_i = 1$ and $w_v = 0$. The definition of a neutral element would not be possible with a mean intensity value estimated from a given neighborhood and it helps to straightforwardly and smoothly control the degree of abstraction of the applied diversification.

During application, a fixed set of global statistic weights $\mathbf{w} = (w_i, w_v)$ is chosen and for each voxel $\mathbf{x}$ a random intensity is drawn from the assigned distribution $\tilde{I}(\mathbf{x})$. The intensity weight w_i allows to control the brightness of the resulting image, while the variance weight w_v gives control over the noise content within the image, as shown in Fig. 1. To preserve the normalized intensity

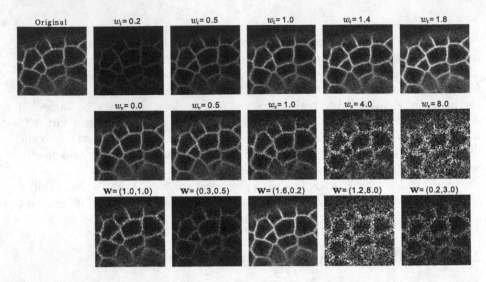

Fig. 1. Examples of an image slice from a publicly available data set [8] (left), and diverse appearances obtained with the proposed method. The upper row shows results for different intensity weights w_i, while $w_v = 0$ is kept neutral. The middle row shows results for different variance weights w_v, while $w_i = 1$ is kept neutral. The lower row shows random examples when jointly changing the statistic weights $\mathbf{w} = (w_i, w_v)$.

value range, the sampled image is value-clipped to $(0,1)$. Once the variance statistics have been determined in a preprocessing step and are available during application, transformation of a given image can be performed fast and on-the-fly, since intensities only have to be drawn from the assigned distributions.

3   Experiments and Results

We experimented with different applications of the proposed method, which range from benchmarking and data augmentation to test-time augmentation approaches. With these experiments we demonstrate the range of usability, while we note that the method is not limited to this choice of applications. We used a publicly available annotated data set of 3D image stacks showing fluorescently labeled cell membranes in *A. thaliana* [8], which was split into plants 2, 4, 8 and 13 for training, and plants 15 and 18 for testing. Furthermore, to impose a more complex challenge, we used the same test data set (plants 15 and 18) with synthetically decreased quality, which was published in [1]. As segmentation approach we employed a 3D extension [2] of the Cellpose instance segmentation approach [7] and used the intersection-over-union (IoU) score as a metric to assess the segmentation quality. To assess more details, IoU thresholds were fixed to determine if a segmentation was accurately predicted or not. This allows to calculate the ratio of instance segmentation (accuracy) with an IoU score higher than the threshold, ultimately leading to insights into how segmentations of

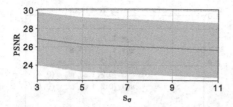 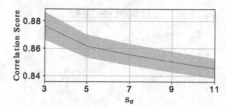

Fig. 2. Peak signal-to-noise ratio (PSNR, left) and correlation score (right) for different neighborhood extents s_σ used to determine the local intensity variance $\sigma_\mathbf{x}$. Default weights $w_i = w_v = 1$ were used to augment images from a publicly available data set [8], and shaded regions show the score standard deviation.

different IoU levels were influenced by the proposed approaches. Models were trained for 500 epochs with patches of size (128, 128, 64). Extracting variance statistics from larger neighborhood sizes s_σ, resulted in decreasing peak signal-to-noise ratios (PSNR) and correlation scores between the sampled image and the original image, exemplary assessed for default weights $w_i = 1$ and $w_v = 1$ (Fig. 2). We empirically chose $s_\sigma = 5$ as a reasonable trade-off between loss of similarity to the original image and size of the influencing neighborhood, *i.e.*, significance of the estimated intensity variance $\sigma_\mathbf{x}$. Consequently, the intensity variance for each voxel was estimated from 125 local intensity values for the used 3D image data set.

3.1 Data Augmentation

In order to render segmentation approaches more robust to difficult image characteristics, such as low PSNR and low intensity (or a combination of both), the proposed diversification can be utilized as data augmentation method in different experimental setups. Details of each experiment are explained in the following.

Single Augmentation. During training, weights $\mathbf{w} = (w_i, w_v)$ were limited to predefined ranges and individually drawn from a normal distribution centered around the respective neutral elements ($w_i = 1$, $w_v = 0$). Furthermore, the normal distribution was scaled, such that the weight limit furthest away from the neutral element was located at the distance that matches three times the standard deviation. This is followed by a truncation of the distribution to the predefined, potentially asymmetric, weight range, to prevent drawing of outliers. Different experiments with multiple weight limits were conducted, with results being shown in Fig. 3.

Stacked Diversification. Since the proposed method transforms intensities in a given image without imposing geometrical changes, the target segmentation masks remain unchanged. In this experiment we wanted to exploit this fact and created a stack including the original patch and a predefined number n_{div} of

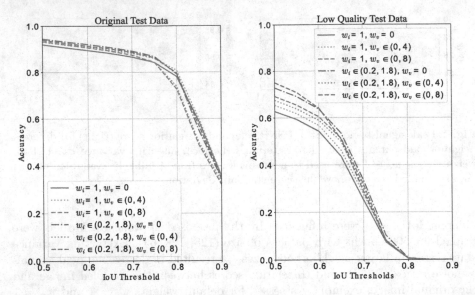

Fig. 3. Obtained accuracy over different IoU thresholds for the single augmentation experiment. Results are shown for the original (left) and low quality (right) test data.

diversified patch appearances, leading to a total number of $b = n_{div} + 1$ patches. Statistic weights $\mathbf{w} = (w_i, w_v)$ were chosen with two different strategies. As a first experiment, $w_i \in [0.2, 1.8]$ and $w_v \in [0, 8]$ were randomly and uniformly drawn from the specified value ranges, which we refer to as *random strategy*. As another experiment, $w_i \in [0.2, 1.8]$ and $w_v \in [0, 8]$ were selected, such that the resulting appearance stack included patches transformed by the full range of possible weight values, *i.e.*, the weight limits and uniformly distributed weights in between. In the special case when only one additional patch is desired ($b = 2$), the weights were fixed to default values $w_i = w_v = 1$. We refer to this experiment as *structured strategy*. In addition to the usual losses proposed in [2], comparing prediction and ground truth target for each patch, consistency is assessed during training, by computing losses among predictions for the diverse patch appearances. Since the resulting stack of patches effectively increases the batch size to b, we conducted a *baseline* experiment by simply increasing the batch size without using any transformations. Results for all experiments on the original and low quality test data are shown in Fig. 4.

Curriculum Learning. In order to guide a segmentation model to be more robust towards challenging appearances, the weight ranges can be continuously increased during training. This allows to start training with the original image diversity of the given data set, while adding more complex challenges as the training progresses. To configure this process we defined a parameter δ_{full}, indicating the number of epochs until the maximum weight range should be reached. Within this interval, the weights are continuously moved away from the neutral

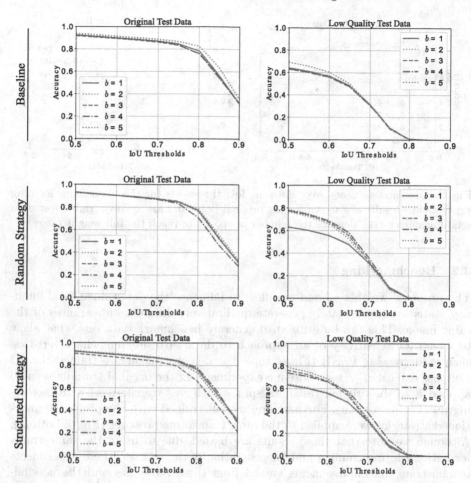

Fig. 4. Obtained accuracy over different IoU thresholds for the stacked diversification experiments, including the *baseline* setup (top), *random strategy* (middle) and *structured strategy* (bottom). Results are shown for the original (left) and low quality (right) test data sets. Parameter b denotes the effective number of patches per batch.

element to the predefined limits. This experiment was limited to the *random strategy*, since this proved to reliably increase robustness of the segmentation model. Results obtained for the original and low quality test data using different δ_{full} are shown in Fig. 5. The case $\delta_{full} = 0$ equals the regular random strategy.

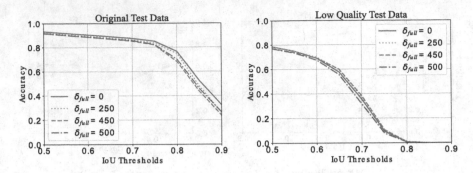

Fig. 5. Obtained accuracy over different IoU thresholds for the curriculum learning experiment. Results are shown for the original (left) and low quality (right) test data sets. Parameter δ_{full} denotes the number of epochs to reach the full weight range.

3.2   Benchmarking

The proposed weights w_i and w_v allow to influence the determined local intensity statistics, to ultimately generate qualitatively different appearances of the same image. This can be utilized to generate benchmark data sets, that allow to assess the sensitivity of an approach to data with different characteristics, such as decreasing PSNR (Fig. 6, top). For demonstration, we trained the 3D Cellpose extension [2] as a baseline experiment on the original training set and applied it to the original test data split, which was transformed with increasing w_v (Fig. 6, bottom). Furthermore, models trained with the previously mentioned strategies were applied to the same transformed test set (Fig. 6, bottom). Although we note that these results are biased, due to using the same transformations during training and for generation of the test set, these experiments demonstrate the improvements gained from those strategies and the possibility to generate benchmark data. This benchmark concept can be extended by including changes in intensity or a combination of both, changes in intensity and PSNR.

3.3   Test-Time Augmentation

Different local intensity characteristics impose different challenges for segmentation approaches. Since the proposed method aims at diversifying image characteristics, we experimented with a test-time augmentation strategy to offer a variety of challenges, which in combination help to find an overall robust segmentation result. During inference of the segmentation model that was trained with the original training data split, each test patch was diversified into n_{tta} different appearances. Weights $w_i \in [0.2, 1.8]$ and $w_v \in [0, 8]$ were chosen similar to the previously mentioned *structured strategy*, *i.e.*, they included the weight limits and uniformly distributed values in between. The final consensus was computed as an average of the raw network outputs, and the postprocessing

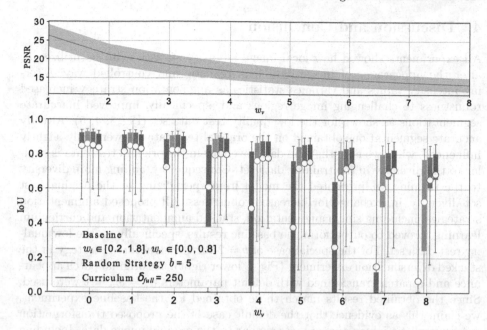

Fig. 6. PSNR (top) and IoU scores of obtained segmentations (bottom) for images augmented with increasing w_v. Segmentation approaches include the baseline approach without using any transformations, the single augmentation approach with $w_i \in [0.2, 1.8]$ and $w_v \in [0, 8]$, the stacked diversification approach using the *random strategy* with $b = 5$ and the curriculum approach with $\delta_{full} = 250$. IoU scores are shown as boxplots with whiskers showing the 5th and 95th percentile, boxes indicating the inter-quartile range, and mean scores being highlighted as circles.

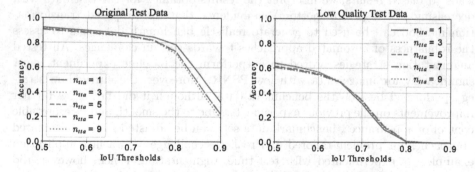

Fig. 7. Obtained accuracy over different IoU thresholds for the test-time augmentation experiment. Results are shown for the original (left) and low quality (right) test data sets. Parameter n_{tta} denotes the number of different appearances processed to generate the averaged output. For $n_{tta} = 1$ only the original appearance was used.

to obtain instance segmentations (as explained in [2]) was performed using the final aggregated prediction. Experimental results for different n_{tta} are shown in Fig. 7.

4   Discussion and Conclusion

All experiments showed how local image intensity statistics can be utilized to alter the appearance of image data in a realistic and controlled way. Altering intensity values and variance statistics as augmentation strategy increased robustness to challenging image regions and, specifically, improved inaccurate segmentations as shown for the low quality test data set (Fig. 3, 4, 5). Already accurate segmentations obtained on the original test data set were only slightly influenced, while we note that the data diversity in the original test data is similar to the diversity in the training data set. Consequently, adding more diversity to the training set prevented the model from specializing to the original test set diversity, in exchange for increased robustness. All proposed augmentation strategies, including single augmentation, stacked augmentation and curriculum learning, proved to outperform the baseline results, specifically on the low quality test data set. For the special case of $b = 2$ for the structured strategy in the stacked diversification experiment (Fig. 4, lower right), the original patch appearance and a patch transformed with default parameters $w_i = w_v = 1$ were used. Since the obtained results match those obtained for the baseline experiment, we claim this as evidence that the default case of the proposed transformation creates realistic image appearances similar to the original image data. Including a curriculum strategy to the training process, however, did not improve results upon the stacked augmentation training strategy (Fig. 5), but it improved upon the baseline results and is valued as an incentive for further research.

Furthermore, we demonstrated that statistic weights can be smoothly altered to, *e.g.*, continuously decrease the PSNR of images (Fig. 6, top). Although we note, that using the same transformation strategy for the training and test data leads to biased results, we interpret the results obtained for the test data with decreasing PSNR (Fig. 6, bottom) as evidence that the proposed transformation method can be used to generate realistic benchmark data sets to assess the robustness of automated approaches towards certain challenges. All tested augmentation strategies proved to outperform the baseline experiment, most significantly for image data with low PSNR. Moreover, the curriculum strategy performed best on the benchmark data, although it did not show further improvements on the previous experiments. Due to the smooth and interpretable control of appearances, benchmark data sets can be adjusted to test automated approaches for problem-tailored and realistic challenges. As a last application example, we experimented with test-time augmentation, which, however, did not have a large impact on the final results, but it, nevertheless, states another application case up for further research.

In conclusion, we demonstrated with different applications, that the proposed transformation allows to realistically increase image data diversity to enhance the efficacy of available annotations and that it helps to assess robustness of automated approaches to realistic image data challenges. Since the transformation does not come with further annotation costs, we envision that it is straightforwardly applicable to other image processing tasks besides automated segmentation and we will further test applicability to different data sets.

References

1. Eschweiler, D., Rethwisch, M., Jarchow, M., Koppers, S., Stegmaier, J.: 3D fluorescence microscopy data synthesis for segmentation and benchmarking. PLoS ONE **16**(12), e0260509 (2021)
2. Eschweiler, D., Stegmaier, J.: Robust 3D cell segmentation: extending the view of cellpose. In: IEEE International Conference in Image Processing (2022)
3. Meijering, E.: A bird's-eye view of deep learning in bioimage analysis. Comput. Struct. Biotechnol. J. **18**, 2312 (2020)
4. Meyer, M.I., de la Rosa, E., Pedrosa de Barros, N., Paolella, R., Van Leemput, K., Sima, D.M.: A contrast augmentation approach to improve multi-scanner generalization in MRI. Front. Neurosci. 1048 (2021)
5. Moshkov, N., Mathe, B., Kertesz-Farkas, A., Hollandi, R., Horvath, P.: Test-time augmentation for deep learning-based cell segmentation on microscopy images. Sci. Rep. **10**(1), 1–7 (2020)
6. Shorten, C., Khoshgoftaar, T.M.: A survey on image data augmentation for deep learning. J. Big Data **6**(1), 1–48 (2019)
7. Stringer, C., Wang, T., Michaelos, M., Pachitariu, M.: Cellpose: a generalist algorithm for cellular segmentation. Nat. Methods **18**(1), 100–106 (2021)
8. Willis, L., et al.: Cell size and growth regulation in the arabidopsis thaliana apical stem cell niche. Proc. Natl. Acad. Sci. **113**(51), E8238–E8246 (2016)
9. Zhao, A., Balakrishnan, G., Durand, F., Guttag, J.V., Dalca, A.V.: Data augmentation using learned transformations for one-shot medical image segmentation. In: IEEE/CVF Conference on Computer Vision and Pattern Recognition, pp. 8543–8553 (2019)
10. Zhou, Z., Sodha, V., Pang, J., Gotway, M.B., Liang, J.: Models genesis. Med. Image Anal. **67**, 101840 (2021)

Pathology Synthesis of 3D Consistent Cardiac MR Images Using 2D VAEs and GANs

Sina Amirrajab[1](✉), Cristian Lorenz[2], Juergen Weese[2], Josien Pluim[1], and Marcel Breeuwer[1,3]

[1] Biomedical Engineering Department, Eindhoven University of Technology, Eindhoven, The Netherlands
s.amirrajab@tue.nl
[2] Philips Research Laboratories, Hamburg, Germany
[3] Philips Healthcare, MR R&D - Clinical Science, Best, The Netherlands

Abstract. We propose a method for synthesizing cardiac MR images with plausible heart shapes and realistic appearances for the purpose of generating labeled data for deep-learning (DL) training. It breaks down the image synthesis into label deformation and label-to-image translation tasks. The former is achieved via latent space interpolation in a VAE model, while the latter is accomplished via a conditional GAN model. We devise an approach for label manipulation in the latent space of the trained VAE model, namely pathology synthesis, aiming to synthesize a series of pseudo-pathological synthetic subjects with characteristics of a desired heart disease. Furthermore, we propose to model the relationship between 2D slices in the latent space of the VAE via estimating the correlation coefficient matrix between the latent vectors and utilizing it to correlate elements of randomly drawn samples before decoding to image space. This simple yet effective approach results in generating 3D consistent subjects from 2D slice-by-slice generations. Such an approach could provide a solution to diversify and enrich the available database of cardiac MR images and to pave the way for the development of generalizable DL based image analysis algorithms. The code will be available at https://github.com/sinaamirrajab/CardiacPathologySynthesis.

Keywords: Pathology synthesis · Cardiac MRI · GANs · VAEs · Image synthesis

1 Introduction

Deep generative modeling has gained attention in medical imaging research thanks to its ability to generate highly realistic images that may alleviate medical data scarcity [1]. The most successful family of generative models known as generative adversarial networks (GANs) [2] and Variational Autoencoders (VAEs) [3] are widely used for medical image synthesis and segmentation [4, 5]. Many studies have proposed generative models to synthesize realistic and diversified images for brain [6, 7] and heart [8, 9]

Supplementary Information The online version contains supplementary material available at https://doi.org/10.1007/978-3-031-16980-9_4.

among other medical applications [10]. However, the generated data using most mentioned approaches are often unlabeled and therefore not suitable for training a supervised deep learning algorithm, for instance, for medical image segmentation.

1.1 Contributions

We propose to break down the task of cardiac image synthesis into 1) learning the deformation of anatomical content of the ground truth (GT) labels using VAEs and 2) translating GT labels to realistic CMR images using conditional GANs. We devise a strategy, namely **Pathology Synthesis**, to deform labels via interpolation in the latent space of the VAE for the purpose of generating virtual subjects with a target heart disease that affects the heart geometry, e.g. synthesizing a pseudo-pathological subject with thickened myocardium for hypertrophic cardiomyopathy. The synthetic subjects in this study are labeled by design and therefore suitable for medical data augmentation.

Furthermore, we propose a method to generate 3D consistent volumes of synthetic subjects by modeling the correlation between 2D slices in the latent space. The relationship between the slices is captured via estimating the covariance matrix calculated for all latent vectors across all slices. The estimated covariance matrix is used to correlate the elements of a randomly drawn sample. This technique results in a coherent sampling from the latent space and in turn reconstruction of more consistent 3D volume by stacking 2D slices generated from the 2D model.

2 Method

Image Synthesis Model: The synthesis model architecture includes a ResNet encoder [11] for extracting the style of an input image and a label conditional decoder based on Spatially Adaptive Normalization (SPADE) layer [12]. The model employs SPADE normalization layers throughout the generator architecture to preserve the anatomical content of the GT labels [12, 13]. After successful training of the model with pairs of real images and corresponding labels, the generator can translate GT labels to realistic CMR images. To alter the heart anatomy of the synthesized image, we can simply deform the labels. In the previous studies new subjects are synthesized by applying simple transformations such as random elastic deformation, morphological dilation, and erosion on GT labels [13, 14]. We utilize the same synthesis network with default training parameters for this study and here we focus on label deformation to generate heart pathology using a VAE model.

Label Deformation Model: We propose a DL based approach using a VAE model to generate plausible anatomical deformations via latent space manipulation to generate subjects with characteristics of heart pathologies. The VAE model consists of an encoder and a decoder network trained on the ground truth label masks and tries to learn underlying geometrical factors of the heart present in the data. The changes in the heart geometry can be associated with a specific type of disease. For instance, thickening and thinning of the left ventricular myocardium can be an indicating factor of hypertrophic cardiomyopathy and dilated cardiomyopathy, respectively. The goal here is to learn the effects of these factors on the heart geometry presented in the GT labels and to explore the latent space of the VAE to generate new labels with plausibly deformed anatomies. Additionally, we model the characteristics of a particular heart disease in the latent space and generate new samples with heart geometries that represent these disease characteristics.

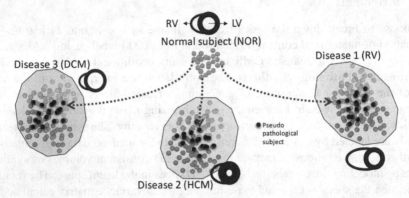

Fig. 1. Strategy to traverse and interpolate in the latent space to perform label deformation using the trained VAE. Each encoded slice of a subject is represented as a dot in the low-dimensional latent space for this schematic view. The statistics of pathological subjects are estimated to draw a sample (pseudo pathological subject) for pathology synthesis. Intermediate latent codes between normal subject (NOR) and the random pseudo-pathological subjects are linearly interpolated (indicated as a dotted blue arrow) to incrementally add pathological features to the heart. (Color figure online)

2.1 Pathology Synthesis

Pathology synthesis is designed to generate subjects with informed characteristics of a heart pathology and its effects on the geometry of the heart, given that the pathology is manifested in the ground truth labels. The assumption here is that subjects with a common pathological class have similar heart characteristics and hence they are encoded to the same area in the latent space, as shown in Fig. 1.

Suppose we wish to generate subjects with a target pathology, for instance with characteristics of hypertrophic cardiomyopathy (HCM), potentially thickening of the myocardium. Note that we want to preserve the identity of a normal subject (NOR) and only generate disease characteristics such as thickening of the left myocardium for HCM. To this end, assuming that the disease features can be grouped to a neighboring location in the latent space, we encode all subjects with the desired pathology into the latent space and estimate mean, standard deviation, minimum, and maximum across all subjects for all interpolated slices; $(\mu, \sigma, min, max)_{HCM}$. These statistics are calculated on the mean of the posterior distribution which is the output of the encoder. The matrix size for these parameters is $(n_s \times n_z)$, where n_s is the number of interpolated slices (32 in our case) and n_z is the size of the latent vector. Note that we equalize the number of slices for each subject via slice interpolation in the latent space. A sample is drawn from a truncated normal distribution parameterized by these statistics, which we call pseudo-pathology sample; $x_{pHCM} \sim TN(\mu, \sigma, min, max)_{HCM}$. The sample generated with statistics of all HCM subjects should potentially represent heart features of a HCM subject: abnormally thick myocardium. We expect to observe an incremental progression of this anatomical feature on a normal heart by performing linear interpolation between a NOR subject and a pseudo-HCM sample.

To model dependency of variables, the correlation between the dimensions of the latent code for all pathological subjects is measured using Kendall rank correlation coefficient. The uncorrelated generated sample is then transformed in the latent space according to the overall correlation coefficient $(n_z \times n_z)$ estimated from the training data to account for relationship between elements of the latent code. The elements of latent vector are correlated using Cholesky matrix decomposition as explained in supplementary material. However, the relationship between different slices of one subject has not yet been modeled. This can lead to generating inconsistent heart geometries in slice direction of one subject as a consequence of slice-by-slice 2D synthesis.

2.2 Modeling Slice Relationship

We propose a simple statistical modeling to account for the relationship between slices in the latent space. The goal here is to generate consistent 3D volume of labels by stacking 2D reconstructed slices from the decoder part of the VAE model. The 2D VAE model is trained as normal while we attempt to take advantage of the correlation between slices of a given subject in the latent space and reconstruct a consistent 3D volume during the inference. In pathology synthesis, we want to perform a linear interpolation between a NOR subject (x_{NOR}) and the random pseudo-pathological sample (x_{pHCM}) derived from the previous section in the latent space. Although different slices of the NOR subject are inherently correlated in the latent space, the random sample does not contain any information about the relationship between slices. To model this relationship, we estimate the correlation between slices of the x_{NOR} and construct the associated correlation coefficient matrix $(n_s \times n_s)$. Given this matrix, we correlate the slices of the x_{pHCM} using the Cholesky matrix decomposition. The procedure is explained in more detail in the supplementary material.

The interaction between latent vectors as well as the relationship between different slices is modeled to generate more realistic correlated samples in the latent space. We found that both latent correlation matrix $(n_z \times n_z)$ and slice correlation matrix $(n_s \times n_s)$ are important for consistent synthesis. This simple yet effective approach to sampling would better respect the relationship between features presented in the training data and result in generating 3D consistent subjects, despite utilizing 2D models. A similar idea for modeling the distribution of 3D brain MRI data via estimating the correlation in the latent space of a 2D slice VAE has recently been explored in [15].

2.3 Data and Implementation

We utilize ACDC challenge data [16] including normal cases (NOR) and three disease classes such as dilated cardiomyopathy (DCM), hypertrophic cardiomyopathy (HCM) and abnormal right ventricle (RV). All 100 ACDC subjects are resampled to 1.5 × 1.5 mm in-plane resolution and cropped to 128 × 128 pixels around the heart using the provided ground truth labels. Percentile based intensity normalization is applied as a post-processing and the intensity range is mapped to the interval of −1 and 1.

The input of the VAE model is a one-hot encoding version of the label map including three channels for heart classes of right ventricle, left ventricle, myocardium, and one background class. The encoder part of the model includes four convolutional blocks with three convolutional layers each followed by batch normalization (BN) and LeakyReLU activation function. The encoded features are fed to four sequential fully connected layers to output the parameters of a Gaussian distribution over the latent representation. The decoder part of the model is comprised of four convolutional blocks each with one up sampling layer followed by two convolutional layers with BN and LeakyReLU. The last additional block of the decoder includes one convolutional layer followed by BN and another convolution with four channel outputs and Softmax activation function. The VAE model is trained using a combination of cross-entropy loss as the reconstruction loss and Kullback-Leibler divergence (KLD) with weighting factor of β for regularization of the

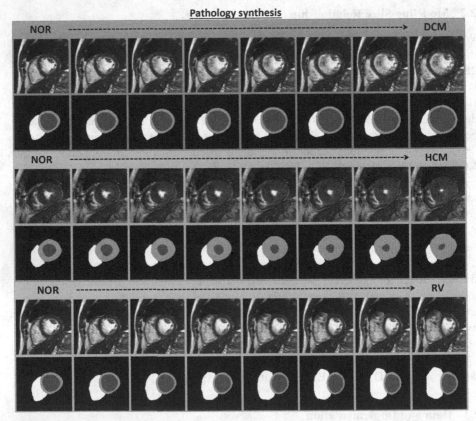

Fig. 2. Pathology synthesis to generate the transition between a normal subject (NOR) to a target pathology such as dilated cardiomyopathy (DCM), hypertrophic cardiomyopathy (HCM) and dilated right ventricle (RV). The effects of a disease on the heart geometry of a subject are respectively left ventricle dilation, myocardial thickening and right ventricle dilation.

latent space capacity [17]. We experimentally identify the size of the latent vector ($n_z =$ 16) and weight of KLD ($\beta = 15$) by inspecting the quality of the label reconstruction and the outcome of interpolation.

3 Results

3.1 Pathology Synthesis

The results for pathology synthesis with three target heart diseases namely DCM, HCM, and RV diseases are shown in Fig. 2. The characteristics of a particular heart disease are linearly added to the latent code of a normal subject (NOR). The heart shape characteristics of subjects with DCM, dilation of the left ventricle, is progressively appearing on the NOR subject through interpolation from left to right. The same is observed for thickening of the myocardium in the case of NOR to HCM and dilation of the right ventricle for NOR to RV. Note that in pathology synthesis the identity of the NOR subject is not changing while the disease features are manifested on the geometry of the subject's heart and the image appearance stays the same. Interestingly, the detailed structures of the papillary muscles and myocardial trabeculations inside the left and right ventricles are generated despite not being present in the ground truth labels.

We generate synthetic data including five pathological versions of each NOR case, e.g. by interpolating between NOR and HCM subject (synth_HCM). To visualize the anatomical variation of the synthesized data in comparison with the real data, we calculated the ejection fraction (EF) for RV and LV using the ground truth labels ($EF(\%) = \frac{EDV-ESV}{EDV} * 100$), where EDV and ESV are end-diastolic and end-systolic volumes. As can be seen from Fig. 3, there is a considerable overlap between the EF distribution of the synthesized data and the real data.

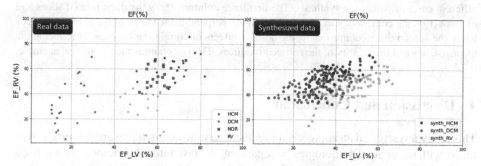

Fig. 3. Distribution of calculated ejection fraction (EF) using the ground truth labels for right-ventricle (EF_RV) and left-ventricle (EF_LV) for the real and synthesized data with pathology.

3.2 Modeling the Slice Relationship

Our proposed 2D model synthesizes images slice-by-slice with high visual fidelity and realism. However, the synthetic subject that is composed of stacking multiple 2D slices is not generated coherently by the network when we look at the generated slices from perpendicular directions. The reason is that random samples in the latent space contain no information about the relationship between different slices of one subject, i.e. generated slices are uncorrelated. Synthesis examples with target pathologies and the positive effects of the proposed slice correlation on generating 3D consistent subject is shown in Fig. 4 with three-dimensional rendering of the synthesized labels. The irregularities in the slice direction are substantially reduced for the correlated slices for synthesizing different pathological cases. We notice that some real images may originally be hampered by slice misalignment artifact and our correlated sampling cannot reduce this artifact.

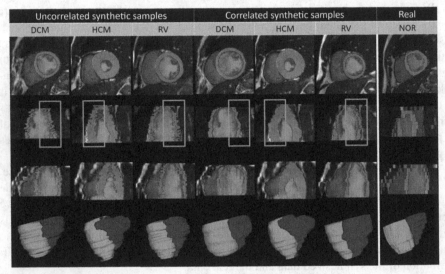

Fig. 4. Three-dimensional rendering of the labels for uncorrelated and correlated synthesis for different cases of pathology synthesis. The first three columns show the uncorrelated slices and its impact on the consistency of the anatomy in the perpendicular views of the short axis slices while the second three columns show the positive effects of correlating samples on reducing the inconsistency and irregularity of the consecutive slices. The last column shows one real example.

4   Discussion and Conclusion

This study investigated an approach for realistic cardiac magnetic resonance image synthesis with target heart pathologies by separating the task into label deformation using a VAE and image generation using a label-conditional GAN. The pathology synthesis was designed to generate subjects with heart characteristics of a particular disease through sampling in the latent space with statistics of a target pathology via performing linear interpolation between a normal subject and pseudo pathological sample in the latent space of the trained VAE.

Furthermore, to tackle one of the important challenges of 3D medical image synthesis, we demonstrated that modeling the correlation between slices in the latent space can be a simple yet effective way to generate consistent 3D subjects from 2D models.

A limitation of our study is the lack of quantitative evaluation of the quality of synthesized images as well as of the 3D consistency of the synthesized subjects. This aspect will be explored in the future work. Visualizations of the synthesized images and the distribution of the heart ejection fractions on the synthesized data nonetheless show encouraging results. Our approach could provide a solution to diversify and enrich an available database of cardiac MR images and to pave the way for the development of generalizable DL based image analysis algorithms. The methods proposed in this study could be extended for other applications in medical image synthesis such as brain MR image generation and simulation of lesion progression.

Acknowledgments. This research is a part of the OpenGTN project, supported by the European Union in the Marie Curie Innovative Training Networks (ITN) program under project No. 76446.

References

1. Yi, X., Walia, E., Babyn, P.: Generative adversarial network in medical imaging: a review. Med. Image Anal. **58**, 101552 (2019)
2. Goodfellow, I.J., et al.: Generative adversarial networks. Commun. ACM **63**(11), 139–144 (2014)
3. Kingma, D.P., Welling, M.: Auto-encoding variational bayes. In: 2nd International Conference on Learning Representations, ICLR 2014 - Conference Track Proceedings
4. Joyce, T., Kozerke, S.: 3D medical image synthesis by factorised representation and deformable model learning. In: Burgos, N., Gooya, A., Svoboda, D. (eds.) SASHIMI 2019. LNCS, vol. 11827, pp. 110–119. Springer, Cham (2019). https://doi.org/10.1007/978-3-030-32778-1_12
5. Kazeminia, S., et al.: GANs for medical image analysis. Artif. Intell. Med. **109**, 101938 (2020)
6. Kwon, G., Han, C., Kim, D.-S.: Generation of 3D brain MRI Using auto-encoding generative adversarial networks. In: Shen, D., et al. (eds.) MICCAI 2019. LNCS, vol. 11766, pp. 118–126. Springer, Cham (2019). https://doi.org/10.1007/978-3-030-32248-9_14
7. Dar, S.U.H., Yurt, M., Karacan, L., Erdem, A., Erdem, E., Cukur, T.: Image synthesis in multi-contrast mri with conditional generative adversarial networks. IEEE Trans. Med. Imaging **38**(10), 2375–2388 (2019)
8. Chartsias, A., Joyce, T., Dharmakumar, R., Tsaftaris, S.A.: Adversarial image synthesis for unpaired multi-modal cardiac data. In: Tsaftaris, S.A., Gooya, A., Frangi, A.F., Prince, J.L. (eds.) SASHIMI 2017. LNCS, vol. 10557, pp. 3–13. Springer, Cham (2017). https://doi.org/10.1007/978-3-319-68127-6_1
9. Rezaei, M.: Generative adversarial network for cardiovascular imaging. In: Machine Learning in Cardiovascular Medicine, pp. 95–121 (2021)
10. Armanious, K., et al.: MedGAN: Medical Image Translation using GANs. Comput. Med. Imaging Graph. **79**,(2018)
11. He, K., Zhang, X., Ren, S., Sun, J.: Deep residual learning for image recognition. In: Proceedings CVPR IEEE Computer Society Conference on Computer Vision and Pattern Recognition, pp. 770–778 (2016)
12. Park, T., Liu, M.Y., Wang, T.C., Zhu, J.Y.: Semantic image synthesis with spatially-adaptive normalization. In: IEEE Computer Society Conference on Computer Vision and Pattern Recognition, pp. 2332–2341 (2019)

13. Lustermans, D.R., Amirrajab, S., Veta, M., Breeuwer, M., Scannell, C.M.: Optimized Automated Cardiac MR Scar Quantification with GAN-Based Data Augmentation, Submitted Peer Review (2021)
14. Al Khalil, Y., Amirrajab, S., Pluim, J., Breeuwer, M.: Late fusion U-net with GAN-based augmentation for generalizable cardiac MRI segmentation. In: Puyol Antón, E., et al. (eds.) STACOM 2021. LNCS, vol. 13131, pp. 360–373. Springer, Cham (2022). https://doi.org/10.1007/978-3-030-93722-5_39
15. Volokitin, A., et al.: Modelling the distribution of 3D brain MRI using a 2D slice VAE. In: Martel, A.L., et al. (eds.) MICCAI 2020. LNCS, vol. 12267, pp. 657–666. Springer, Cham (2020). https://doi.org/10.1007/978-3-030-59728-3_64
16. Bernard, O., et al.: Deep learning techniques for automatic MRI cardiac multi-structures segmentation and diagnosis: is the problem solved? IEEE Trans. Med. Imaging 37(11), 2514–2525 (2018)
17. Higgins, I., et al.: beta-VAE: learning basic visual concepts with a constrained variational framework. In: ICLR conference (2016)

HealthyGAN: Learning from Unannotated Medical Images to Detect Anomalies Associated with Human Disease

Md Mahfuzur Rahman Siddiquee[1,2]([envelope]), Jay Shah[1,2], Teresa Wu[1,2], Catherine Chong[2,3], Todd Schwedt[2,3], and Baoxin Li[1,2]

[1] Arizona State University, Tempe, AZ, USA
mrahmans@asu.edu
[2] ASU-Mayo Center for Innovative Imaging, Tempe, AZ, USA
[3] Mayo Clinic, Phoenix, AZ, USA

Abstract. Automated anomaly detection from medical images, such as MRIs and X-rays, can significantly reduce human effort in disease diagnosis. Owing to the complexity of modeling anomalies and the high cost of manual annotation by domain experts (e.g., radiologists), a typical technique in the current medical imaging literature has focused on deriving diagnostic models from healthy subjects only, assuming the model will detect the images from patients as outliers. However, in many real-world scenarios, unannotated datasets with a mix of both healthy and diseased individuals are abundant. Therefore, this paper poses the research question of how to improve unsupervised anomaly detection by utilizing (1) an unannotated set of mixed images, in addition to (2) the set of healthy images as being used in the literature. To answer the question, we propose HealthyGAN, a novel one-directional image-to-image translation method, which learns to translate the images from the mixed dataset to only healthy images. Being one-directional, Healthy-GAN relaxes the requirement of cycle-consistency of existing unpaired image-to-image translation methods, which is unattainable with mixed unannotated data. Once the translation is learned, we generate a difference map for any given image by subtracting its translated output. Regions of significant responses in the difference map correspond to potential anomalies (if any). Our HealthyGAN outperforms the conventional state-of-the-art methods by significant margins on two publicly available datasets: COVID-19 and NIH ChestX-ray14, and one institutional dataset collected from Mayo Clinic. The implementation is publicly available at https://github.com/mahfuzmohammad/HealthyGAN.

Keywords: Anomaly detection · COVID-19 detection · Thoracic disease detection · Migraine detection · Image-to-Image translation

1 Introduction

Supervised learning from a large annotated dataset is becoming easier [10,15], due to deep neural networks. For problems like anomaly detection (e.g., rare disease

C. Zhao et al. (Eds.): SASHIMI 2022, LNCS 13570, pp. 43–54, 2022.
https://doi.org/10.1007/978-3-031-16980-9_5

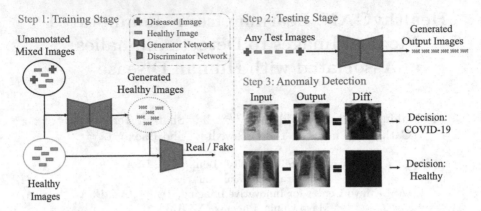

Fig. 1. Overview of the proposed anomaly detection method. At the training stage, our proposed HealthyGAN learns to generate healthy images utilizing an unannotated dataset mixed with both healthy and potential diseased/anomalous images, in addition to, a set of healthy images. At the testing stage, the absolute difference between the translated healthy image and the input image reveals the presence of an anomaly.

detection in medical images), however, it may often be challenging to obtain large enough datasets of annotated samples, making it impractical to rely on supervised learning for the task. Therefore, many recent attempts to develop diagnostic models learn only from the images of healthy (i.e. normal) subjects [1,2,7,9,11,25–28,34,35]. However, in practice, *unannotated* anomalous samples (mixed with normal samples) are usually available and what is missing is the elaborated annotation. In this research, we seek to answer the question: *How can we utilize an unannotated mixed dataset, in addition to the set of normal images, to improve the performance of anomaly detection?*

The answer to the question has been explored in the distant past for lesion detection in vascular CT images using SVM [40]. To the best of our knowledge, we have not seen any deep learning approach designed to address this question. Therefore, aiming to achieve a more generalized solution, in this paper we have developed a novel one-directional unpaired image-to-image translation network, termed HealthyGAN, based on Generative Adversarial Network [12,13] (GAN). The proposed HealthyGAN learns to translate any images from a mixed dataset to normal images (a.k.a. healthy images) and detect abnormalities based on the differences between the input and the output images as illustrated in Fig. 1. We want to highlight that existing unpaired image-to-image translation methods [8,16,20–22,30,33,36–39] are not suitable for solving this problem since they are (1) bi-directional, requiring both abnormal-to-normal and normal-to-abnormal translation to ensure cycle-consistency [39]; or (2) require the images to be annotated as normal vs. abnormal *prior* to training. However, the translation of normal images back to abnormal images is not a feasible approach while using unannotated datasets. To address this challenge, HealthyGAN employs two important properties for improving anomaly detection: (1) unpaired image-to-image translation; and (2) one-directional image-to-image translation. To achieve these properties, we introduce a novel reconstruction loss that ensures effective cycle-consistency during the one-directional translation. Specifically, unlike traditional cycle-consistency loss [39], our reconstruction loss utilizes learned attention-masks to generate the reconstructed images for cycle-consistency. Since all the image manipulation for backward-cycle occurs using basic mathematical operations, there is no need for image annotation (see Sect. 2).

Through extensive experiments, we demonstrate that HealthyGAN outperforms existing state-of-the-art anomaly detection methods by significant margins on two public datasets: COVID-19 and NIH ChestX-ray14; and one single institute dataset for Migraine detection. This performance is attributed to Healthy-GAN's capability of utilizing unannotated diseased/anomalous images during training. In summary, we make the following contributions:

- We introduce a novel one-directional unpaired image-to-image translation method for anomaly detection that utilizes unannotated mixed datasets with images from healthy subjects and patients.
- We develop a novel reconstruction loss for ensuring cycle-consistency without requiring annotated inputs.
- With three challenging medical datasets, we perform extensive experiments comparing the proposed method, HealthyGAN, against the conventional state-of-the-art anomaly detection methods, and we report significant performance improvements and provide detailed analysis.

2   HealthyGAN: The Proposed Method

2.1   Network Architecture

The proposed HealthyGAN consists of a discriminator network and a generator network. The discriminator network follows PatchGAN [18,19,39] architecture and is similar to the ones used in [8,24]. Our discriminator distinguishes whether the input image is a real or a fake (i.e. generated) healthy image.

The generator network takes any images without knowing their labels and translates them to only healthy images. For training, we use a mixed dataset (Set A) containing both diseased and healthy images, and another dataset (Set B) containing only healthy images. The generated images of these corresponding Sets are denoted as A' and B', respectively. The generator does not generate the A' and B' images directly; rather, it generates intermediate healthy images B_{int} and masks M. The masks' values are in the range [0–1], where 0 means background pixel, and 1 means foreground pixel. Then we produce the final generated image B' following Eq. 1 and similarly, A' following Eq. 2.

$$B' = B_{int} \odot M + A \odot (1 - M) \tag{1}$$
$$A' = A \odot M + B_{int} \odot (1 - M) \tag{2}$$

If the image from Set A is diseased, we expect the mask M to activate the diseased region as foreground; otherwise, we expect M to be empty/zero. It is worth

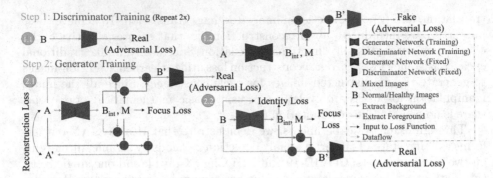

Fig. 2. A single training iteration of HealthyGAN, each of which consists of 2 sub-steps: (1) discriminator training and (2) generator training. The discriminator learns to distinguish real healthy images from the generated ones while the generator tries to fool the discriminator by generating realistic healthy images. Please see Sect. 2 for training details, Appendix A for hyper-parameters, and Appendix B for the network architectures.

noting the similarity between Eq. 2 and the cycle-consistency concept introduced in [39]. Since the proposed method is controlling the image generation, partially, by the mask M, it neither requires a label nor an additional generator network to generate A' (Fig. 2). As the generator network translates the input images to a single direction, we call it a one-directional image-to-image translation method.

2.2 Training

Figure 2 depicts the detailed training methodology of HealthyGAN. We train the generator and the discriminator network, alternately, like any GAN model. At each training step, we update the weights of the generator once for every two weight updates of the discriminator network and repeat until convergence.

The discriminator is trained to learn the healthy images in B as real and any images from the generator to be fake using an *adversarial loss* defined in Eq. 3.

$$\mathcal{L}_{adv}^{D} = \mathbb{E}_{x \in A}[D_{real/fake}(G(x))] - \mathbb{E}_{x \in B}[D_{real/fake}(x)] \\ + \lambda_{gp}\mathbb{E}_{\hat{x}}[(\|\nabla_{\hat{x}}D_{real/fake}(\hat{x})\|_2 - 1)^2] \tag{3}$$

Here, $G(x)$ denotes the output of the generator and is obtained by Eq. 1. $D_{real/fake}(x)$ denotes the output of the discriminator network. Eq. 3 is the revised adversarial loss based on the Wasserstein GAN [3] and an added gradient penalty [14] with weight λ_{gp} which helps to stabilize the training.

The objective of the generator is to translate any input image to the corresponding healthy image. To be specific, if the input image is a healthy image, the generator is expected to behave like an autoencoder. If the input is a diseased image, the generator should remove anomalous parts and produce a healthy image in the output. The *adversarial loss* for the generator is defined in Eq. 4.

$$\mathcal{L}_{adv}^{G} = - \sum_{x \in \{A,B\}} \mathbb{E}_x[D_{real/fake}(G(x))] \tag{4}$$

For the known healthy image set, B, the generator should behave like an autoencoder. Hence, we apply an *identity loss* (defined in Eq. 5) for these images.

$$\mathcal{L}_{id} = \mathbb{E}_{x \in B}[||G_{int}(x) - x||_1] \tag{5}$$

Here, G_{int} denotes the generated images before applying the masks (B_{int} in Fig. 2). Since we train HealthyGAN using unpaired images we add a *reconstruction loss* (Eq. 6) to ensure that the generated images are close to the input images.

$$\mathcal{L}_{rec} = \mathbb{E}_{x \in A, y \in A'}[||x - y||_1] \tag{6}$$

To control the size of the masks, we have adopted the *focus loss* of Eq. 7 from [23].

$$\mathcal{L}_f = \lambda_{fs}(\sum_{i=1}^{n} M_i/n)^2 + \lambda_{fz}\frac{1}{n}\sum_{i=1}^{n}\frac{1}{|M_i - 0.5| + \epsilon} \tag{7}$$

Here, n denotes the number of pixels in the mask M and M_i denotes a pixel in it. The first component controls the size of the mask and the second component forces the values to be close to 0/1. λ_{fs} and λ_{fz} are relative weights of these components, respectively.

Combining all losses, the final full objective function for the discriminator and generator can be described by Eq. 8 and Eq. 9, respectively.

$$\mathcal{L}_D = \mathcal{L}_{adv}^{D} \tag{8}$$

$$\mathcal{L}_G = \mathcal{L}_{adv}^{G} + \lambda_{rec}\mathcal{L}_{rec} + \lambda_{id}\mathcal{L}_{id} + \lambda_f\mathcal{L}_f \tag{9}$$

where λ_{rec}, λ_{id}, and λ_f determine the relative importance of the *reconstruction loss*, *identity loss*, and *focus loss*, respectively.

2.3   Detecting Anomalies

Figure 1 provides an overview of the proposed anomaly detection method. Given an unannotated mixed dataset containing a mixture of both diseased and healthy images A and another dataset containing only healthy images B, we train the HealthyGAN as described in Sect. 2.2. Once trained, we first translate each of the test images into healthy images, and then we compute the absolute difference between the generated healthy images and the input images. We expect the resultant difference images to show the diseased regions if the input is a diseased image; otherwise, we expect the difference image to contain only pixels with a value of zero or very close to zero. Therefore, we detect the presence of the disease by checking the mean value of the difference images. Please note that the difference images indicate the presence of the disease/anomaly, and can also serve to localize image regions that associate with the disease/anomaly. However, the proposed HealthyGAN does not guarantee the detection of all the disease-specific features. Identifying only a subset of the disease-specific features is sufficient to serve the purpose of this study.

3   Experiments and Results

Competing Methods. We have compared the proposed HealthyGAN with 6 state-of-the-art anomaly detection methods currently in use. We have selected these methods as they are the most recent. Among them, ALAD [34], ALOCC [26], f-AnoGAN [28], and Ganomaly [1] are methodologically the closest to the proposed HealthyGAN. We have excluded other methodologically similar works such as EGBAD [35] and AnoGAN [27] from our competing methods' list since ALAD and f-AnoGAN are improved versions of these methods, respectively. However, we have included PatchCore [25] and PaDiM [9], though methodologically different than the proposed HealthyGAN, as they are state of the art for novelty detection in natural image dataset like MVTec AD [4,5].

Evaluation. We have compared the proposed HealthyGAN for anomaly detection with the conventional methods using the AUC score from the receiver operating characteristic (ROC) curve. In addition, we have reported precision, recall, specificity, and F1 scores. To get the prediction score for HealthyGAN, we first take the absolute difference between the input image and its translated image. Then we compute the mean value of the resultant difference image. We found the mean to be more robust than the maximum. For the conventional methods, we have used the anomaly score generation method proposed by their corresponding authors.

3.1   COVID-19 Detection

Dataset. We have utilized the COVIDx dataset from [31]. The original dataset contains a training set with 15,464 Chest X-rays (1,670 COVID-19 positives, 13,794 healthy) and a testing set with 200 Chest X-rays (100 positives and 100 healthy). For our experiments, we have randomly taken 10,031 healthy images for the known healthy training set. For the mixed unannotated training set, we have randomly taken 3,663 healthy and 1,570 COVID-19 positive images.

Results. The top section in Table 1 summarizes the COVID-19 detection results. As seen, HealthyGAN achieves COVID-19 detection AUC of 0.84 outperforming all the conventional methods by a large margin. It also achieves the best precision, specificity, and F1 scores of 0.76. In contrast, f-AnoGAN, the top performing among the competing methods, achieves an AUC score of only 0.64 which is 0.20 points lower than the proposed HealthyGAN. f-AnoGAN achieves precision, recall, specificity, and F1 scores of 0.55, 0.53, 0.56, and 0.54, respectively. Fig. 3 shows qualitative results of COVID-19 detection by HealthyGAN.

3.2   Chest X-ray 14 Diseases Detection

Dataset. We have utilized only the Posterior Anterior (PA) X-rays from the ChestX-ray14 dataset [32] for this experiment. The dataset contains X-rays with one or more of 14 thoracic diseases. For ease of evaluation, we selected the X-rays having only one disease. From the resultant X-rays, we used 10,000 healthy

Table 1. Summary of the anomaly detection results. We have compared HealthyGAN with 6 state-of-the-art anomaly detection methods using 5 metrics on 3 medical imaging datasets. The best results are in **bold** and the second best results are <u>underlined</u>.

Datasets	Metrics	ALAD	ALOCC	f-AnoGAN	Ganomaly	Padim	PatchCore	HealthyGAN
COVID-19	AUC	0.58	0.63	<u>0.64</u>	0.58	0.56	0.52	**0.84**
	Prec.	0.49	<u>0.63</u>	0.55	0.59	0.56	0.52	**0.76**
	Rec.	**0.89**	0.63	0.53	0.60	0.56	0.53	<u>0.76</u>
	Spec.	0.09	<u>0.63</u>	0.56	0.59	0.56	0.51	**0.76**
	F1	<u>0.64</u>	0.63	0.54	0.60	0.56	0.52	**0.76**
X-ray 14 diseases	AUC	0.53	0.48	<u>0.55</u>	0.49	0.54	0.53	**0.56**
	Prec.	0.53	0.48	**0.55**	0.49	<u>0.54</u>	0.53	**0.55**
	Rec.	0.53	0.48	**0.55**	0.49	<u>0.54</u>	0.53	**0.55**
	Spec.	0.53	0.48	**0.55**	0.49	<u>0.54</u>	0.53	**0.55**
	F1	0.53	0.48	**0.55**	0.49	<u>0.54</u>	0.53	**0.55**
Migraine	AUC	0.60	0.40	0.50	<u>0.70</u>	0.35	0.60	**0.75**
	Prec.	0.60	0.40	0.50	<u>0.70</u>	0.36	0.60	**0.78**
	Rec.	0.60	0.40	0.50	<u>0.70</u>	0.40	0.60	**0.70**
	Spec.	0.60	0.40	0.50	<u>0.70</u>	0.30	0.60	**0.80**
	F1	0.60	0.40	0.50	<u>0.70</u>	0.38	0.60	**0.74**

X-rays for the known healthy training set; 5,000 healthy X-rays, and 3,195 diseased X-rays for the mixed unannotated training set. For the validation set, we used 4,000 healthy and 4,000 diseased X-rays and for the testing set, we used 10,000 healthy and 10,000 diseased X-rays.

Results. The middle section of Table 1 summarizes the 14 diseases detection results. As seen, HealthyGAN achieves the best detection AUC score of 0.56 while f-AnoGAN performs the second best with an AUC score of 0.55. They both achieve precision, recall, specificity, and F1 scores of 0.55. Figure 3 contains qualitative results of the 14 diseases detection by HealthyGAN.

3.3   Migraine Detection

Dataset. Our migraine dataset, collected by our collaborators at Mayo Clinic, contains 96 brain MRIs of migraine patients and 104 brain MRIs of healthy participants. We randomly selected 10 migraine patients and 10 healthy participants for each of the validation and test sets. The rest of the 76 migraine patients and 84 healthy participants were used as the mixed unannotated training set. For the known healthy set, we used 424 participants from the IXI public dataset [6].

Results. The last section of Table 1 summarizes the results for migraine detection. HealthyGAN outperforms all the conventional methods by achieving an AUC score of 0.75. It also achieves the best precision, recall, specificity, and F1 scores of 0.78, 0.70, 0.80, and 0.74, respectively. In contrast, the top performing conventional method, Ganomaly, achieves AUC, precision, recall, specificity, and F1 scores of only 0.70. Figure 3 shows qualitative results of HealthyGAN.

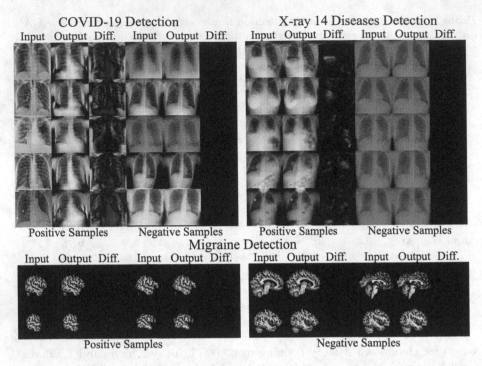

Fig. 3. Qualitative results of COVID-19, Chest X-ray 14 diseases detection, and Migraine detection by HealthyGAN. As seen, HealthyGAN has resulted in a high response in the difference maps for positive samples compared to the negative samples.

4   Conclusion

We have introduced a novel one-directional unpaired image-to-image translation method for anomaly detection from medical images, named HealthyGAN. We have devised a methodology to utilize an unannotated mixed dataset with both normal and anomalous images during the training of the proposed HealthyGAN. It has been possible due to the proposed novel reconstruction loss that ensures effective cycle-consistency without requiring input image annotations. Our extensive evaluation has demonstrated the proposed HealthyGAN's superiority over the existing state-of-the-art anomaly detection methods. The superior performance is attributed to HealthyGAN's capability of utilizing unannotated anomalous images during training.

Acknowledgments. This research has been supported by the United States Department of Defense W81XWH-15-1-0286 and W81XWH1910534, National Institutes of Health K23NS070891, National Institutes of Health - National Institute of Neurological Disorders and Stroke, Award Number 1R61NS113315-01, and Amgen Investigator Sponsored Study 20187183. We thank Arizona State University Research (ASURC) Computing for hosting our computing resources.

A   Implementation Details

We have resized the input images to 256×256 for the experiments on COVID-19 and Migraine detection in Sect. 3.1 and Sect. 3.3, respectively. For the X-ray 14 diseases detection in Sect. 3.2, we have resized the images to 128×128. We have set $\lambda_{gp} = 10$, $\lambda_{id} = 1$, $\lambda_{rec} = 1$, $\lambda_f = 0.1$, $\lambda_{fz} = 1$, and $\lambda_{fs} = 1$ for all the experiments. For COVID-19 and Migraine detection, we have used a batch-size of 16. For X-ray 14 diseases, we have used 32. We trained the models for 400,000 iterations. We have used Adam optimizer with a learning rate of $1e^{-4}$. The learning rate has been decayed for the last 100,000 iterations. Once trained, we have picked the best model using Fréchet inception distance (FID) [17,29]. The network architecture details are provided in Appendix B.

B   Network Architectures

B.1   Discriminator

See Table 2.

Table 2. Discriminator network architecture. OC, KS, S, P, and NS stand for output channels, kernel size, stride, padding, and negative slope, respectively. The network architecture is adopted from [8,24] with slight modification.

Type	Operations	Input shape	Output shape
Input layer	Conv2d (OC = 64, KS = 4, S = 2, P = 1), LeakyReLU (NS = 0.01)	$(h, w, 3)$	$(\frac{h}{2}, \frac{w}{2}, 64)$
Hidden layers	Conv2d (OC = 128, KS = 4, S = 2, P = 1), LeakyReLU (NS = 0.01)	$(\frac{h}{2}, \frac{w}{2}, 64)$	$(\frac{h}{4}, \frac{w}{4}, 128)$
	Conv2d (OC = 256, KS = 4, S = 2, P = 1), LeakyReLU (NS = 0.01)	$(\frac{h}{4}, \frac{w}{4}, 128)$	$(\frac{h}{8}, \frac{w}{8}, 256)$
	Conv2d (OC = 512, KS = 4, S = 2, P = 1), LeakyReLU (NS = 0.01)	$(\frac{h}{8}, \frac{w}{8}, 256)$	$(\frac{h}{16}, \frac{w}{16}, 512)$
	Conv2d (OC = 1024, KS = 4, S = 2, P = 1), LeakyReLU (NS = 0.01)	$(\frac{h}{16}, \frac{w}{16}, 512)$	$(\frac{h}{32}, \frac{w}{32}, 1024)$
	Conv2d (OC = 2048, KS = 4, S = 2, P = 1), LeakyReLU (NS = 0.01)	$(\frac{h}{32}, \frac{w}{32}, 1024)$	$(\frac{h}{64}, \frac{w}{64}, 2048)$
Output layer (D_{src})	Conv2d (OC = 1, KS = 3, S = 1, P = 1)	$(\frac{h}{64}, \frac{w}{64}, 2048)$	$(\frac{h}{64}, \frac{w}{64}, 1)$

B.2   Generator

See Table 3.

Table 3. Generator network architecture. OC, KS, S, P, and IN stand for output channels, kernel size, stride, padding, and instance norm, respectively. The network architecture is adopted from [8, 24] with slight modification.

Type	Operations	Input shape	Output shape
Encoder	Conv2d (OC = 64, KS = 7, S = 1, P = 3), IN, ReLU	$(h, w, 3)$	$(h, w, 64)$
	Conv2d (OC = 128, KS = 4, S = 2, P = 1), IN, ReLU	$(h, w, 64)$	$(\frac{h}{2}, \frac{w}{2}, 128)$
	Conv2d (OC = 256, KS = 4, S = 2, P = 1), IN, ReLU	$(\frac{h}{2}, \frac{w}{2}, 128)$	$(\frac{h}{4}, \frac{w}{4}, 256)$
Bottleneck	Residual Block: Conv2d (OC = 256, KS = 3, S = 1, P = 1), IN, ReLU	$(\frac{h}{4}, \frac{w}{4}, 256)$	$(\frac{h}{4}, \frac{w}{4}, 256)$
	Residual Block: Conv2d (OC = 256, KS = 3, S = 1, P = 1), IN, ReLU	$(\frac{h}{4}, \frac{w}{4}, 256)$	$(\frac{h}{4}, \frac{w}{4}, 256)$
	Residual Block: Conv2d (OC = 256, KS = 3, S = 1, P = 1), IN, ReLU	$(\frac{h}{4}, \frac{w}{4}, 256)$	$(\frac{h}{4}, \frac{w}{4}, 256)$
	Residual Block: Conv2d (OC = 256, KS = 3, S = 1, P = 1), IN, ReLU	$(\frac{h}{4}, \frac{w}{4}, 256)$	$(\frac{h}{4}, \frac{w}{4}, 256)$
	Residual Block: Conv2d (OC = 256, KS = 3, S = 1, P = 1), IN, ReLU	$(\frac{h}{4}, \frac{w}{4}, 256)$	$(\frac{h}{4}, \frac{w}{4}, 256)$
	Residual Block: Conv2d (OC = 256, KS = 3, S = 1, P = 1), IN, ReLU	$(\frac{h}{4}, \frac{w}{4}, 256)$	$(\frac{h}{4}, \frac{w}{4}, 256)$
Decoder	ConvTranspose2d (OC = 128, KS = 4, S = 2, P = 1), IN, ReLU	$(\frac{h}{4}, \frac{w}{4}, 256)$	$(\frac{h}{4}, \frac{w}{4}, 128)$
	ConvTranspose2d (OC = 64, KS = 4, S = 2, P = 1), IN, ReLU	$(\frac{h}{2}, \frac{w}{2}, 128)$	$(h, w, 64)$
	ConvTranspose2d (OC = 4, KS = 7, S = 1, P = 3), Tanh	$(h, w, 64)$	$(h, w, 4)$

References

1. Akcay, S., Atapour-Abarghouei, A., Breckon, T.P.: GANomaly: semi-supervised anomaly detection via adversarial training. In: Jawahar, C.V., Li, H., Mori, G., Schindler, K. (eds.) ACCV 2018. LNCS, vol. 11363, pp. 622–637. Springer, Cham (2019). https://doi.org/10.1007/978-3-030-20893-6_39
2. Alex, V., et al.: Generative adversarial networks for brain lesion detection. In: Medical Imaging 2017: Image Processing, vol. 10133, p. 101330G. International Society for Optics and Photonics (2017)
3. Arjovsky, M., et al.: Wasserstein generative adversarial networks. In: International Conference on Machine Learning, pp. 214–223 (2017)

4. Bergmann, P., et al.: MVTec AD-a comprehensive real-world dataset for unsupervised anomaly detection. In: Proceedings of the IEEE/CVF Conference on CVPR, pp. 9592–9600 (2019)

5. Bergmann, P., et al.: The MVTec anomaly detection dataset: a comprehensive real-world dataset for unsupervised anomaly detection. Int. J. Comput. Vision **129**(4), 1038–1059 (2021)

6. IXI dataset. http://brain-development.org/ixi-dataset/

7. Chen, X., et al.: Unsupervised detection of lesions in brain MRI using constrained adversarial auto-encoders. arXiv preprint arXiv:1806.04972 (2018)

8. Choi, Y., et al.: StarGAN: unified generative adversarial networks for multi-domain image-to-image translation. In: The IEEE Conference on CVPR, June 2018

9. Defard, T., Setkov, A., Loesch, A., Audigier, R.: PaDiM: a patch distribution modeling framework for anomaly detection and localization. In: Del Bimbo, A., et al. (eds.) ICPR 2021. LNCS, vol. 12664, pp. 475–489. Springer, Cham (2021). https://doi.org/10.1007/978-3-030-68799-1_35

10. Esteva, A., et al.: Dermatologist-level classification of skin cancer with deep neural networks. Nature **542**(7639), 115–118 (2017)

11. Gherbi, E., et al.: An encoding adversarial network for anomaly detection. In: Asian Conference on Machine Learning, pp. 188–203. PMLR (2019)

12. Goodfellow, I., et al.: Generative adversarial nets. In: Advances in Neural Information Processing Systems, pp. 2672–2680 (2014)

13. Goodfellow, I., et al.: Generative adversarial networks. Commun. ACM **63**(11), 139–144 (2020)

14. Gulrajani, I., et al.: Improved training of Wasserstein GANs. In: Advances in Neural Information Processing Systems, pp. 5767–5777 (2017)

15. He, K., et al.: Delving deep into rectifiers: Surpassing human-level performance on imagenet classification. In: Proceedings of the IEEE International Conference on Computer Vision, pp. 1026–1034 (2015)

16. He, Z., et al.: AttGAN: facial attribute editing by only changing what you want. IEEE Trans. Image Process. **28**(11), 5464–5478 (2019)

17. Heusel, M., et al.: GANs trained by a two time-scale update rule converge to a local nash equilibrium. In: Advances in Neural Information Processing Systems, vol. 30 (2017)

18. Isola, P., et al.: Image-to-image translation with conditional adversarial networks. In: Proceedings of the IEEE Conference on CVPR, pp. 1125–1134 (2017)

19. Li, C., Wand, M.: Precomputed real-time texture synthesis with Markovian generative adversarial networks. In: Leibe, B., Matas, J., Sebe, N., Welling, M. (eds.) ECCV 2016. LNCS, vol. 9907, pp. 702–716. Springer, Cham (2016). https://doi.org/10.1007/978-3-319-46487-9_43

20. Liu, M., et al.: STGAN: a unified selective transfer network for arbitrary image attribute editing. In: Proceedings of the IEEE Conference on CVPR, pp. 3673–3682 (2019)

21. Liu, M.Y., et al.: Unsupervised image-to-image translation networks. In: Advances in Neural Information Processing Systems, pp. 700–708 (2017)

22. Mejjati, Y.A., et al.: Unsupervised attention-guided image-to-image translation. In: Advances in Neural Information Processing Systems, pp. 3693–3703 (2018)

23. Nizan, O., et al.: Breaking the cycle-colleagues are all you need. In: Proceedings of the IEEE/CVF Conference on CVPR, pp. 7860–7869 (2020)

24. Rahman Siddiquee, M.M., et al.: Learning fixed points in generative adversarial networks: from image-to-image translation to disease detection and localization. In: Proceedings of the IEEE International Conference on Computer Vision, pp. 191–200 (2019)
25. Roth, K., et al.: Towards total recall in industrial anomaly detection. arXiv preprint arXiv:2106.08265 (2021)
26. Sabokrou, M., et al.: Adversarially learned one-class classifier for novelty detection. In: Proceedings of the IEEE Conference on CVPR, pp. 3379–3388 (2018)
27. Schlegl, T., Seeböck, P., Waldstein, S.M., Schmidt-Erfurth, U., Langs, G.: Unsupervised anomaly detection with generative adversarial networks to guide marker discovery. In: Niethammer, M., et al. (eds.) IPMI 2017. LNCS, vol. 10265, pp. 146–157. Springer, Cham (2017). https://doi.org/10.1007/978-3-319-59050-9_12
28. Schlegl, T., et al.: f-AnoGAN: fast unsupervised anomaly detection with generative adversarial networks. Med. Image Anal. **54**, 30–44 (2019)
29. Seitzer, M.: PyTorch-FID: FID Score for PyTorch, version 0.1.1, August 2020. https://github.com/mseitzer/pytorch-fid
30. Shen, W., et al.: Learning residual images for face attribute manipulation. In: Proceedings of the IEEE Conference on CVPR, pp. 4030–4038 (2017)
31. Wang, L., et al.: COVID-Net: a tailored deep convolutional neural network design for detection of COVID-19 cases from chest X-ray images. Sci. Rep. **10**(1), 19549 (2020)
32. Wang, X., et al.: ChestX-ray8: hospital-scale chest X-ray database and benchmarks on weakly-supervised classification and localization of common thorax diseases. In: Proceedings of the IEEE Conference on CVPR, pp. 2097–2106 (2017)
33. Yi, Z., et al.: DualGAN: unsupervised dual learning for image-to-image translation. In: ICCV, pp. 2868–2876 (2017)
34. Zenati, H., et al.: Adversarially learned anomaly detection. In: 2018 IEEE International Conference on Data Mining (ICDM), pp. 727–736. IEEE (2018)
35. Zenati, H., et al.: Efficient GAN-based anomaly detection. arXiv preprint arXiv:1802.06222 (2018)
36. Zhang, G., et al.: Generative adversarial network with spatial attention for face attribute editing. In: Proceedings of the ECCV, pp. 417–432 (2018)
37. Zhao, Y., et al.: Unpaired image-to-image translation using adversarial consistency loss. arXiv preprint arXiv:2003.04858 (2020)
38. Zhu, J.Y., et al.: Toward multimodal image-to-image translation. In: Advances in Neural Information Processing Systems, pp. 465–476 (2017)
39. Zhu, J.Y., et al.: Unpaired image-to-image translation using cycle-consistent adversarial networks. arXiv preprint (2017)
40. Zuluaga, M.A., Hush, D., Delgado Leyton, E.J.F., Hoyos, M.H., Orkisz, M.: Learning from only positive and unlabeled data to detect lesions in vascular CT images. In: Fichtinger, G., Martel, A., Peters, T. (eds.) MICCAI 2011. LNCS, vol. 6893, pp. 9–16. Springer, Heidelberg (2011). https://doi.org/10.1007/978-3-642-23626-6_2

Bi-directional Synthesis of Pre- and Post-contrast MRI via Guided Feature Disentanglement

Yuan Xue[1(✉)], Blake E. Dewey[1], Lianrui Zuo[1,5], Shuo Han[3], Aaron Carass[1], Peiyu Duan[3], Samuel W. Remedios[2], Dzung L. Pham[6], Shiv Saidha[4], Peter A. Calabresi[4], and Jerry L. Prince[1]

[1] Department of Electrical and Computer Engineering, Johns Hopkins University, Baltimore, MD 21218, USA
yuanxue@jhu.edu
[2] Department of Computer Science, Johns Hopkins University, Baltimore, MD 21218, USA
[3] Department of Biomedical Engineering, Johns Hopkins School of Medicine, Baltimore, MD 21287, USA
[4] Department of Neurology, Johns Hopkins School of Medicine, Baltimore, MD 21287, USA
[5] Laboratory of Behavioral Neuroscience, National Institute on Aging, National Institutes of Health, Baltimore, MD 20892, USA
[6] Center for Neuroscience and Regenerative Medicine, Henry M. Jackson Foundation, Bethesda, MD 20817, USA

Abstract. Magnetic resonance imaging (MRI) with gadolinium contrast is widely used for tissue enhancement and better identification of active lesions and tumors. Recent studies have shown that gadolinium deposition can accumulate in tissues including the brain, which raises safety concerns. Prior works have tried to synthesize post-contrast T1-weighted MRIs from pre-contrast MRIs to avoid the use of gadolinium. However, contrast and image representations are often entangled during the synthesis process, resulting in synthetic post-contrast MRIs with undesirable contrast enhancements. Moreover, the synthesis of pre-contrast MRIs from post-contrast MRIs which can be useful for volumetric analysis is rarely investigated in the literature. To tackle pre- and post- contrast MRI synthesis, we propose a BI-directional Contrast Enhancement Prediction and Synthesis (BICEPS) network that enables disentanglement of contrast and image representations via a bi-directional image-to-image translation (I2I) model. Our proposed model can perform both pre-to-post and post-to-pre contrast synthesis, and provides an interpretable synthesis process by predicting contrast enhancement maps from the learned contrast embedding. Extensive experiments on a multiple sclerosis dataset demonstrate the feasibility of applying our bidirectional synthesis and show that BICEPS outperforms current methods.

Keywords: Multi-modal MRI Synthesis · Contrast Enhancement · Feature Disentanglement · Multiple Sclerosis

C. Zhao et al. (Eds.): SASHIMI 2022, LNCS 13570, pp. 55–65, 2022.
https://doi.org/10.1007/978-3-031-16980-9_6

1   Introduction

Gadolinium-based contrast agents (GBCAs) have been widely applied in magnetic resonance imaging (MRI) to enhance tissue contrast [25] and to better identify active lesions in multiple sclerosis (MS) [13] and tumors [22]. Although GBCAs are generally considered safe [12], recent research indicates that gadolinium can accumulate in the brain [3]. Such gadolinium deposition may cause health issues, which raises safety concerns in the use of GBCAs [20]. To avoid the use of GBCAs, deep learning based image synthesis models [1,2,6,10,16] have been proposed to simulate post-contrast MRIs from pre-contrast MRIs without compromising diagnostic ability. The feasibility of such methods is also corroborated by research on predicting lesions from pre-contrast MRIs [14].

To simulate post-contrast MRIs from pre-contrast MRIs, UNets [19] and conditional generative adversarial networks (cGANs) [9] have been proposed as the image synthesis models. Taking multiple pre-contrast MRI sequences of the same subject as input, image-to-image translations (I2I) generate post-contrast T1-weighted MRIs (post-T_1w). Past efforts on simulating post-contrast MRIs have had promising results, though few works have focused on interpreting the synthesis process. Kleesiek et al. [10] introduced a 3D UNet [4] model to predict a contrast enhancement map along with an uncertainty map. Although the model provides some level of interpretability, the disentanglement of contrast and image signal has not been investigated. Additionally, there has been limited work [21] on synthesizing pre-contrast T1-weighted MRIs (pre-T_1w) from post-contrast. In clinical practice, there are cases where only post-T_1w is acquired due to time and cost. Since most image analysis pipelines [8] are developed for pre-T_1w, missing such data limits the use of these algorithms.

In this paper, we propose a BI-directional Contrast Enhancement Prediction and Synthesis (BICEPS) model which can perform both pre-T_1w to post-T_1w and post-T_1w to pre-T_1w synthesis using a single model. The bi-directional synthesis is achieved by first disentangling contrast and image features via a feature encoder and generating a corresponding post-contrast MRI and contrast enhancement map (CE-map) via a dual-path decoder. The disentanglement enables a more interpretable synthesis process and better alignment between the contrast and image features. Depending on the target MRI sequence, the synthesis process of BICEPS can be interpreted as a combination of a prediction process and a reconstruction process. When the inputs contain a pre-T_1w, BICEPS will try to simulate the post-T_1w and recover the input pre-T_1w. Similarly, given inputs with post-T_1w, BICEPS aims to simulate the pre-T_1w and recover the input post-T_1w. The network can also take as input other pre-contrast tissue contrasts (e.g., T_2w and FLAIR), if they are available, to provide complementary information for a better synthesis. We further train BICEPS with input dropout, so that not all input tissue contrasts are needed during the inference. The disentanglement of contrast and image features encourages better alignment between pre-T_1w and post-T_1w sequences, and provides an interpretable CE-map. The bi-directional synthesis requires multi-task learning of the network and thus improves the robustness and generalizability of our proposed model.

To the best of our knowledge, this work is the first to exploit feature disentanglement for bi-directional synthesis between pre- and post-contrast MRIs.

2   Methodology

Network Architecture. The overall framework of BICEPS is outlined in Fig. 1. Our backbone network is similar to Pix2Pix [9] with 3D convolutional kernels and additional residual blocks [7]. Input to the network is 3D patches during training, with full volumes used during inference. The network takes four input patches from three different tissue contrasts: T_1w, T_2w, and FLAIR. A zero patch is also used for bi-directional synthesis. For pre-to-post synthesis, the T_1w image is pre-T_1w and for post-to-pre synthesis, the T_1w image is post-T_1w. If one or both of the T_2w and FLAIR images is missing, then the input can be replaced by zeros. The T_1w image (pre- or post-) is always required. The encoder network consists of two down-sampling layers via a 3D convolution. Four consecutive residual blocks are applied before each down-sampling layer. The architecture of our residual block is the same as in [2], where the number of channels is reduced to $1/4$ of the input channel dimension in the residual block. The decoder network takes the encoded image feature maps and contrast feature maps from the encoder network and outputs both the post-T_1w and the CE-map through two paths. In the image path, contrast features are fused with image features via a contrast-aware synthesis (CAS) block. While in the contrast path, only contrast features are used to generate the CE-map. The two paths encourages the disentanglement of the image and contrast features to ease the bi-directional synthesis and ensure better alignment between the image and contrast features. To get pre-T_1w, the predicted CE-map and post-T_1w are subtracted.

For bi-directional synthesis, we design two specific input channels for pre-T_1w or post-T_1w. For pre-to-post, the post-T_1w input channel is set to all zeros. In this case, the image feature is extracted from the input and the contrast feature is synthesized from multiple input channels (*i.e.*, multiple MRI tissue contrasts such as T_2w or FLAIR). The image path in the decoder synthesizes the target post-T_1w,

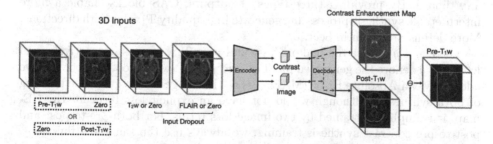

Fig. 1. Overview of our proposed BICEPS model. The network takes four 3D inputs the first two of which are always a T_1w image (pre- or post-) and a zero image. The second two inputs are T_2w and FLAIR images, either of which or both can be replaced by zeros if missing. The outputs are the same regardless of the inputs.

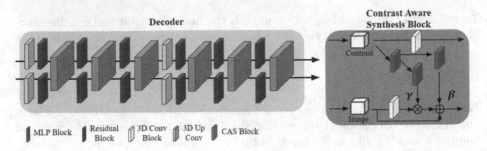

Fig. 2. The architecture of our proposed decoder network and Contrast Aware Synthesis (CAS) block. Regardless of encoder inputs, the decoder takes the contrast and image embeddings learned from the encoder and generates CE-maps and post-T_1w images.

and the predicted pre-T_1w means to reconstruct the corresponding input. Similarly, for post-to-pre, the pre-T_1w input channel is set to all zeros. The encoder then tries to extract both image and contrast features from the input MRIs. The image path will try to recover the target post-T_1w, and predict the pre-T_1w by subtracting the predicted CE-map. During inference, the network automatically detects the input sequences and performs the corresponding synthesis tasks.

Contrast-Aware Synthesis. The architecture of our decoder network and CAS block are in Fig. 2. The decoder network consists of two up-sampling layers via 3D transposed convolutional layers with multiple residual and CAS blocks. The decoder takes two inputs, the learned contrast and image latent embeddings from the encoder network, and outputs a CE-map as well as a post-T_1w image. For the image path, which synthesizes the post-T_1w, contrast and image features are fused within the CAS block. The design of the CAS block is inspired by [5] and [15]. Different from [15] which used a fixed conditional input, our CAS block gradually refines a learned contrast embedding and incorporates it into the image features. γ and β are spatial maps with the same dimension as the input contrast or image feature. Intuitively, γ and β contain both position and intensity features of the CE-map and thus can guide the synthesis of the post-T_1w image. By providing three types of outputs, CAS blocks enable a more interpretable synthesis process and generate high quality T_1w for both directions. More details are given in Sect. 3.

Let x and y denote the real pre-T_1w and post-T_1w images, respectively, and let $\hat{x}$ and $\hat{y}$ denote the generated pre-T_1w and post-T_1w images, respectively. We adopt a Mean Absolute Error (MAE) loss as the image loss to guide the training of both syntheses. Although we do not have an explicit loss term for the CE-map, it is implicitly trained by two image loss terms. For both pre-to-post and post-to-pre contrast synthesis training, we always use the same loss functions. The image loss is defined as $\mathcal{L}_{\text{img}} = ||x - \hat{x}||_1 + ||y - \hat{y}||_1$.

Disentanglement. To better disentangle contrast and image features, we include an additional discriminator network, D, and adopt an adversarial loss to adaptively learn the difference between the paired synthetic images and the groundtruth. D follows the DCGAN [17] architecture where 3D convolutional kernels are used for 3D image input. Let x' denote other non-T_1w input images including T_2w and FLAIR images. The adversarial objective is defined as,

$$\max_{\theta_D} \min_{\theta_G} \mathcal{L}_{\text{adv}} = \mathbb{E}_{x,x',y} \log \sigma(D(x,x',y)) + \mathbb{E}_{x,x',y} \log(1 - \sigma(D(\hat{x}, x', \hat{y}))), \quad (1)$$

where $\sigma(\cdot)$ is the sigmoid function and θ_D represents the parameters of the conditional discriminator network D, θ_G represents the parameters of the bi-directional synthesis network G. For the second term, the input of the synthesis network is either x or y depending on the task. The adversarial loss ensures better matching between synthesized outputs and thus implicitly encourages better disentanglement between contrast and image features. The overall loss function for training our model is $\mathcal{L} = \lambda \mathcal{L}_{\text{img}} + \mathcal{L}_{\text{adv}}$, where λ is a scaling factor.

Input Dropout. While BICEPS by default takes 3 input tissue contrasts, we further boost the flexibility of BICEPS by allowing missing input contrasts for inference. This is achieved by randomly replacing one input channel with a zero image during training, which we call *input dropout*. During inference, missing MRI sequences will be replaced with zero images to maintain the same input dimension. Compared with previous methods [1,2] which handle a different number of input sequences by training multiple models, our trained model can perform bi-directional synthesis with either full sequences or partial sequences using the same model. Note that in the adversarial loss term, we always include all available MRI sequences regardless of whether they are used as inputs or not.

Implementation Details. The encoder network of BICEPS consists of two down-sampling with 3D convolution kernel size $3 \times 3 \times 3$ and stride 2. Four consecutive residual blocks with $3 \times 3 \times 3$ convolution, BatchNormalization, and LeakyReLU activation as in [2] are placed before each down-sampling layer. The last down-sampling layer is followed by 4 additional residual blocks to generate the contrast and image embeddings in the latent space. The decoder network consists of two up-sampling 3D transposed convolutional layers with kernel size $3 \times 3 \times 3$ and stride 2. MLP layer in the CAS block is implemented as a $1 \times 1 \times 1$ convolution. A $1 \times 1 \times 1$ convolution is also applied before the output. We disable tracking the running mean and std. dev. in the BatchNormalization step since the input to the network could contain zero images due to the bi-directional synthesis and input dropout. λ is set to 100. We adopt a three-layer DCGAN [17] discriminator with 3D convolutional kernel size $4 \times 4 \times 4$. LSGAN [11] is used as the adversarial loss for stabilizing the training. During training, T_2w and FLAIR images are randomly replaced with zero images with probability $1/4$. We alternatively train the network with one iteration pre-to-post, then an iteration post-to-pre. We use the `AdamW` optimizer with $(\beta_1, \beta_2) = (0.5, 0.999)$, weight decay 10^{-2}, and initial learning rate 10^{-3}. The learning rate is decayed every time the validation loss does not decrease for 20 epochs with a rate of 0.8. The batch size is 16 and the maximum number of training epochs is 500.

All MRIs were center cropped to $224 \times 256 \times 224$, then randomly extracted 3D patches of size $56 \times 64 \times 56$ were used as input to the network during the training.

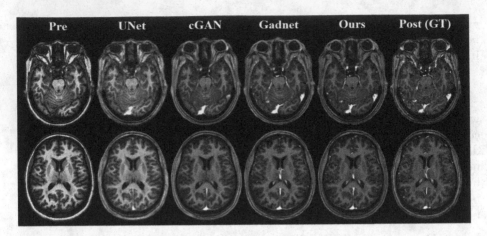

Fig. 3. Pre-to-post synthesis: The two rows show (from L to R) the pre-T_1w image, the results from four different synthesis methods, and the ground truth post-T_1w image.

Random horizontal flipping was also applied for data augmentation. At inference, whole image volumes are input to the network with no further processing.

3   Experiments and Results

Dataset. We conducted experiments on an MS dataset, containing 59 subjects collected on a Philips Achieva 3.0T scanner. Each scan contained multiple structural images including two 3D T_1w images (acquired at resolution $1.1 \times 1.1 \times 1.18$ mm, TE = 6 ms, TR = 3 s, TI = 840 ms), a 2D FLAIR image (acquired at resolution $0.83 \times 0.83 \times 2.2$ mm, TE = 68 ms, TR = 11s, TI = 2.8s) and a 2D T_2weighted (T_2w) image (acquired at resolution $1.1 \times 1.1 \times 2.2$ mm, TE = 12 ms/80 ms, TR = 4.2 s). T_1w and T_2w images were reconstructed on the scanner with 0.83×0.83 mm in-plane. Three-dimensional T_1w images were obtained both before and after contrast administration. Gadolinium dosage was 0.1 mmol per kg of subject weight. Within the 59 subjects, we randomly select 40 for training, 6 for validation, and 13 for our test set. All comparisons are done on the test set.

For preprocesing, images went through inhomogeneity correction using N4 [23]. 2D acquired images (T_2w, FLAIR) were super-resolved and anti-aliased using SMORE [26]. All contrasts for subjects were rigidly registered to the pre-T_1w image. After registration, images were gain-corrected by linearly adjusting the intensities to align the white matter histogram peaks [18], since it showed better performance in synthesis tasks than other normalizations.

Result Analysis. We evaluated the BICEPS model for both pre-to-post and post-to-pre contrast synthesis. For pre-to-post synthesis, we compare BICEPS with state-of-the-art post contrast synthesis methods including 2D UNet [19], 2D cGAN [9,16], and 3D Gadnet [2]. 2D networks are applied on axial slices. Quantitative and qualitative comparisons can be found in Table 1 two columns under

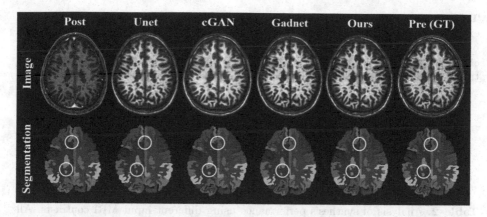

Fig. 4. Post-to-pre synthesis: The top row shows the images and the second row shows their associated SLANT segmentation. The pre-T_1w segmentation is treated as the groundtruth. White circles highlight regions where BICEPS leads to better segmentation than other synthesis methods.

pre- to post- contrast and Fig. 3, respectively. SSIM and PSNR are calculated on 3D volumes. From Table 1, one can observe that even though BICEPS was trained to perform synthesis in both directions, it outperforms the other methods in both metrics. As illustrated in Fig. 3, UNet and cGAN fail to capture the detailed contrast enhancement of the synthesized post-T_1w. Both Gadnet and BICEPS generate post-T_1w which contain correct contrast enhancement information, yet Gadnet slightly overestimates the contrast enhancement.

While no prior works have been done for post-to-pre synthesis, we adopted the same methods used for pre-to-post synthesis as baselines to compare with our model. We would emphasize that all baseline methods were trained separately for different tasks, while BICEPS uses the same trained model for both tasks. To validate the clinical usefulness of post-to-pre synthesis when only post-contrast is available, we ran the SLANT [8] whole brain segmentation model which was designed for pre-contrast images on all synthetic pre-T_1w. As a reference, we also ran SLANT on both the real pre-T_1w and real post-T_1w. The Dice coefficient between real post-T_1w segmentation and pre-T_1w segmentation is 88.73 ± 1.25. From the last three columns of Table 1, BICEPS achieves comparable performance in terms of SSIM and PSNR to cGAN and Gadnet. While all methods achieve considerably better segmentation results than using the real post-T_1w, pre-T_1w generated from our method has a segmentation result that agrees more with the real pre-T_1w segmentation, which further validates the utility of our model. As shown in Fig. 4, BICEPS clearly leads to more accurate brain segmentation results when comparing to the other methods ($p < 0.025$ compared to cGAN which is the second best method using the paired Wilcoxon signed rank test).

Input Dropout Testing. To validate our proposed input dropout, we test BICEPS with different input sequences using the **same** trained model. Compared with previous methods using **different** trained models, our trained

Table 1. Quantitative comparisons between synthesis methods. For post- to pre-T_1w experiments, Dice is calculated using SLANT [8] whole brain segmentation results between the original and synthesized pre-T_1w. The Dice of the original post-T_1w is 88.73 ± 1.25. Note that BICEPS uses a single model for both directions, other methods train two separate models.

Methods	Pre- to Post- contrast		Post- to Pre- contrast		
	SSIM↑ (%)	PSNR↑ (dB)	SSIM↑ (%)	PSNR↑ (dB)	Dice↑ (%)
UNet 2D [19]	83.60 ± 2.50	28.96 ± 1.59	87.11 ± 2.06	30.34 ± 1.39	92.04 ± 1.06
cGAN [9,16]	85.55 ± 2.14	27.44 ± 1.15	91.19 ± 1.68	33.98 ± 1.18	93.06 ± 1.27
Gadnet [2]	87.74 ± 2.56	31.40 ± 1.58	91.35 ± 1.76	**35.38 ± 1.40**	92.38 ± 0.99
BICEPS (Ours)	**89.93 ± 2.08**	**32.59 ± 1.25**	91.84 ± 2.44	32.38 ± 1.68	**93.41 ± 1.10**

Table 2. Analysis of synthesis performance using different input MRI contrasts. All results are from the same BICEPS model trained using input dropout.

Inputs	Pre- to Post- contrast		Post- to Pre- contrast	
	SSIM↑ (%)	PSNR↑ (dB)	SSIM↑ (%)	PSNR↑ (dB)
T_1w	77.21 ± 2.32	28.27 ± 1.66	68.06 ± 3.15	28.30 ± 2.37
T_1w + T_2w	82.55 ± 3.03	30.81 ± 1.63	83.15 ± 2.58	27.87 ± 1.12
T_1w + FLAIR	83.53 ± 2.73	29.35 ± 1.59	90.19 ± 2.50	**32.42 ± 2.32**
Full	**89.93 ± 2.08**	**32.59 ± 1.25**	**91.84 ± 2.44**	32.38 ± 1.68

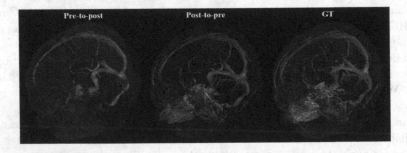

Fig. 5. MIP rendering visualization of CE-maps, defined as the differece between post-T_1w and pre-T_1w. From left to right: our method in pre-to-post synthesis, our method in post-to-pre synthesis, and the groundtruth.

BICEPS model eliminates the effect of randomization in the training and thus has a more accurate understanding of contributions from different input sequences in different tasks. From Table 2, we conclude that in pre-to-post synthesis, all input sequences play an important role in the synthesis. On the other hand, FLAIR contributes more towards post-to-pre synthesis than the T_2w image.

Other Applications. We also explore the potential of applying BICEPS to other tasks such as dural sinuses segmentation. We use the maximum intensity projection (MIP) [24] to render the CE-map learned by BICEPS as well as the groundtruth. In Fig. 5, we compare the groundtruth CE-map, with the post-to-pre output of BICEPS. Our method correctly highlights all dural sinuses, which indicates that our method successfully separates contrast and image features. For pre-to-post synthesis, predicting the CE-map is more challenging since the contrast must be estimated from the input. Although the visualization of our pre-to-post CE-map is not as close to the groundtruth as in post-to-pre, major sinuses including superior sagittal sinus, straight sinus, and transverse sinuses are still clearly visible. Based on such observations, we believe BICEPS can be instructional in dural sinuses segmentation.

4 Conclusion

In this paper, we propose a novel bi-directional synthesis model for both pre-to-post and post-to-pre MRI synthesis via disentangling image and contrast features from the input. We demonstrate that our proposed BICEPS outperforms current methods in both tasks on an MS dataset. In the future, we plan to investigate the potential of applying BICEPS and incorporating T2* weighted images to the detection of active MS lesions and dural sinuses segmentations.

Acknowledgements. This research was in part supported by the Intramural Research Program of the NIH, National Institute on Aging.

References

1. Bône, A., et al.: Contrast-enhanced brain mri synthesis with deep learning: key input modalities and asymptotic performance. In: 2021 IEEE 18th International Symposium on Biomedical Imaging (ISBI), pp. 1159–1163. IEEE (2021)
2. Calabrese, E., Rudie, J.D., Rauschecker, A.M., Villanueva-Meyer, J.E., Cha, S.: Feasibility of simulated postcontrast MRI of glioblastomas and lower-grade gliomas by using three-dimensional fully convolutional neural networks. Radiol. Artif. Intell. **3**(5), e200276 (2021)
3. Choi, J.W., Moon, W.J.: Gadolinium deposition in the brain: current updates. Korean J. Radiol. **20**(1), 134–147 (2019)
4. Çiçek, Ö., Abdulkadir, A., Lienkamp, S.S., Brox, T., Ronneberger, O.: 3D U-Net: learning dense volumetric segmentation from sparse annotation. In: Ourselin, S., Joskowicz, L., Sabuncu, M.R., Unal, G., Wells, W. (eds.) MICCAI 2016. LNCS, vol. 9901, pp. 424–432. Springer, Cham (2016). https://doi.org/10.1007/978-3-319-46723-8_49
5. Dumoulin, V., Shlens, J., Kudlur, M.: A learned representation for artistic style. arXiv preprint arXiv:1610.07629 (2016)
6. Gong, E., Pauly, J.M., Wintermark, M., Zaharchuk, G.: Deep learning enables reduced gadolinium dose for contrast-enhanced brain mri. J. Magn. Reson. Imaging **48**(2), 330–340 (2018)

7. He, K., Zhang, X., Ren, S., Sun, J.: Deep residual learning for image recognition. In: Proceedings of the IEEE Conference on Computer Vision- and Pattern Recognition, pp. 770–778 (2016)
8. Huo, Y., et al.: 3d whole brain segmentation using spatially localized atlas network tiles. Neuroimage **194**, 105–119 (2019)
9. Isola, P., Zhu, J.Y., Zhou, T., Efros, A.A.: Image-to-image translation with conditional adversarial networks. In: Proceedings of the IEEE Conference on Computer Vision and Pattern Recognition, pp. 1125–1134 (2017)
10. Kleesiek, J., et al.: Can virtual contrast enhancement in brain MRI replace gadolinium?: a feasibility study. Invest. Radiol. **54**(10), 653–660 (2019)
11. Mao, X., Li, Q., Xie, H., Lau, R.Y., Wang, Z., Paul Smolley, S.: Least squares generative adversarial networks. In: ICCV, pp. 2794–2802 (2017)
12. Matsumura, T., et al.: Safety of gadopentetate dimeglumine after 120 million administrations over 25 years of clinical use. Magn. Reson. Med. Sci. **12**, 297–304 (2013)
13. McFarland, H.F., et al.: Using gadolinium-enhanced magnetic resonance imaging lesions to monitor disease activity in multiple sclerosis. Ann. Neurol. **32**(6), 758–766 (1992)
14. Narayana, P.A., Coronado, I., Sujit, S.J., Wolinsky, J.S., Lublin, F.D., Gabr, R.E.: Deep learning for predicting enhancing lesions in multiple sclerosis from noncontrast MRI. Radiology **294**(2), 398–404 (2020)
15. Park, T., Liu, M.Y., Wang, T.C., Zhu, J.Y.: Semantic image synthesis with spatially-adaptive normalization. In: Proceedings of the IEEE/CVF Conference on Computer Vision and Pattern Recognition, pp. 2337–2346 (2019)
16. Preetha, C.J., et al.: Deep-learning-based synthesis of post-contrast t1-weighted mri for tumour response assessment in neuro-oncology: a multicentre, retrospective cohort study. Lancet Digit. Health **3**(12), e784–e794 (2021)
17. Radford, A., Metz, L., Chintala, S.: Unsupervised representation learning with deep convolutional generative adversarial networks. arXiv preprint arXiv:1511.06434 (2015)
18. Reinhold, J.C., Dewey, B.E., Carass, A., Prince, J.L.: Evaluating the impact of intensity normalization on MR image synthesis. In: Medical Imaging 2019: Image Processing. vol. 10949, pp. 890–898. SPIE (2019)
19. Ronneberger, O., Fischer, P., Brox, T.: U-net: convolutional networks for biomedical image segmentation. In: Navab, N., Hornegger, J., Wells, W.M., Frangi, A.F. (eds.) MICCAI 2015. LNCS, vol. 9351, pp. 234–241. Springer, Cham (2015). https://doi.org/10.1007/978-3-319-24574-4_28
20. Semelka, R.C., Ramalho, M., AlObaidy, M., Ramalho, J.: Gadolinium in humans: a family of disorders. Am. J. Roentgenol. **207**(2), 229–233 (2016)
21. Simona, B., et al.: Homogenization of brain Mri from a clinical data warehouse using contrast-enhanced to non-contrast-enhanced image translation with u-net derived models. In: Medical Imaging 2022: Image Processing. vol. 12032, pp. 576–582. SPIE (2022)
22. Tuncbilek, N., Karakas, H.M., Okten, O.O.: Dynamic contrast enhanced mri in the differential diagnosis of soft tissue tumors. Eur. J. Radiol. **53**(3), 500–505 (2005)
23. Tustison, N.J., et al.: N4itk: improved n3 bias correction. IEEE Trans. Med. Imaging **29**(6), 1310–1320 (2010)
24. Wallis, J.W., Miller, T.R., Lerner, C.A., Kleerup, E.C.: Three-dimensional display in nuclear medicine. IEEE Trans. Med. Imaging **8**(4), 230–297 (1989)

25. Yankeelov, T.E., Gore, J.C.: Dynamic contrast enhanced magnetic resonance imaging in oncology: theory, data acquisition, analysis, and examples. Current Medical Imaging **3**(2), 91–107 (2007)
26. Zhao, C., Dewey, B.E., Pham, D.L., Calabresi, P.A., Reich, D.S., Prince, J.L.: Smore: a self-supervised anti-aliasing and super-resolution algorithm for mri using deep learning. IEEE Trans. Med. Imaging **40**(3), 805–817 (2020)

Morphology-Preserving Autoregressive 3D Generative Modelling of the Brain

Petru-Daniel Tudosiu[1]([✉])(iD), Walter Hugo Lopez Pinaya[1](iD),
Mark S. Graham[1](iD), Pedro Borges[1](iD), Virginia Fernandez[1](iD), Dai Yang[2],
Jeremy Appleyard[2], Guido Novati[3], Disha Mehra[2], Mike Vella[4],
Parashkev Nachev[5](iD), Sebastien Ourselin[1](iD), and Jorge Cardoso[1](iD)

[1] Department of Biomedical Engineering, School of Biomedical Engineering
& Imaging Sciences, King's College London, London, UK
petru.tudosiu@kcl.ac.uk
[2] NVIDIA, Santa Clara, USA
[3] DeepMind, London, UK
[4] Oxford Nanopore Technologies, Gosling Building, Oxford Science Park,
Edmund Halley Road, Littlemore, Oxford OX4 4DQ, UK
[5] Queen Square Institute of Neurology, University College London, London, UK

Abstract. Human anatomy, morphology, and associated diseases can be studied using medical imaging data. However, access to medical imaging data is restricted by governance and privacy concerns, data ownership, and the cost of acquisition, thus limiting our ability to understand the human body. A possible solution to this issue is the creation of a model able to learn and then generate synthetic images of the human body conditioned on specific characteristics of relevance (e.g., age, sex, and disease status). Deep generative models, in the form of neural networks, have been recently used to create synthetic 2D images of natural scenes. Still, the ability to produce high-resolution 3D volumetric imaging data with correct anatomical morphology has been hampered by data scarcity and algorithmic and computational limitations. This work proposes a generative model that can be scaled to produce anatomically correct, high-resolution, and realistic images of the human brain, with the necessary quality to allow further downstream analyses. The ability to generate a potentially unlimited amount of data not only enables large-scale studies of human anatomy and pathology without jeopardizing patient privacy, but also significantly advances research in the field of anomaly detection, modality synthesis, learning under limited data, and fair and ethical AI. Code and trained models are available at: https://github.com/AmigoLab/SynthAnatomy.

Keywords: Transformers · VQ-VAE · Generative modelling · Neuroimaging · Neuromorphology

G. Novati and M. Vella—Work done while at NVIDIA.

C. Zhao et al. (Eds.): SASHIMI 2022, LNCS 13570, pp. 66–78, 2022.
https://doi.org/10.1007/978-3-031-16980-9_7

1   Introduction

Current advances in the application of deep learning (DL) in medical imaging were driven by substantial initiatives and challenges such as UK Biobank (UKB) [1], Alzheimer's Disease Neuroimaging Initiative (ADNI) [2], and the Medical Segmentation Decathlon [3]. However, these are relatively small compared to computer vision datasets. Owing to the lack of access to sufficient data due to privacy concerns, medical imaging data is not fully leveraging DL's full potential and this hinders its translation from research to the clinical environment. State-of-the-art (SOTA) algorithms rely on a handful of highly curated datasets which could lead to biases due to imbalanced demographics or acquisition parameters, that may negatively affect their performance for certain populations. A solution to this problem could come from the generative modelling of the underlying available data to balance the prevalence of confounding variables in the training dataset.

While semi-supervised 3D generative modelling of the brain has been steadily explored and improved [4–6], progress in unsupervised generative modelling has been more limited. Generative Adversarial Network (GAN) based approaches, which suffer from memory constraints and stability issues, have mostly been trained on low-resolution 3D images [7–9], having only recently been able to synthesise full resolution images via learning partial sub-volumes [10]. Whereas previous methods quantify sample diversity using classic metrics such as Multi-Scale Structural Similarity Index (MS-SSIM) [11], distribution alignment via Fréchet Inception Distance (FID) [12] and Maximum Mean Discrepancy (MMD) [13], none have quantified if the generated data preserves the morphological characteristics of the data – crucial if we are to use such methods.

Recently, autoregressive models have achieved SOTA results synthesising high resolution natural images [14–16]. This was accomplished by employing a compression model, namely a Vector Quantised-Variational Autoencoder (VQ-VAE) [14,17], to project the images into a discrete latent representation where the images' likelihood becomes tractable. An attention-based Transformer network [18,19] is then used to model the product of conditional distributions by maximising the expected log-likelihood of the training data.

Following [20] as part of the Synthetic Data Desiderata, a good synthetic dataset should share many if not all statistical properties of the real dataset. One such property, if not the most important, of synthetic structural medical images is their morphological correctness. Covariates of interest such as demographic and pathological ones determine the phenotype of each subject which in turn contributes to the population-level morphological statistics. Without it, any development done on the synthetic data as part of the Train on Synthetic, Test on Real [21] paradigm could suffer from higher domain distribution shifts slowing down the development. Furthermore, without morphological assessment, any hypothesis tested on the synthetic data would be rendered highly uncertain.

In this study, we scale and optimise VQ-VAE and Transformer models for high-resolution volumetric data, aiming to learn the data distribution of both radiologically healthy and pathological brains. A thorough morphological evaluation is employed by using Voxel-Based Morphometry (VBM) [22] and volumetric analysis using Geodesic Information Flows (GIF) [23], demonstrating that synthetic data generated by the proposed model preserves the morphological characteristics and phenotype of the data.

2   Background

Our model is based on the two-stage architecture introduced by [14,17] and extended by [15], where a VQ-VAE model is used to project a high-resolution image into a compressed latent representation and a transformer is trained to maximize the likelihood of the flattened representations.

2.1   VQ-VAE

The VQ-VAE [14,17] is comprised of an encoder E that projects the input image $\mathbf{x} \in \mathbb{R}^{H \times W \times D}$ to a latent representation space $\widehat{\mathbf{z}} \in \mathbb{R}^{h \times w \times d \times n_z}$ where n_z is the latent embedding vector's dimensionality. Afterwards, an element-wise quantization is done for each spatial code $\widehat{\mathbf{z}}_{ijk} \in \mathbb{R}^{n_z}$ onto its nearest vector $e_k \in \mathbb{R}^{n_z}, k \in 1, ..., K$ from a codebook, where K denotes the vocabulary size of the codebook, obtaining $\widehat{\mathbf{z}}_q$. The codebook's elements are learned in an online manner, together with the other model's parameters. Based on the quantized latent space, a decoder G tries to reconstruct the observations $\widehat{\mathbf{x}} \in \mathbb{R}^{H \times W \times D}$. By replacing each of the codebook elements vector $\widehat{\mathbf{z}}_q \in \mathbb{R}^{h \times w \times d \times n_z}$ with their associated index k, the latent discrete representation is obtained.

2.2   Transformer

Transformers models and their associated self-attention mechanisms can capture the interactions between inputs regardless of their relative positioning. Due to this, the attention mechanism scales quadratically with the size of the input sequence. Since the VQ-VAE's latent discrete representation when applied to volumetric medical data is 3D and thus large in scale, standard transformers do not scale to the necessary sequence length. Recently, multiple advances have made Transformers more efficient [24]; models such as the Performer, with its FAVOR+ linear scaling attention approximation [19] offers a good compromise between accurately modelling long-sequences while preserving a reasonable computational complexity [24]. Thus the Performer is used to model the latent sequences; by minimizing the conditional distribution of codebook indices $p(s_i) = p(s_i|s_{<i})$ on the flattened 1D sequences of the 3D latent discrete representations, the data log-likelihood is maximized in an autoregressive fashion.

3   Methods

3.1   Descriptive Quantization for Transformer Usage

To create a Transformer-based generative model of the brain, the image volume needs to be transformed into a 1D sequence of tokens. To achieve this, a VQ-VAE model that reduces the overall spatial size by a factor of 4096, allowing an input image of size X to be represented by a sequence of 1400 tokens. This 1400-long token sequence is learnt in an online fashion together with the VQ-VAE model by using the Exponential Moving Average (EMA) algorithm [14,17] as per Eq. 1.

$$\mathcal{L}_{VQ-VAE}(\mathbf{x}, G(\widehat{\mathbf{z}}_{\mathbf{q}})) = \mathcal{L}_{Rec} + \mathcal{L}_{Adv} + \|sg[E(\mathbf{x})] - \widehat{\mathbf{z}}_{\mathbf{q}}\|_2^2 + \beta\|sg[\widehat{\mathbf{z}}_{\mathbf{q}}] - E(\mathbf{x})\|_2^2 \quad (1)$$

$$N_i^{(t)} := N_i^{(t-1)} * \gamma + n_i^{(t)}(1-\gamma), \quad m_i^{(t)} := m_i^{(t-1)} * \gamma + \sum_j^{n_i^{(t)}} E(x)_{i,j}^{(t)}(1-\gamma), \quad \widehat{\mathbf{z}}_{qi}^{(t)} := \frac{m_i^{(t)}}{N_i^{(t)}} \quad (2)$$

where sg stands for the stop-gradient operation. As per [14,17], the third loss component in Eq. 1 is replaced by Eq. 2, where $n_i^{(t)}$ stands for the number of vectors in $E(\mathbf{x})$ that will be quantized to codebook element $\widehat{\mathbf{z}}_{qi}$. The hyper-parameters γ and β control the decay of the EMA and the commitment of the encoder output to a certain quantized element respectively.

For the codebook to be perceptually rich, a loss similar to [15,25] which is formed by the first and second elements of Eq. 1 as defined bellow:

$$\mathcal{L}_{Rec} = \|\mathbf{x} - \widehat{\mathbf{x}}\|_1 + \||FFT(\mathbf{x})| - |FFT(\widehat{\mathbf{x}})|\|_2 + \mathcal{LPIPS}_{0.5}(\mathbf{x}, \widehat{\mathbf{x}}) \quad (3)$$

Where the first term is a pixel-space L1 norm, the second term is the L2 norm of the image's Fourier representations based on [26] which aims at facilitating high-frequency feature preservation, the third term is the LPIPS [27] loss using AlexNet applied on 50% of slices on each axis. Lastly, the $\mathcal{L}_{Adv}$ is based on a Patch-GAN discriminator-based adversarial loss [15,28], replacing the original loss by the LS-GAN [29] one (see Eq. 4):

$$\min_D \mathcal{L}_{LSGAN}(D) = \frac{1}{2}\mathbb{E}_{\mathbf{x}\sim p_{data}(\mathbf{x})}\left[(D(\mathbf{x}) - 1)^2\right] + \frac{1}{2}\mathbb{E}_{\mathbf{x}\sim p_{data}(\mathbf{x})}\left[(D(G(\widehat{\mathbf{x}})))^2\right]$$
$$\min_G \mathcal{L}_{LSGAN}(G) = \frac{1}{2}\mathbb{E}_{\mathbf{x}\sim p_{\mathbf{x}}(\mathbf{z})}\left[(D(G(\widehat{\mathbf{x}})) - 1)^2\right] \quad (4)$$

Each of these losses independently contributes to model training stability and reconstruction quality.

3.2 Autoregressive Modelling of the Brain

The VQ-VAE model was first trained on T1w MRI images of neurologically healthy subjects from UKB [1] until convergence, and then their z_q representations were extracted. Afterwards, further fine-tuning on the pathological dataset formed from the baseline T1w MRI scans of ADNI [2] subjects was done until over-fitting was noticed, at which point the ADNI subjects' z_q representation was also extracted. This paradigm was chosen since in [30] it was shown to either be on par or better compared to training a VQ-VAE model only on the pathological dataset. Furthermore, we aim also to highlight that the pre-trained model can be fine-tuned and learn new morphology, in this case, a pathological one, thus increasing the usefulness of the UKB trained VQ-VAE as a pretrained model for the community.

In order to ensure a higher quality of the Transformer's samples, the top 1% generated samples, based on the score obtained by averaging the Patch-GAN discriminator output, were used in this work.

As the VQ-VAE representations cover all phenotypes, a separate Transformer model has been trained on the latent representations of different sub-populations to model individual morphological subgroups. More specifically, to demonstrate the morphological phenotype preservation, the UKB [1] dataset was partitioned into young vs. old sub-populations, and small vs. big ventricles sub-populations. We defined all of these groups based on the first and last of five quantiles based on "age when attended assessment centre" (21003-2.0) and "volume of the ventricular cerebrospinal fluid" (25004-2.0) UKB variables, respectively. To test the preservation of disease morphology, we split the ADNI dataset into cognitively normal (CN) and Alzheimer's disease (AD) subgroups based on the "diagnosis/scan category assignment field".

4 Experiments and Results

The performance of the proposed model is assessed in two ways: first, the quality of generated samples is measured according to image fidelity metrics commonly used in generative models; second, we verify if the morphological characteristics of a population and the differences between sub-populations are preserved when comparing real and synthetic data. We compared our model to a baseline volumetric VAE model. The models by [8,9,29,31] underwent extensive hyper-parameter exploration at the original resolutions but failed to converge on our data. Only the VAE results are thus presented as a baseline.

4.1 Quantitative Image Fidelity Evaluation

Similarly to [8,9], we use the FID [12] to assess the visual quality of the generated images. Since originally the metric is based on a pretrained Inception V3 network on 2D natural images, it cannot be applied on 3D volumes directly, so here it is applied on the middle slice of each axis and reported individually. To measure the quality of the 3D samples, batch-wise MMD with a dot product as the kernel is being used as suggested in [8,9]. Briefly, MMD quantifies the distance between the distributions with finite sample estimates in kernel functions in

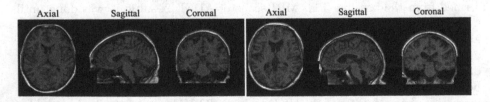

Fig. 1. Synthetic samples. On the left UKB small ventricles and on the right UKB big ventricles.

the reproducing kernel Hilbert space [13]. Lastly, to estimate the diversity of the generated images, MS-SSIM is being used in a pair-wise fashion between the generated synthetic samples as in [8,9]. For easy comparison, all metrics have also been calculated between each sub-population's real images such that a ground truth baseline is also offered.

Across the board, as is described in Table 1, both in regards to the sub-populations and axial, coronal and sagittal slices, the FID of the VQ-VAE model outperforms the VAE baseline by a high margin, showcasing the realistic appearance of the sampled synthetic brains as seen in Fig. 3. The same can be said for the $bMMD^2$, where the VQ-VAE is one order of magnitude smaller for UKB sub-populations and substantially better for the ADNI sub-populations. The difference in $bMMD^2$ performance between VQ-VAE's UKB and ADNI sub-populations might be because the ADNI dataset is considerably smaller than the UKB one, and to circumvent that, the VQ-VAE compression model was firstly trained on the UKB dataset and then fine-tuned on the ADNI one. Thus, the z_q representation fed into the Transformer, which is the generative model per se, is not specialised for ADNI, but instead, it tries to encompass it. Finally, MS-SSIM shows that the VQ-VAE achieves a life-like high diversity of samples across all sub-populations, significantly surpassing the VAE. The peculiar case of the ADNI AD sub-population might be attributed to the same cause as the $bMMD^2$.

4.2 Morphological Evaluation

To evaluate the morphological correctness of the synthetic samples, Voxel-Based Morphometry (VBM) [22] was used to investigate the focal differences in the

Table 1. The $bMMD^2$ and MS-SSIM were calculated on 3D generated images while FID was done middle-slices-wise of generated volumes.

Model	Dataset	Population	FID (Ax—Cor—Sag)	$bMMD^2$	MS-SSIM
Real	UKB	Young	0.35 | 0.85 | 0.42	$0.00208_{\pm0.00026}$	$0.65_{\pm0.08}$
VQ-VAE (ours)	UKB	Young	31.04 | 57.19 | 57.19	$0.00903_{\pm0.00090}$	$0.68_{\pm0.03}$
VAE	UKB	Young	193.56 | 302.74 | 251.34	$0.02757_{\pm0.00091}$	$0.15_{\pm0.001}$
Real	UKB	Old	1.16 | 1.42 | 0.37	$0.00217_{\pm0.00045}$	$0.65_{\pm0.07}$
VQ-VAE (ours)	UKB	Old	33.68 | 60.60 | 78.82	$0.00887_{\pm0.00104}$	$\mathbf{0.67_{\pm0.03}}$
VAE	UKB	Old	234.86 | 289.21 | 242.18	$0.02622_{\pm0.00044}$	$0.15_{\pm0.001}$
Real	UKB	Small ventricles	1.74 | 1.99 | 0.87	$0.00220_{\pm0.00044}$	$0.67_{\pm0.07}$
VQ-VAE (ours)	UKB	Small ventricles	28.33 | 58.23 | 76.68	$0.00892_{\pm0.00106}$	$\mathbf{0.70_{\pm0.04}}$
VAE	UKB	Small ventricles	206.92 | 318.37 | 258.17	$0.02836_{\pm0.00078}$	$0.14_{\pm0.001}$
Real	UKB	Big ventricles	1.15 | 1.44 | 0.53	$0.00231_{\pm0.00041}$	$0.64_{\pm0.05}$
VQ-VAE (ours)	UKB	Big ventricles	36.02 | 57.76 | 76.51	$0.00937_{\pm0.00069}$	$0.68_{\pm0.04}$
VAE	UKB	Big ventricles	215.37 | 293.97 | 244.84	$0.02738_{\pm0.00058}$	$0.16_{\pm0.001}$
Real	ADNI	Cognitively normal	21.49 | 17.31 | 9.34	$0.00123_{\pm0.00021}$	$0.56_{\pm0.05}$
VQ-VAE (ours)	ADNI	Cognitively normal	53.88 | 93.62 | 112.32	$0.01558_{\pm0.00348}$	$0.71_{\pm0.08}$
VAE	ADNI	Cognitively normal	233.59 | 397.52 | 421.04	$0.02562_{\pm0.00119}$	$0.14_{\pm0.05}$
Real	ADNI	Alzheimer's diseased	9.08 | 16.85 | 13.49	$0.00167_{\pm0.00034}$	$0.55_{\pm0.13}$
VQ-VAE (ours)	ADNI	Alzheimer's diseased	87.75 | 51.74 | 90.95	$0.01562_{\pm0.00304}$	$0.61_{\pm0.11}$
VAE	ADNI	Alzheimer's diseased	235.33 | 332.70 | 340.78	$0.02804_{\pm0.00177}$	$0.12_{\pm0.06}$

brain anatomy of the sub-populations. At the core of VBM stands the application of a generalised linear model and associated statistical tests across all voxels of a group-aligned population, to identify morphological differences in modulated tissue compartment between the selected groups.

The VBM analysis did not factor out any covariates available in the real datasets since the generative process was unconditioned. All t-statistics maps have been corrected to minimise the effects of low variance areas following [32]. As shown in Fig. 2 the t-statistics maps between synthetic images generated by the VQ-VAE strongly agree with the VBM maps of real data, primarily when compared with the VAE baseline. In the UKB small ventricles vs. big ventricles experiment, VQ-VAE again successfully models the ventricular differences correctly compared to the real-data VBM maps, while the VAE model strongly emphasizes them or exacerbates the subarachnoid CSF. Lastly, the morphological differences between cognitively normal vs. AD subjects on the ADNI dataset on the VQVAE generated data strongly preserve the known temporal lobe and hippocampal atrophy patterns associated with AD, producing a VBM t-map that strongly resembles the one from real data. Conversely, the VAE fails to show coherent structural differences in the GM.

Furthermore, we compared the volumes of key brain regions between populations of real and synthetic data. All images were segmented using GIF [23], a robust multi-atlas based probabilistic segmentation model of the human brain which segments the brain into non-overlapping hierarchical 155 regions. Based on probabilistic segmentations, the total volume of each tissue was calculated, and then we ran a two-sided t-test to assess if there was a statistically significant

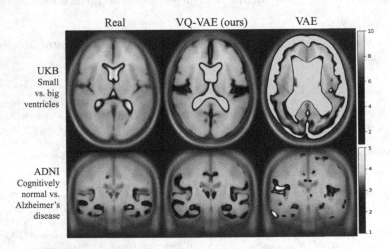

Fig. 2. Thresholded uncorrected VBM t-statistics maps processed as per [32] showcasing the morphological differences between two populations based on real samples, VQ-VAE synthetic samples, and VAE synthetic samples. For UKB small vs. big ventricles modulated CSF tissue segments were used, while for ADNI, cognitively normal vs. AD modulated GM tissue segments were used.

difference between the tissue volumes of the real vs. synthetic populations. The Bonferroni-corrected target p-value was 2.083e–05.

Table 2. Tissue volumes based on GIF's probabilistic tissue segmentations. Mean and standard deviations were rounded to the nearest 10^3. The bold values indicate the two-sided t-tests did not pass the statistical significance threshold compared to the real data.

Model	Dataset	Population	Gray Matter	White Matter	CSF	Deep Gray Matter
Real	UKB	Young	$595_{\pm 32}$	$460_{\pm 29}$	$280_{\pm 21}$	$40_{\pm 3}$
VQ-VAE (ours)	UKB	Young	$\mathbf{587_{\pm 24}}$	$\mathbf{472_{\pm 20}}$	$\mathbf{283_{\pm 11}}$	$40_{\pm 2}$
VAE	UKB	Young	$576_{\pm 1}$	$444_{\pm 1}$	$234_{\pm 1}$	$34_{\pm 0}$
Real	UKB	Old	$587_{\pm 31}$	$457_{\pm 29}$	$283_{\pm 22}$	$40_{\pm 3}$
VQ-VAE (ours)	UKB	Old	$\mathbf{576_{\pm 22}}$	$\mathbf{465_{\pm 20}}$	$310_{\pm 14}$	$\mathbf{39_{\pm 2}}$
VAE	UKB	Old	$560_{\pm 1}$	$434_{\pm 1}$	$250_{\pm 1}$	$33_{\pm 0}$
Real	UKB	Small ventricles	$596_{\pm 30}$	$462_{\pm 27}$	$270_{\pm 17}$	$41_{\pm 3}$
VQ-VAE (ours)	UKB	Small ventricles	$\mathbf{594_{\pm 19}}$	$\mathbf{477_{\pm 18}}$	$280_{\pm 12}$	$\mathbf{41_{\pm 2}}$
VAE	UKB	Small ventricles	$572_{\pm 1}$	$444_{\pm 1}$	$235_{\pm 1}$	$35_{\pm 0}$
Real	UKB	Big ventricles	$589_{\pm 34}$	$459_{\pm 30}$	$283_{\pm 19}$	$41_{\pm 3}$
VQ-VAE (ours)	UKB	Big ventricles	$574_{\pm 20}$	$\mathbf{467_{\pm 17}}$	$307_{\pm 15}$	$39_{\pm 2}$
VAE	UKB	Big ventricles	$570_{\pm 1}$	$442_{\pm 1}$	$246_{\pm 1}$	$34_{\pm 0}$
Real	ADNI	Cognitively normal	$530_{\pm 51}$	$430_{\pm 40}$	$309_{\pm 32}$	$40_{\pm 5}$
VQ-VAE (ours)	ADNI	Cognitively normal	$\mathbf{554_{\pm 19}}$	$\mathbf{458_{\pm 18}}$	$\mathbf{299_{\pm 12}}$	$\mathbf{39_{\pm 2}}$
VAE	ADNI	Cognitively Normal	$518_{\pm 5}$	$440_{\pm 4}$	$258_{\pm 3}$	$34_{\pm 1}$
Real	ADNI	Alzheimer's diseased	$526_{\pm 47}$	$443_{\pm 36}$	$330_{\pm 28}$	$38_{\pm 3}$
VQ-VAE (ours)	ADNI	Alzheimer's diseased	$\mathbf{532_{\pm 38}}$	$\mathbf{446_{\pm 20}}$	$298_{\pm 27}$	$\mathbf{37_{\pm 3}}$
VAE	ADNI	Alzheimer's diseased	$510_{\pm 5}$	$443_{\pm 4}$	$269_{\pm 4}$	$34_{\pm 1}$

Overall, no significant volume differences were found between real and VQ-VAE samples for most subgroups and tissue types, while significant differences were found for most VAE statistics, demonstrating that the proposed method strongly preserves tissue volumes. The CSF volumes of the VQ-VAE UKB small and big ventricle populations were found to be statistically significantly different from their real counterparts as shown in Table 2, following the VBM results from Fig. 2, and which could explain the increase in the t-statistic observed in the ventricular regions of the synthetic samples. On the other hand, the GM volumes were not statistically significantly different, corroborating the idea that the synthetic t-statistics are closer in magnitude to the real ones. Note that the VAE samples were also found not to be statistically significant in the ADNI AD/CT subset, but this is primarily due to the larger variance and the conservative Bonferroni correction.

5   Conclusion

In this work, we propose a scalable and high-resolution volumetric generative model of the brain that preserves morphology. VBM [22] and GIF [23] were used to assess the morphological preservation, while FID [12] and $bMMD^2$ [13] to measure distribution alignment between synthetic and real samples. We have shown that the synthetic samples preserve healthy and pathological morphology and that they are realistic images that closely align with the distribution of the real samples. Future work should address the lack of conditioning and the top 1% pruning to increase diversity and provide sampling control. Furthermore, the generative model could be extended for disease progression modelling, disentanglement of style and content, have its privacy preserving capabilities examined, and scaled to include multiple pathologies. To the best of our knowledge, this is the first morphologically preserving generative model of the brain, which paves the way for an unlimited amount of clinically viable data without jeopardizing patient privacy.

Acknowledgements. WHLP, MG, PB, MJC and PN are supported by Wellcome [WT213038/Z/18/Z]. PTD is supported by the EPSRC Research Council, part of the EPSRC DTP [EP/R513064/1]. FV is supported by Wellcome/ EPSRC Centre for Medical Engineering [WT203148/Z/16/Z], Wellcome Flagship Programme [WT213038/Z/18/Z], The London AI Centre for Value-based Healthcare and GE Healthcare. PB is also supported by Wellcome Flagship Programme [WT213038/Z/18/Z] and Wellcome EPSRC CME [WT203148/Z/16/Z]. PN is also supported by the UCLH NIHR Biomedical Research Centre. The models in this work were trained on NVIDIA Cambridge-1, the UK's largest supercomputer, aimed at accelerating digital biology.

6   Appendix

6.1   VQ-VAEs

The VQ-VAE model has a similar architecture with [33] but in 3D. The encoder uses strided convolutions with stride 2 and kernel size 4. There are four downsamplings in this VQ-VAE, giving the downsampling factor $f = 2^4$. After the downsampling layers, there are three residuals blocks ($3 \times 3 \times 3$ Conv, ReLU, $1 \times 1 \times 1$ Conv, ReLU). The decoder mirrors the encoder and uses transposed convolutions with stride 2 and kernel size 4. All convolution layers have 256 kernels. The β in Eq. 1 is 0.25 and the γ in Eq. 2 is 0.5. The codebook size was 2048 while each element's size was 32.

6.2   Transformers

Performer's[1] [19] has $L = 24$ layers, $d = 256$ embedding size, 16 multi-head attention modules (8 are local attention heads with window size of 420), and ReZero gating [34]. Before the raster style ordering input was RAS+ canonical voxel representation oriented.

---

[1] Implementation used: https://github.com/lucidrains/performer-pytorch.

6.3 Losses

VQ-VAE's pixel-space loss weight is 1.0, perceptual loss' weight is 0.001, frequency loss' weight is 1.0. The LPIPS uses AlexNet. Adam has been used as optimizer with an exponential decay of 0.99999. VQ-VAE's learning rate was 0.000165, discriminator's learning rate was 0.00005 and Performer's CrossEntropy learning rate was 0.001.

6.4 Datasets

All datasets have been split into training and testing sub-sets. The VQ-VAE UKB sub-sets had 31740 and 3970 subjects respectively, while VQ-VAE ADNI had 648 and 82. All datasets have been first processed with a rigid body registration such that they roughly fit the same field of view. Afterwards, all samples are passed through the following transformations before being fed into the VQ-VAE during training: first, they are being normalized to [0, 1], then tightly spatially cropped resulting in an image of size (160, 224, 160), random affine (rotation range 0.04, translation range 2, scale range 0.05), random contrast adjustment (gamma [0.99, 1.01]), random intensity shift (offsets [0.0, 0.05]), random Gaussian noise (mean 0.0, standard deviation 0.02), and finally, the images were thresholded to be in the range [0, 1.0]. For the Transformer, the UKB and ADNI datasets were split into sub-populations. UKB was split into small ventricles (6388 and 108), big ventricles (6321 and 156), young (6633 and 113), old (5137 and 106), while ADNI was split into cognitively normal (118 and 29) and Alzheimer's disease (151 and 36). For the Transformer training, each ADNI sample has been augmented 100 times and each augmentation's index-based representation was used for training it.

6.5 VBM Analysis

For the Voxel-Based Morphometry (VBM), Statistical Parametric Mapping (SPM) [35] package version 12.7486 was used with MATLAB R2019a. Before running the statistical tests, the images must first undergo unified segmentation where they were spatially normalized to a common template and simultaneously segmented into the Gray Matter (GM), White Matter (WM), and Cerebrospinal fluid (CSF) tissue segments based on prior probability maps and voxel intensities. The unified segmentation was done with the default parameters: Bias Regularisation (light regularisation 0.001), Bias FWHM (60 mm cutoff), MRF Parameter (1), Clean Up (Light Clean), Warping Regularisation ([0, 0.001, 0.5, 0.05, 0.2]), Affine Regularisation (ICBM space template - European brains), Smoothness (0), Sampling Distance (3). As per standard practice when using VBM, the group-aligned segmentations were modulated to preserve tissue volume, and a smoothing kernel was applied to the modulated tissue compartments to make the data conform to the Gaussian field model that underlines VBM and to increase the sensitivity to detect structural changes. The smoothing was also done with the default parameters with FWHM ([8, 8, 8]). For the VBM analysis, a Two-sample t-test Design was used, with the following parameters: Independence (Yes), Variance (Unequal), Grand mean scaling (No) and ANCOVA (No). No covariates, masking or global normalisation have been used.

Appendix F - Additional Samples

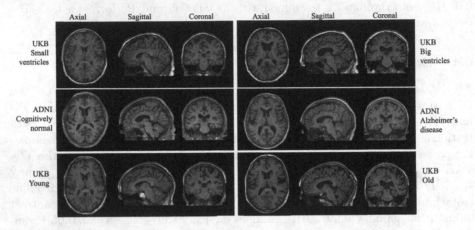

Fig. 3. Synthetic samples

References

1. Sudlow, C., et al.: UK biobank: an open access resource for identifying the causes of a wide range of complex diseases of middle and old age. PLoS Med. **12**(3) (2015)
2. Clifford, R., Jack Jr., et al.: The Alzheimer's disease neuroimaging initiative (ADNI): MRI methods. J. Magn. Reson. Imaging **27**(4), 685–691 (2008)
3. Simpson, A.L., et al.: A large annotated medical image dataset for the development and evaluation of segmentation algorithms. arXiv preprint arXiv:1902.09063 (2019)
4. Chong, C.K., Ho, E.T.W.: Synthesis of 3D MRI brain images with shape and texture generative adversarial deep neural networks. IEEE Access **9**, 64747–64760 (2021)
5. Lin, W., et al.: Bidirectional mapping of brain MRI and pet with 3D reversible GAN for the diagnosis of Alzheimer's disease. Front. Neurosci. **15**, 357 (2021)
6. Rusak, F., et al.: 3D Brain MRI GAN-based synthesis conditioned on partial volume maps. In: Burgos, N., Svoboda, D., Wolterink, J.M., Zhao, C. (eds.) SASHIMI 2020. LNCS, vol. 12417, pp. 11–20. Springer, Cham (2020). https://doi.org/10.1007/978-3-030-59520-3_2
7. Segato, A., et al.: Data augmentation of 3d brain environment using deep convolutional refined auto-encoding alpha GAN. IEEE Trans. Med. Robot. Bion. **3**(1), 269–272 (2020)
8. Kwon, G., Han, C., Kim, D.: Generation of 3D brain MRI using auto-encoding generative adversarial networks. In: Shen, D., et al. (eds.) MICCAI 2019. LNCS, vol. 11766, pp. 118–126. Springer, Cham (2019). https://doi.org/10.1007/978-3-030-32248-9_14
9. Xing, S., et al.: Cycle consistent embedding of 3D brains with auto-encoding generative adversarial networks. In: Medical Imaging with Deep Learning (2021)

10. Sun, L., et al.: Hierarchical amortized training for memory-efficient high resolution 3D GAN. arXiv preprint arXiv:2008.01910 (2020)
11. Wang, Z., et al.: Multiscale structural similarity for image quality assessment. In: The Thrity-Seventh Asilomar Conference on Signals, Systems & Computers, 2003, vol. 2, pp. 1398–1402. IEEE (2003)
12. Heusel, M., et al.: GANs trained by a two time-scale update rule converge to a local Nash equilibrium. In: Advances in Neural Information Processing Systems, vol. 30 (2017)
13. Gretton, A., et al.: A kernel two-sample test. J. Mach. Learn. Res. **13**(1), 723–773 (2012)
14. Razavi, A., et al.: Generating diverse high-fidelity images with VQ-VAE-2. In: Proceedings of the 33rd International Conference on Advances in Neural Information Processing Systems, vol. 32 (2019)
15. Esser, P., et al.: Taming transformers for high-resolution image synthesis. In: Proceedings of the IEEE/CVF Conference on Computer Vision and Pattern Recognition, pp. 12873–12883 (2021)
16. Yu, J., et al.: Vector-quantized image modeling with improved VQGAN. arXiv preprint arXiv:2110.04627 (2021)
17. Van Den Oord, A., Vinyals, O., et al.: Neural discrete representation learning. In: Proceedings of the 31st International Conference on Advances in Neural Information Processing Systems, vol. 30 (2017)
18. Vaswani, A., et al.: Attention is all you need. In: Advances in Neural Information Processing Systems, vol. 30 (2017)
19. Krzysztof, C., et al.: Rethinking attention with performers. In: Proceedings of ICLR (2021)
20. Jordon, J., et al.: Synthetic data-what, why and how? arXiv preprint arXiv:2205.03257 (2022)
21. Esteban, C., et al.: Real-valued (medical) time series generation with recurrent conditional GANs. arXiv preprint arXiv:1706.02633 (2017)
22. Ashburner, J., Friston, K.J.: Voxel-based morphometry-the methods. Neuroimage **11**(6), 805–821 (2000)
23. Cardoso, M.J., et al.: Geodesic information flows: spatially-variant graphs and their application to segmentation and fusion. IEEE Trans. Med. Imaging **34**(9):1976–1988 (2015)
24. Tay, V., et al.: Long range arena: a benchmark for efficient transformers. In: International Conference on Learning Representations (2020)
25. Graham, M.S., et al.: Transformer-based out-of-distribution detection for clinically safe segmentation. In: Conference on Medical Imaging with Deep Learning (2022)
26. Dhariwal, P., et al.: Jukebox: a generative model for music. arXiv preprint arXiv:2005.00341 (2020)
27. Zhang, R., et al.: The unreasonable effectiveness of deep features as a perceptual metric. In: Proceedings of the IEEE Conference on Computer Vision and Pattern Recognition, pp. 586–595 (2018)
28. Isola, P., et al.: Image-to-image translation with conditional adversarial networks. In: Proceedings of the IEEE Conference on Computer Vision and Pattern Recognition, pp. 1125–1134 (2017)
29. Mao, X., et al.: Least squares generative adversarial networks. In: Proceedings of the IEEE International Conference on Computer Vision, pp. 2794–2802 (2017)
30. Tudosiu, P.-D., et al.: Neuromorphologicaly-preserving volumetric data encoding using VQ-VAE. arXiv preprint arXiv:2002.05692 (2020)

31. Gulrajani, I., et al.: Improved training of Wasserstein GANs. In: Conference on Advances in Neural Information Processing Systems, vol. 30 (2017)
32. Ridgway, G.R., et al.: The problem of low variance voxels in statistical parametric mapping; a new hat avoids a 'haircut'. Neuroimage **59**(3), 2131–2141 (2012)
33. Pinaya, W.H.L., et al.: Unsupervised brain anomaly detection and segmentation with transformers. In: Conference on Medical Imaging with Deep Learning, pp. 596–617. PMLR (2021)
34. Bachlechner, T., et al.: ReZero is all you need: Fast convergence at large depth. In: Uncertainty in Artificial Intelligence, pp. 1352–1361. PMLR (2021)
35. Ashburner, J., et al.: SPM12 Manual. Wellcome Trust Centre for Neuroimaging, London (2014)

Can Segmentation Models Be Trained with Fully Synthetically Generated Data?

Virginia Fernandez(✉) [iD], Walter Hugo Lopez Pinaya [iD], Pedro Borges [iD],
Petru-Daniel Tudosiu [iD], Mark S. Graham [iD], Tom Vercauteren [iD],
and M. Jorge Cardoso [iD]

King's College London, London WC2R 2LS, UK
virginia.fernandez@kcl.ac.uk

Abstract. In order to achieve good performance and generalisability, medical image segmentation models should be trained on sizeable datasets with sufficient variability. Due to ethics and governance restrictions, and the costs associated with labelling data, scientific development is often stifled, with models trained and tested on limited data. Data augmentation is often used to artificially increase the variability in the data distribution and improve model generalisability. Recent works have explored deep generative models for image synthesis, as such an approach would enable the generation of an effectively infinite amount of varied data, addressing the generalisability and data access problems. However, many proposed solutions limit the user's control over what is generated. In this work, we propose brainSPADE, a model which combines a synthetic diffusion-based label generator with a semantic image generator. Our model can produce fully synthetic brain labels on-demand, with or without pathology of interest, and then generate a corresponding MRI image of an arbitrary guided style. Experiments show that brainSPADE synthetic data can be used to train segmentation models with performance comparable to that of models trained on real data.

1 Background

In recent years, there has been a growing interest in applying deep learning models to medical image segmentation. Indeed, Convolutional Neural Networks are a good surrogate for manual segmentation [29], which is time-consuming and requires anatomical and radiological expertise. However, deep learning models typically require large and heterogeneous training data to achieve good and generalisable results [16]. Yet, the access to sizeable medical imaging datasets is limited. Not only do they require specialised and costly equipment to acquire, but they are also subject to strict regulations, reduced accessibility, and complex maintenance in terms of data curation [27]. Even when these datasets are accessible, labels are often scarce and task-specific, increasing the domain shift between

---

Supplementary Information The online version contains supplementary material available at https://doi.org/10.1007/978-3-031-16980-9_8.

C. Zhao et al. (Eds.): SASHIMI 2022, LNCS 13570, pp. 79–90, 2022.
https://doi.org/10.1007/978-3-031-16980-9_8

datasets. A model which can generate images and associated labels with arbitrary contrasts and pathologies would democratise medical image segmentation research and improve model accuracy and generalisability.

Brain magnetic resonance imaging (MRI) datasets are heterogeneous as they tend to arise from a diversity of image acquisition protocols, and are partially labelled. As certain pathologies tend to be more perceptible in some MRI contrasts than others, different acquisition protocols are often followed depending on the nature of the study [1]. Furthermore, there is a significant lack of label consistency across datasets: namely, the annotated regions in any given dataset will be tailored to the study for which they were acquired [4].

To address the lack of comprehensive labelled data for many brain MRI segmentation tasks, domain adaptation (DA) and multi-task learning techniques can be used to create models that are robust to small or incomplete datasets [9,15]. Another approach is to augment the data by applying simple transformations on individual images or by modelling the data distribution along relevant directions of variability [2]. Generative modelling, typically using unsupervised learning methods [12], yields a representation of the input data distribution that does not require the user to have substantial prior knowledge about it. Some of these DL models are stochastic, allowing for continuous sampling of varied data, making them suitable for data augmentation. Such is the case for Generative Adversarial Networks (GANs) [12] and Variational Auto-Encoders (VAEs) [19]. In addition, some generative models allow for conditioning [6,24,25,31,33,34], opening the door to models that provide data as a function of the user's query.

Conditional generative models have been previously applied to augment data for brain MRI segmentation tasks [26], but they require non-synthetic input segmentation maps. To this end, we propose brainSPADE, a fully synthetic model of the neurotypical and diseased human brain, capable of generating unlimited paired data samples to train models for the segmentation of healthy regions and pathologies. Our model, brainSPADE is comprised of two sub-models: 1) a synthetic label generator; 2) a semantic image generator conditioned on the labels arising from the label generator. Our image generator provides the user with control over the content and contrast of the output images independently. We show that segmentation models trained on the fully synthetic data produced by the proposed generative model do not only generalise well to real data but also generalise to out-of-domain distributions.

2 Materials and Methods

2.1 Materials

Data: We trained our models on T1-weighted and FLAIR MRI images from several datasets, which all have been aligned to the MNI152-T1 template:

- Training of label generator: We used quality-controlled semi-automatically generated labels from a subset of 200 patients from the Southall and Brent Revisited cohort (SABRE) [18], and from a set of 128 patients from the Brain Tumour Segmentation Challenge (BRATS) [23]. Healthy labels were obtained using [5], and are in the form of partial volume (PV) maps of five anatomical regions: cerebrospinal fluid (CSF), white matter (WM), grey matter (GM), deep grey matter and brainstem. Tumour labels were provided with BRATS.
- Training the image generator: we used the images and associated labels from the same SABRE and BRATS datasets, plus a subset of 38 volumes from the Alzheimer's Disease Neuroimaging Initiative 2 (ADNI2) [3].
- Validation experiments: a hold-out set of the SABRE and BRATS datasets were used for validation, plus a subset of 30 FLAIR volumes from the Open Access Series of Imaging Studies (OASIS) [20] and 34 T1 volumes from the Autism Brain Imaging Data Exchange (ABIDE) dataset [21]. The labelling mechanism for all datasets was the same as for the training process [5] except for the BRATS tumour labels, where we used the challenge manual segmentations, and the ABIDE dataset, where the CSF, GM and WM labels were generated with SPM12 (version r7771, running on MATLAB R2019a).

Slicing Process: The proposed model works in 2D (192×256). For the healthy label generator, 7008 random label slices were sampled from SABRE, and for the lesion generator, 8636 label slices (2/3 containing at least 20 lesion tumour pixels, 1/3 containing none at all) were sampled from BRATS. For the image generator, 2765 random label slices and their equivalent multi-contrast images were sampled from SABRE, ADNI2, and BRATS. Only slices containing at least 10% of brain pixels were considered, leaving out the upper and lowermost slices.

The code for this work was written in PyTorch (1.10.2) and will be released upon publication. The networks were trained using an NVIDIA Quadro RTX 8000 GPU and an NVIDIA DGX SuperPOD cluster.

2.2 Methods

The full model, comprising label and image generators, is depicted in Fig. 1.
Label Generator: Segmentations contain the morphological characteristics of the patient, thus constituting Protected Health Information (PHI) [32] and requiring patient consent for sharing [11]. The development of a generative model of segmentations can, however, mitigate these. Segmentations are rich in phenotype information, but they lack local textures, making them challenging for standard generative models like GANs, by aggravating their considerable training instability.

To address the intrinsic limitations of GANs for label map generation, we chose to apply state-of-the-art latent diffusion models (LDMs), a generative model that samples noise from a Gaussian distribution and denoises it via a Markov chain process [14,28]. Coupled with a VAE, LDMs can become efficient and reliable generative models by performing the denoising process in the latent space. Based on [28], first, we train a spatial VAE with two downsamplings and a latent space dimension

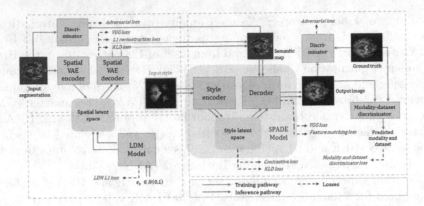

Fig. 1. brainSPADE pipeline: Random noise $e \in \mathcal{N}(0, \mathbf{I})$ is sampled by the LDM and incrementally denoised into a latent representation that the VAE decodes into a synthetic label. An image of the desired style is fed through the SPADE encoder, producing a latent style that, in combination with the semantic label, is decoded into the final image. Training losses have been annotated according to where they are used. Each dashed rectangle represents a different training stage.

of $48 \times 64 \times 3$, optimising the loss $L_{VAE} = D_{KLD}(E(l)\|\mathcal{N}(0, \mathbf{I})) + L_{perc.}(l, \hat{l}) + L_{adv}(D(l), D(\hat{l})) + L_{l1}(\hat{l}, l)$, where l is the input ground truth segmentation maps, $\hat{l}$ is the reconstructed probabilistic partial volume segmentation map, KLD is the Kullback-Leibler Distance (KLD) [19], L_{perc} is a perceptual loss, L_{adv} is an adversarial loss, computed using D, a patch-based discriminator based on [10] and L_{l1} is the L1-norm.

As a spatial VAE latent representation has a semantic context, it cannot be generated by sampling from a Gaussian distribution. Thus, an instance from that latent representation is sampled and denoised via the LDM model and then decoded with the VAE. The LDM model is based on a time-conditioned U-Net [28] with 1000 time steps. Similar to [14], we use a fixed variance and the reparametrized approach that predicts the added noise at each time step ϵ. An L1-loss between the added noise and the predicted added noise was used to optimise the model. Two different LDM models were trained on healthy and tumour-affected semantic label slices.

Image Generator: SPADE [25] is an image synthesis model that generates high-quality images from semantic maps. The network is a VAE-GAN, in which the encoder yields a latent space representation of an input style image conveying the desired style, which is then used by the decoder, along with the semantic map to create an output image. The semantic maps are fed via special normalisation blocks that imprint the desired content on the output at different upsampling levels. We trained SPADE using the original losses from [25]: an adversarial Hinge loss based on a Patch-GAN discriminator, a perceptual loss, a KLD loss, and a regulariser feature matching loss. The ground truths for the losses corresponded to images matching the content of the input semantic map and input style image. The weights of these losses were tuned empirically.

While the original SPADE model was found to produce high-quality outputs, the following limitations were identified:

1. The latent space encoding the styles is solely optimised with the KLD loss, with no specific clustering enforcement. In our scenario, the style images are MRI contrasts that link the appearance of tissue to its magnetic properties, and thus one needs to ensure that the latent space is clustered based on the contrast, and not on aspects such as the slice number.
2. SPADE is designed to accept categorical segmentations. However, previous work on MRI synthesis [30] shows that partial volume maps, that associate probability of belonging to each class to each pixel, result in finer details on the output images.
3. As explained previously, SPADE is designed to handle the style and content at different stages of the network. However, the original training process uses paired semantic maps and images to calculate the losses, making it impossible to rule out that the style latent space does not hold some information about the content of the output image.

To address limitation 1, we added two losses. First, a modality and dataset discrimination loss $L_{mod,dat}$, calculated by forward passing the generated images through a modality and dataset discriminator $D_{mod-dat}$ pre-trained on real data:

$$L_{mod,dat} = \alpha_{mod} \times BCE(mod_{\hat{i}}, mod_i) + \alpha_{dat} \times BCE(dat_{\hat{i}}, dat_i); \qquad (1)$$

where BCE is the binary cross entropy loss, mod and dat the modality and dataset (SABRE, ADNI2 etc.) predicted by $D_{mod-dat}$, $\hat{i}$ is the generated image and i its equivalent ground truth. We varied α_{mod} and α_{dat} across the training, always keeping $\alpha_{mod} > \alpha_{dat}$. Secondly, a contrastive learning loss on the latent space based on [7] is introduced as $L_{contrastive} = cosim(E_s(i), E_s(T(i)))$, where cosim is the cosine similarity index, E_s is the style encoder, i the input style image and T a random affine transformation implemented with MONAI [8].

Limitation 2 is addressed by replacing categorical labels by probabilistic partial volume maps, which we also used to train our label generator (see Sect. 2.2).

Finally, to address limitation 3, we enforce the separation of the style and content generation pipelines by using different brain slices from the same volume as the style image and semantic map during training.

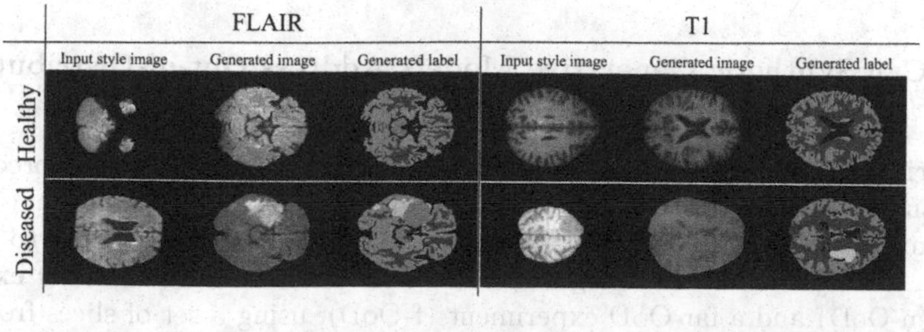

Fig. 2. Example synthetic labels and associated synthetic T1 and FLAIR images produced by our model for both our experiments, given an input style image.

Appendix A provides further information about the training process and hyperparameters. Generated neurotypical and diseased images from different modalities are displayed in Fig. 2.

2.3 Segmentation Network Used for the Experiments

For our segmentation experiment, we used trained instances of 2D nnU-Net [17] until convergence, keeping the default parameters and loss functions.

3 Experiments

To test whether fully synthetic datasets can be used to train segmentation models, we propose three experiments; training segmentation models on synthetic data for healthy tissue segmentation, out-of-distribution healthy tissue segmentation and tumour segmentation. All models are then tested on real data.

3.1 Can We Learn to Segment Healthy Regions Using Synthetic Data?

Experiment Set-Up: In this experiment, we train two models on T1 images to segment three regions, CSF, GM and WM: 1) R_{iod}, trained on 7008 paired data slices from SABRE, sampled from 180 volumetric subjects; and 2) S_{iod}, trained on 20000 synthetic partial volume maps and the corresponding generated images. The models were tested on a set of 25 holdout volumes from SABRE, and the Dice score was calculated for the volumes made up of the aggregated 2D segmentations performed by nnU-Net.

Results: Table 1 summarises the Dice scores per region obtained by both models on the test set. Example segmentations are depicted in Appendix B. We compared the results using a two-sided t-test. Even though for all regions the performance of R_{iod} was significantly better (p-value < 0.05), the Dice scores obtained for S_{iod} were comparable to performances achieved in the literature [22]. It is important to note that the ground truth labels used for R_{iod} and the ground truth labels for our test set were obtained with GIF, whereas the labels for S_{iod} were obtained using the label generator, potentially creating a gap between label distributions that could explain the difference in performance.

3.2 Can Synthetic Generative Models Address Out-of-Distribution Segmentation?

Experiment Set-Up: As an extension of Experiment 3.1, we explored the potential of our model when it comes to handling out-of-distribution (OoD) style images, as it is able to translate between modalities and capture, to some extent, the style of unseen images. For this, we performed a near-OoD experiment (n-OoD) and a far-OoD experiment (f-OoD), using a set of slices from 25

T1 ABIDE volumes (representing n-OoD) and a set of 25 OASIS FLAIR volumes (representing f-OoD) as test target datasets. Both R_{iod} and S_{iod} from 3.1 were tested on these datasets. We also trained models R_{n-ood} and R_{f-ood} on 580 slices from five paired volumes sourced from the targets n-OoD and f-OoD distributions, serving as a reference; and models S_{n-ood} and S_{n-ood}, on 20000 brainSPADE generated images, using the styles of unpaired images from the target n-OoD and f-OoD distributions during inference.

Table 1. Mean and standard deviations of Dice for each region, for experiment 3.1 (in-of-distribution (IoD)). Bold values represent statistically best performances.

Tissue dice	IoD (experiment 3.1)	
	R_{iod}	S_{iod}
CSF	**0.953 ± 0.008**	0.919 ± 0.023
GM	**0.952 ± 0.006**	0.925 ± 0.008
WM	**0.965 ± 0.005**	0.945 ± 0.006

Table 2. Mean and standard deviations of Dice for each region, for experiment 3.2 (out-of-distribution (OoD)). Bold values represent statistically best performances.

Experiment 3.2 Near out of distribution (n-OoD)				
Tissue	R_{iod}	S_{iod}	S_{n-ood}	R_{n-ood}
CSF	0.782 ± 0.002	0.825 ± 0.023	0.841 ± 0.017	**0.914 ± 0.022**
GM	0.774 ± 0.019	0.881 ± 0.008	0.895 ± 0.010	**0.971 ± 0.011**
WM	0.652 ± 0.036	0.873 ± 0.007	0.891 ± 0.007	**0.973 ± 0.009**
Experiment 3.2 Far out of distribution (f-OoD)				
Tissue	R_{iod}	S_{iod}	S_{f-ood}	R_{f-ood}
CSF	0.711 ± 0.042	0.736 ± 0.054	0.792 ± 0.034	**0.830 ± 0.050**
GM	0.531 ± 0.033	0.592 ± 0.033	0.784 ± 0.027	**0.826 ± 0.047**
WM	0.447 ± 0.180	0.433 ± 0.178	0.809 ± 0.031	**0.862 ± 0.038**

Results: The Dice scores obtained for the different structures are reported in Table 2. Example segmentations can be found in Appendix B. Both S_{iod} and R_{iod} experienced a drop in performance when tested on n-OoD and f-OoD data, whereas S_{n-ood} and S_{f-ood} were significantly better (p-value < 0.0001), with dice scores closer to those achieved by models trained on paired data from the target distributions, yet significantly lower. This shows that brainSPADE has some potential for domain adaptation.

3.3 Can We Learn to Segment Pathologies from Synthetic Data?

Experiment Set-Up: In this experiment, we train models on T1 and FLAIR images to segment tumours from a holdout set of sites from BRATS, unseen by brainSPADE. We trained three models: R_{les} on 1064 slices from 5 paired subjects belonging to the target set; S_{les} on 20000 sampled slices from brainSPADE, using the style of target T1 and FLAIR images; and H_{les}, combining both the training sets of R_{les} and S_{les}. The labels for S_{les} were sampled using lesion-conditioning, ensuring a balance between negative and positive samples. The resulting models were tested on 30 test volumes from the target dataset, similarly to 3.1 and 3.2, yielding dice scores on tumours, accuracy, precision and recall.

Results: The results are reported in Table 3, with visual examples available in Appendix B. The hybrid model achieved the top performance for all metrics, having significantly better recall than S_{les} and R_{les}.

Table 3. Mean and associated standard deviations of Dice, accuracy, precision and recall for the tumour segmentation task, for the four models. Bold values represent statistically best performances.

Model	R_{les}	S_{les}	H_{les}
Dice on tumour	0.813 ± 0.174	0.760 ± 0.187	0.876 ± 0.094
Accuracy	0.995 ± 0.007	0.994 ± 0.006	0.997 ± 0.002
Precision	0.878 ± 0.143	0.864 ± 0.124	0.921 ± 0.061
Recall	0.773 ± 0.209	0.713 ± 0.238	$\mathbf{0.852 \pm 0.137}$

4 Discussion and Conclusion

We have shown that brainSPADE, a fully-synthetic brain MRI generative model, can produce labelled datasets that can be used to train segmentation models that exhibit comparable performances to models trained using real data. The synthetic data generated by brainSPADE can not only replace real data for healthy tissue segmentation but also address pathological segmentation, as evidenced by Experiment 3.3. In addition, because the content pathway is completely separated from the style pathway in the generative pipeline, brainSPADE makes it possible to condition on unlabelled images, producing fully labelled datasets that can help train segmentation models with reasonable performance on that target distribution. The ability to replicate, to some extent, the style of an unseen dataset is shown in Experiment 2, where using OoD images as styles for brainSPADE results in a performance boost on that dataset.

These results open a promising pathway to tackle the lack of data in medical imaging segmentation tasks, where multi-modal synthetic data, conditioned by the user's specifications on the style and content, could not only help for data augmentation but compensate for the unavailability of paired training data.

In the future, our model could be fine-tuned on more modalities and patholo-gies, making it generalisable and capable of addressing more complex segmen-tation tasks, e.g. involving small or multiple lesions. Synthetic medical data has the advantage of not retaining any personal information on the patient, as it introduces variations on the original anatomy that should erase all traceability. Nonetheless, future work should analyse to what extent this model introduces variations on the training data and to what extent it retains it. This is key to, on the one hand, ensure that brainSPADE is stochastic and can produce an almost unlimited amount of data, and on the other hand, ensure that the training data cannot be retrieved from the model via model-inversion attacks [13], a critical point if generative models are used as a public surrogate for real medical data.

A   Training Set-Ups

A.1   Training brainSPADE

Training the Label Generator. We trained the VAE for 800 epochs using a learning rate of 5×10^{-5}, Adam optimizer ($\beta_1 = 0.99, \beta_2 = 0.999$) and a batch size of 256 in an NVIDIA DGX A100 node. The training time was approximately 8 hours. The LDM was trained for 1500 epochs, with a learning rate of 2.5×10^{-5}, Adam Optimizer ($\beta_1 = 0.99, \beta_2 = 0.999$) and a batch size of 384 in an NVIDIA DGX A100 node. The training time was approximately 15 hours.

Training the Image Generator. The weights that were used to balance the different losses were: $Ladv$: 1.0, L_{VGG} : 0.25, $Lfeature - matching$: 0.05, L_{KLD} : 0.001, $L_{contrastive}$: 1.0, $L_{mod-dat}$: $(0.1 - 2.5; 0.05 - 0.75)$. An expo-nentially decaying learning rate starting at 5×10^{-4} was used with an Adam Optimizer ($\beta_1 = 0.5, \beta_2 = 0.99$) for 4800 epochs. The training time was approx-imately 2 weeks, using a batch size of 6 in a NVIDIA Quadro RTX 8000 GPU.

For the training process we used the following MONAI augmentations [8]:

- Random bias field augmentation, with a coefficient range of 0.2–0.6.
- Random contrast adjustment, with a γ coefficient range of 0.85–1.25.
- Random gaussian noise addition, with $\mu = 0.0$ and σ range of 0.05–0.15.

The images were normalised using Z-normalisation.

A.2   Training Segmentation nnU-Nets

We used nnU-Net to perform all our segmentation experiments. nnU-Net per-forms automatic hyperparameter selection based on the task and input data; we downloaded the package from Github[1] and selected the '2d' training option. We modified the number of epochs to ensure convergence for all models.

B   Additional Figures

Figs. 3 and 4 show example segmentations from our experiments.

---

[1] https://github.com/MIC-DKFZ/nnUNet.git.

88   V. Fernandez et al.

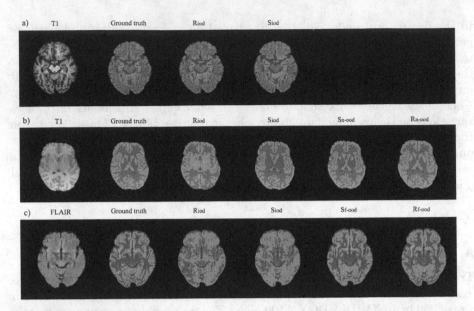

Fig. 3. Example segmentations for Experiments 3.1(a) and 3.2., near-OoD (b) and far-OoD (c); the segmented regions are CSF (red), GM (green) and WM (blue). (Color figure online)

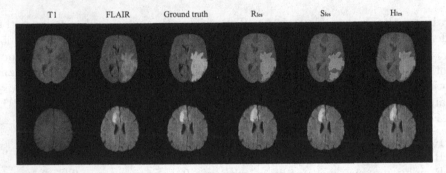

Fig. 4. Example segmentations for Experiment 3.3. From left to right: input T1 and FLAIR images, ground truth, and predictions of tumours made by our models R_{les}, S_{les} and H_{les}, highlighted in red. (Color figure online)

References

1. Abd-Ellah, M.K., et al.: A review on brain tumor diagnosis from MRI images: Practical implications, key achievements, and lessons learned. Magn. Reson. Imaging **61**, 300–318 (2019)
2. Acero, J.C., et al.: SMOD - data augmentation based on statistical models of deformation to enhance segmentation in 2D cine cardiac MRI. In: FIMH (2019)
3. ADNI: Alzheimer's Disease Neuroimaging Initiative. http://adni.loni.usc.edu/

4. Antonelli, M., et al.: The medical segmentation decathlon. Nat. Commun. **13**, 1 13(1), 1–13 (2022)
5. Cardoso, M.J., et al.: Geodesic information flows. Medical image computing and computer-assisted intervention: In: MICCAI ... International Conference on Medical Image Computing and Computer-Assisted Intervention, vol. 15, pp. 262–270 (2012). https://doi.org/10.1007/978-3-642-33418-4_33
6. Chen, D., et al.: StyleBank: an explicit representation for neural image style transfer. In: 2017 IEEE Conference on Computer Vision and Pattern Recognition (CVPR) (2017)
7. Chen, T., et al.: A simple framework for contrastive learning of visual representations. In: Proceedings of the 37th International Conference on Machine Learning, Vienna, Austria, PMLR (2020)
8. Consortium, M.: MONAI: Medical Open Network for AI, March 2020
9. Dorent, R., et al.: Learning joint segmentation of tissues and brain lesions from task-specific hetero-modal domain-shifted datasets. Med. Image Anal. **67** (2021)
10. Esser, P., et al.: Taming transformers for high-resolution image synthesis (2020)
11. European Commission: Regulation (EU) 2016/679 of the European Parliament and of the Council of 27 April 2016 on the protection of natural persons with regard to the processing of personal data and on the free movement of such data, and repealing Directive 95/46/EC (General Data Protection Regulation) (Text with EEA relevance) (2016), https://eur-lex.europa.eu/eli/reg/2016/679/oj
12. Goodfellow, I.J., et al.: Generative adversarial nets. In: Proceedings of the 27th International Conference on Neural Information Processing, Systems - Volume 2 NIPS 2014, pp. 2672–2680. MIT Press, Cambridge (2014)
13. Hidano, S., et al.: Model inversion attacks for prediction systems: without knowledge of non-sensitive attributes. In: 2017 15th PST Annual Conference, pp. 115–11509 (2017)
14. Ho, J., et al.: Denoising diffusion probabilistic models. In: Advances in Neural Information Processing Systems 33 (NeurIPS 2020) (2020)
15. Huo, Y., et al.: SynSeg-Net: synthetic segmentation without target modality ground truth. IEEE Trans. Med. Imaging **38**(4), 1016–1025 (2019)
16. Goodfellow, I., Bengio, Y., et al.: Deep Learning Book. Deep Learning. MIT Press, London (2015)
17. Isensee, F.: Jothers: nnU-Net: a self-configuring method for deep learning-based biomedical image segmentation. Nat. Methods **18**(2), 203–211 (2021)
18. Jones, S., et al.: Cohort Profile Update: Southall and Brent Revisited (SABRE) study: a UK population-based comparison of cardiovascular disease and diabetes in people of European, South Asian and African Caribbean heritage. Int. J. Epidemiol. **49**(5), 1441–1442e (2020)
19. Kingma, D.P., Welling, M.: Auto-Encoding Variational Bayes. CoRR (2014)
20. LaMontagne, P.J., et al.: OASIS-3: longitudinal Neuroimaging, clinical, and cognitive dataset for normal aging and Alzheimer disease. medRxiv p. 2019.12.13.19014902 (2019)
21. Martino, A., et al.: The autism brain imaging data exchange: towards a large-scale evaluation of the intrinsic brain architecture in autism. Mol. Psychiatry **10**, 659–667 (2013)
22. Mendrik, A.M., et al.: MRBrainS challenge: online evaluation framework for brain image segmentation in 3T MRI scans. Comput. Intell. Neurosci. **2015** (2015)
23. Menze, B.H., et al.: The multimodal brain tumor image segmentation benchmark (BRATS). IEEE Trans. Med. Imaging **34**(10), 1993–2024 (2015)

24. van den Oord, A., et al.: Neural discrete representation learning. In: Proceedings of the 31st International Conference on Neural Information Processing, Systems, NIPS 2017, pp. 6309–6318, Curran Associates Inc., Red Hook (2017)
25. Park, T., et al.: Semantic image synthesis with spatially-adaptive normalization. In: Proceedings of IEEE CVPR 2019-June, pp. 2332–2341 (2019)
26. Qasim, A.B., et al.: Red-GAN: attacking class imbalance via conditioned generation. Yet another medical imaging perspective. In: Arbel, T., Ben Ayed, I., de Bruijne, M., Descoteaux, M., Lombaert, H., Pal, C. (eds.) Proceedings of the Third Conference on Medical Imaging with Deep Learning. Proceedings of Machine Learning Research, vol. 121, pp. 655–668. PMLR (2020)
27. Rieke, N., et al.: The future of digital health with federated learning. NPJ Digit. Med. **3**(1), 119 (2020)
28. Rombach, R., et al.: High-resolution image synthesis with latent diffusion models (2021)
29. Ronneberger, O., Fischer, P., Brox, T.: U-Net: convolutional networks for biomedical image segmentation. In: Navab, N., Hornegger, J., Wells, W.M., Frangi, A.F. (eds.) MICCAI 2015. LNCS, vol. 9351, pp. 234–241. Springer, Cham (2015). https://doi.org/10.1007/978-3-319-24574-4_28
30. Rusak, F., et al.: 3D Brain MRI GAN-based synthesis conditioned on partial volume maps. In: Burgos, N., Svoboda, D., Wolterink, J.M., Zhao, C. (eds.) SASHIMI 2020. LNCS, vol. 12417, pp. 11–20. Springer, Cham (2020). https://doi.org/10.1007/978-3-030-59520-3_2
31. Shi, Y., et al.: Retrieval-based spatially adaptive normalization for semantic image synthesis (2022)
32. Wachinger, C., et al.: BrainPrint: a discriminative characterization of brain morphology. NeuroImage **109**, 232–248 (2015)
33. Wang, X., Gupta, A.: Generative image modeling using style and structure adversarial networks. In: Leibe, B., Matas, J., Sebe, N., Welling, M. (eds.) ECCV 2016. LNCS, vol. 9908, pp. 318–335. Springer, Cham (2016). https://doi.org/10.1007/978-3-319-46493-0_20
34. Zhu, P., Abdal, R., Qin, Y., Wonka, P.: SEAN: image synthesis with semantic region-adaptive normalization. In: Proceedings of the IEEE Computer Society Conference on Computer Vision and Pattern Recognition, pp. 5103–5112 (2019)

Multimodal Super Resolution with Dual Domain Loss and Gradient Guidance

Anitha Priya Krishnan(✉) , Roshan Reddy Upendra , Aniket Pramanik,
Zhuang Song, Richard A. D. Carano,
and the Alzheimer's Disease Neuroimaging Initiative

Data Analytics and Imaging, Pharma Personalized Healthcare, Genentech Inc.,
South San Francisco, CA 94080, USA
krishnan.anithapriya@gene.com

Abstract. Spatial resolution plays a crucial role in quantitative assessment of various structures in brain MRI. Super resolution (SR) as a post-processing tool holds promise for restoring the high frequency details lost in a low resolution (LR) acquisition with no additional scan time. Prior multicontrast deep learning SR approaches are mostly in 2D and operate in a pre-upsampling or progressive setting. Here we propose an efficient shallow 3D projection based post-upsampling network for anisotropic SR of brain MRI. The network is optimized using losses in the spatial and frequency domains and a complementary high resolution (HR) input to inform SR of the low resolution (LR) input with tighter integration of features. We investigated the benefit of different feature aggregation strategies such as concatenation and multiplicative attention and gradient guidance from the HR target or the additional HR input. The models were trained and evaluated on diverse datasets and performed comparably with MINet, another recently developed multimodal SR model, with approximately half the number of model parameters. The model generalized well to an external test set; performed satisfactorily on acquired LR MRI volumes despite the LR input being simulated from HR volumes during training and resulted in lower high frequency error norm. From the ablation studies, we note that a multimodal network noticeably improves SR compared to a unimodal network and feature aggregation using concatenation and multiplicative attention performed equally well. We also highlight the leakage of information from the complementary HR input to the SR output volume and the limited value of PSNR and SSIM as evaluation metrics in such cases.

Keywords: Super resolution · Multimodal · Deep learning ·
Fourier-domain loss · Gradient guidance · Magnetic Resonance Imaging

1 Introduction

Magnetic Resonance Imaging (MRI) of the brain is widely used in clinic for assessing various neurological disorders. The routinely acquired T1-weighted

R. R. Upendra and A. Pramanik–Work done as Roche Advanced Analytics Network intern.

(T1w) and T2-weighted (T2w) MRI sequences require varying scan times. For disease management in Alzheimer's disease (AD) and Multiple Sclerosis (MS), it is common to acquire a high resolution (HR) T1w MRI with isotropic 1mm resolution and a lower resolution (LR) T2w and/or T2w fluid attenuated inversion recovery (FLAIR) MRI with similar in-plane resolution but increased slice thickness. The spatial resolution of the acquired scans plays an important role in the performance of the downstream analysis such as atrophy and lesion quantification. The LR volumes are frequently interpolated to match the HR acquisition during such analysis. However, such upsampling does not add the missing high-frequency information. Hence, super resolution (SR) methods are needed to enhance the quality of the acquired LR MRI.

Recently, deep learning models have been developed for single image SR (SISR) of brain MRI [1–5]. Residual learning is a popular strategy among these models [2–4] to alleviate the degradation of high frequency details with deep networks by using skip connections locally and/or globally. These methods operate on 2D [3–5] or 3D [1,2] patches but frequently upsample the LR input images with bicubic interpolation. Such pre-upsampling SR approaches significantly increases the memory requirements for 3D models. Models that refine features at LR have been developed for brain MRI in 2D [3,6] and not 3D.

SISR models trained with voxel-wise loss in the image domain while improving the signal-to-noise ratio (SNR) frequently fail to capture the finer details. Gradient guidance has been investigated to improve the reconstruction of high frequency information in SR of brain MRI using image based [7] or DL approaches [8]. Ma et al., combined gradient guidance with generative adversarial networks for SR to reduce fine structural distortions by explicitly reconstructing gradients in HR along with an associated loss on the gradient maps [9] and Guo et al., combined it with a dual reconstruction network that learns the reverse LR mapping [10]. Complementary information from multimodal MRI have been used by concatenation of additional HR image at the input level [2] in pre-upsampling models and by using fusion modules along multiple stages of the network [11] or at an intermediary level that feeds into a refinement sub-network in post-upsampling methods [12]

Here, we propose a 3D variant of deep back-projection network (DBPN) [13] modified to work with multimodal inputs in a post-upsampling setting, which increases memory efficiency. In addition to extending the model with 3D kernels, our main contributions are: 1) inclusion of a reverse mapping module using the features from down-sampling blocks; 2) dual domain losses in frequency and spatial domains; 3) addition of a separate branch to extract and combine relevant features from a complementary HR input at multiple points in the network either by concatenation or multiplicative attention; and 4) gradient guidance by adding a loss term on the estimated edge maps from super resolved images and the high resolution target or the complementary HR input. We hypothesize that this tight integration of features will enable better reconstruction of high frequency information under the assumption that the edge maps from the two input images are similar. We evaluate this architecture for SISR by 3X

of anisotropic T2w-FLAIR brain MRI and investigate the effect of using HR
T1w-MPRAGE to inform SR with and without gradient guidance. Besides peak
SNR (PSNR) and structural similarity index (SSIM) [14], we investigated other
metrics for quantifying restoration of subtle details.

2   Materials and Methods

SISR aims to estimate a HR image (y) from a LR image (x). It is an ill-posed
problem because a LR image could correspond to multiple HR solutions.

$$\boldsymbol{x} = D(B * \boldsymbol{y}) + \varepsilon = g_\theta \boldsymbol{y} + \boldsymbol{\varepsilon}; g_\theta = DB \tag{1}$$

$$\boldsymbol{y} = f_w(\boldsymbol{x}) - \boldsymbol{\varepsilon} \tag{2}$$

The LR image is modeled by (1), where D denotes the downsampling oper-
ation, B is the blur operator, ε is the additive noise and g_θ is the mapping from
HR to LR parametrized by θ. The HR image is modeled by (2) where f_w is the
mapping from LR to HR parametrized by w. Learning based approaches determine an optimal w by minimizing a loss function between the reconstructed and
acquired target HR images. Here, 3D DBPN is used to estimate this mapping.

Network Architecture: DBPN uses iterative up and down projection blocks,
where the projection blocks implement error-correction by iteratively feeding
the projection error forward and backward [13]. Here we extend the model to
3D (Fig. 1). The feature extraction module in the main branch uses $3 \times 3 \times 3$
and $1 \times 1 \times 1$ filters to obtain 32 feature maps in LR. Similar to the original
implementation, we used convolutional and transposed convolutional layers followed by parametric rectified linear units (pReLU) with no batch normalization
layers. For a scale factor of three along the slice dimension (z) we used $7 \times 7 \times 7$
kernels with an anisotropic stride of $1 \times 1 \times 3$. Dense projection units were used
to facilitate easier propagation of gradients. We chose to use a shallow network
with 2 repeats of dense up and down projection units as the deeper versions of
DBPN in [6,13] did not improve the PSNR and SSIM notably. A LR volume
was reconstructed from the concatenated LR features from the down-projection
units and the projection layer in the extraction module, thereby providing reverse
mapping.

For multicontrast SISR, we added another branch for extraction of the relevant features from HR images and combined them with features from the main
LR branch at multiple locations either by concatenation (unidirectional flow of
information from HR complementary input to main LR branch) or by multiplicative attention (MA) (opposed to [11], bidirectional flow of information from
HR complementary input to main LR branch and vice-versa).

$$F_0^{T1w} = F_{t-1}^{T1w} = F_t^{T1w} \tag{3}$$

$$F_t^{T1w} = F_{t-1}^{T1w}(1 + \sigma(conv_{1 \times 1}(F_t^{up}))) \tag{4}$$

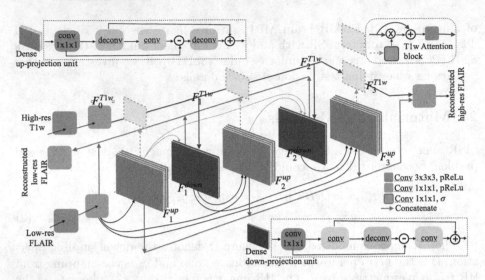

Fig. 1. Architecture of multimodal (MM) DBPN with reverse mapping and a separate branch for extraction and combination of relevant features from another high-resolution input.

where F represents the feature maps, σ is the sigmoid activation, (3) is for combining by concatenation, where the initial extracted features F_0^{T1w} are passed to subsequent stages without additional processing and (4) is for combining with multiplicative attention.

Loss Functions: The networks were trained with L1 loss on both the LR and HR reconstructed volumes in the image domain and weighted L1 loss on the discrete Fourier transform (DFT) coefficients of the model reconstruction and the HR target as introduced in [15] to better capture the high frequency information. The inverse weighting of the Fourier loss with the distance from the center of k-space with low frequencies prevents the amplification of noise. As downsampling of an image corresponds to truncation in the Fourier domain, we used a modified version of Fourier loss function that linearly weights this truncated regions more. For multimodal inputs, we included a loss term that minimizes the L1 loss between the estimated Sobel edges of the reconstructed HR and target HR volume or the additional HR input for gradient guidance.

$$
L_{SR} = \frac{1}{M} \sum_{i=1}^{M} (\alpha \| f_1(\boldsymbol{x}_i) - \boldsymbol{x}_i \|_1 + \beta \| f_2(\boldsymbol{x}_i) - \boldsymbol{y}_i \|_1
$$
$$
+ \gamma \sum_{k=1}^{\frac{N}{2}} \frac{|\hat{\boldsymbol{\mu}}_{ik} - \hat{\boldsymbol{\nu}}_{ik}|^2}{|k|^2} + \eta \| G(f_2(\boldsymbol{x}_i)) - G(\boldsymbol{y}_i) \|_1)
$$
(5)

where M is number of patches in the training set, $\hat{\mu}$ is the DFT coefficient of the reconstructed HR patch, $\hat{\nu}$ is the DFT coefficient of the target HR patch, k is the distance from the center of k-space, G is the Sobel operator in 3D, f_1 is the LR mapping learned from the initial and concatenated down-projection features and f_2 is the forward HR mapping learned from concatenated up-projection and HR complementary input features.

During inference, larger overlapping patches of the input LR FLAIR and HR T1w were forward propagated through the network and stitched with weighted averaging in the overlapping sections. The HR FLAIR or T1w MRI used for gradient guidance is required during training only and not during inference.

3 Experiments

MRI Datasets and Preprocessing: The models were trained on three MRI datasets from patients with AD or MS with T1w and FLAIR sequences acquired with 1mm resolution. For the first dataset, we selected a subset of 142 patients with MS from the UkBioBank [20]. T1w and T2w FLAIR MRI were acquired sagitally with a 3D MPRAGE and SPACE sequence respectively on a Siemens 3T scanner. The second dataset included baseline datasets of 235 patients and a few follow-ups at first year from the Alzheimer's Disease Neuroimaging Initiative (ADNI3)[1]. The MRI datasets were acquired from various scanners and multiple sites but with a standardized protocol. The final real-world (RW) dataset (Flywheel MS, n = 27) was obtained from a novel patient centered study of patients with MS in the US across multiple sites. The training dataset (n = 15) from the MS lesion segmentation challenge [21] was used as the external test set. The LR volumes for training were simulated by: downsampling HR volumes by a scale factor of 3 after gaussian blurring similar to the degradation in [12] or truncating k-space along Z by multiplication with a rect function as in [1,5] but without the anti-ringing Fermi filter [5] and adding gaussian noise at 2–5% of the maximum intensity in the LR volume. The performance on acquired LR FLAIR volumes was assessed qualitatively on a subset (n = 25) of patients from the phase IIIb CHORDS study[2] study with varying lesion loads.

The ADNI3, Flywheel and CHORDS datasets were minimally processed for N4 bias field correction, rigid registration of T1w volumes to FLAIR and skull stripping, with all preprocessing performed using advanced normalization toolkit [22]. We used the preprocessed datasets provided by UKBioBank and MICCAI challenge. A 30% split acted as the internal test-set (n = 136) and the models were trained with a three fold cross-validation with splits at the patient level on the remaining 70%.

Experimental Setup: The models were implemented in Pytorch 1.7.1 [16] and trained with 8 NVIDIA Tesla GPUs with 16GB memory each for 25 epochs on

---

[1] http://adni.loni.usc.edu/adni-3/.
[2] https://clinicaltrials.gov/ct2/show/NCT02637856.

Table 1. Performance comparison of various approaches for 3x anisotropic SISR. MA-multiplicative attention, GG-gradient guidance, HFEN-high frequency error norm

Model/approach	Test set	PSNR↑	SSIM↑	HFEN↓
Bicubic	Internal	27.691 ± 1.328	0.824 ± 0.025	0.451 ± 0.065
	External	28.843 ± 2.477	0.885 ± 0.022	0.458 ± 0.053
MINet [11]	Internal	26.554 ± 2.826	0.883 ± 0.041	0.37 ± 0.131
	External	27.211 ± 2.960	0.907 ± 0.032	0.309 ± 0.100
MA-GG$_{T1w}$	Internal	26.967 ± 2.090	0.890 ± 0.024	0.293 ± 0.068
	External	27.66 ± 2.792	0.912 ± 0.015	0.276 ± 0.037
MA-GG$_{FLAIR}$	Internal	27.283 ± 2.111	0.899 ± 0.023	0.255 ± 0.050
	External	28.039 ± 2.789	0.919 ± 0.015	0.265 ± 0.029

3D patches. The model had 5.4 million parameters and training on one fold took 22 h. The parameters $\alpha, \beta, \gamma, \eta$ were empirically set to 100, 100, 1 and 500 respectively for having a good representation of the various loss terms. The patches were augmented on the fly during batch generation using affine transformations or elastic deformations. The model weights were optimized using Adam optimizer with an initial learning rate of 1e−4. PSNR, SSIM and high frequency error norm (HFEN) [17] were used as evaluation metrics.

$$\zeta_{HFEN} = \frac{\|LoG(F(\boldsymbol{x})) - LoG(\boldsymbol{y})\|_2}{\|LoG(\boldsymbol{y})\|_2} \tag{6}$$

where LoG is the Laplacian of Gaussian filter with a standard deviation of 1.5 voxels. In a few cases, we looked into Fourier radial error spectrum plots (ESP) [18], which plots the error variations with spatial frequencies to further characterize the reconstruction quality. As shown in [11] and in our ablation studies below, multimodal SR approaches perform better than unimodal SR approaches. Hence, we compared our model performance against MINet [11], which is another multimodal super resolution network, on the test-set using the same evaluation metrics. MINet used pixelshuffle layer [19] for learned upsampling of the initial extracted features in LR and as this layer in Pytorch used isotropic scale factors, we replaced it with a transposed convolution layer with 7×7 kernel and a stride of 1×3 for anisotropic upsampling. The resulting model with 10.7 million parameters was trained for SISR along sagittal planes using the default parameter settings.

Results: The performance of the MM DBPN with gradient guidance from the HR target FLAIR and the complementary HR T1w is summarized in Table 1, where the mean and standard deviation are provided. While the DL models improved the SSIM considerably compared to bicubic interpolation in both internal and external test sets, the PSNR decreased marginally. For gradient guidance, using HR FLAIR was nominally better than using HR T1w input.

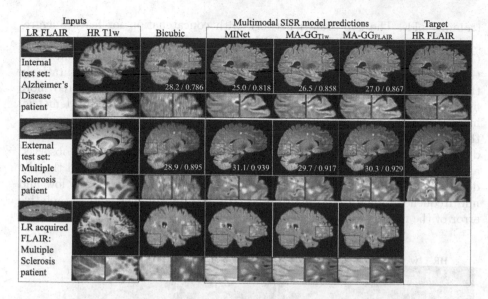

Fig. 2. Representative examples of super resolution of LR FLAIR MRI with HR T1w MRI as the complementary input. PSNR/SSIM values for reconstructed volumes provided. MA-multiplicative attention, GG-gradient guidance

Our MM DBPN models performed marginally better than MINet in improving PSNR and SSIM and consistently decreased HFEN indicating the restoration of fine structural details. The performance on the internal test set is reduced compared to the external test set perhaps due to the higher variability in MRI acquisition. The models performed comparably across the AD and MS disease populations as can be seen in the qualitative results provided in Fig. 2. From the magnified ROIs shown in the bottom panel, we see that the models effectively denoise the images improving the contrast for lesions compared to bicubic interpolated volumes and faithfully adds more fine details in the reconstruction.

Table 2. Ablation studies of 3D DBPN evaluated on the internal test set with gradient guidance from HR target FLAIR volumes. Concat-concatenation, MA-multiplicative attention, Agg-aggregation, GG-gradient guidance, HFEN-high frequency error norm

# branches	Agg	GG	PSNR↑	SSIM↑	HFEN↓
One	-	No	27.117 ± 1.858	0.880 ± 0.022	0.276 ± 0.061
Two	Concat	No	28.079 ± 2.100	0.905 ± 0.023	0.222 ± 0.059
Two	Concat	Yes	26.850 ± 2.041	0.886 ± 0.024	0.274 ± 0.051
Two	MA	Yes	26.942 ± 2.109	0.871 ± 0.022	0.268 ± 0.046

Ablation Studies: To understand the contributions of the various components of the network and loss functions, we performed ablation studies on one of the training folds. The two branch network with concatenation for feature aggregation improved both PSNR and SSIM compared to the one branch network (Table 2). Inclusion of gradient guidance along the main branch and multiplicative attention reduced the overall performance slightly. However qualitatively the addition of gradient guidance and multiplicative attention recovered more fine details (Fig. 3), which was not reflected in either PSNR or SSIM metric, highlighting the need for better metrics to quantify such improvements. From the Fourier ESP we notice that: all DL models have difficulty in capturing the dynamic range of image intensities, lowering the mean values which is observed as the synchronous drop close to the center of k-space (radius $= 0$) and thereby decreasing PSNR; the constant error may be due to denoising in the low and mid frequency ranges that are also present in the LR volumes; and the relative error of the models variants differ mainly for high frequencies.

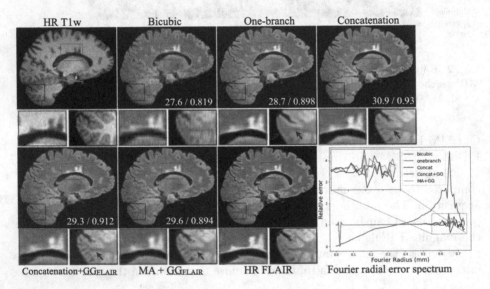

Fig. 3. Ablation studies - effect of complementary input, gradient guidance (GG) and aggregation strategy (Concat - concatenation, MA-multiplicative attention). PSNR/SSIM values for reconstructed volumes provided. Red arrow - edge leakage from T1w to FLAIR; Brown arrow - better reconstruction of edges (Color figure online)

4   Discussion and Conclusion

We have developed an efficient two branch DBPN network for improved anisotropic SISR of 3D brain MRI. Despite training on simulated LR inputs, qualitative evaluation showed that the models performed satisfactorily on acquired LR FLAIR volumes. While there was a clear advantage in using additional information from a complementary HR input, the various aggregation and gradient guidance strategies were equally successful. When using the T1w MRI for gradient guidance, we assume the edge information to be the same as in LR FLAIR MRI. However, this assumption is violated in cases with lesions where their appearance is dissimilar or in some brain regions. We note that the information from T1w MRI leaks into the reconstructed HR FLAIR volumes in the multimodal SISR models. The reduction in SSIM and PSNR in models where the T1w features are more integrated with gradient guidance and multiplicative attention could potentially be driven by this contamination from the complementary input. Hence care must be taken to when choosing the complementary input.

In addition to PSNR and SSIM, we show the utility of HFEN and Fourier ESP as error metrics that provide more insight into reconstruction quality. The models were developed on datasets with standardized protocols for a single scale factor. Extending the networks to multiple scale factors has to be done in a progressive fashion as the convolution operations were designed for a specific scale factor. Future work will involve evaluating the effect of SR on downstream tasks and training the model with non-standardized MRI acquisitions.

Acknowledgement. Aniket Pramanik and Roshan Reddy Upendra were supported by Roche Advanced Analytics Network internship program. Data used in the preparation of this article were also obtained from the Alzheimer's Disease Neuroimaging Initiative (ADNI) database (adni.loni.usc.edu) and the UK Biobank.

References

1. Chen, Y., Xie, Y., Zhou, Z., Shi, F., Christodoulou, AG., Li, D.: Brain MRI super resolution using 3D deep densely connected neural networks. In: IEEE 15th International Symposium on Biomedical Imaging (ISBI 2018), pp. 739–742 (2018)
2. Pham, CH., et al.: Multiscale brain MRI super-resolution using deep 3D convolutional networks. Comput. Med. Imaging Graph. **77**, Article 101647 (2019)
3. Shi, J., et al.: MR image super-resolution via wide residual networks with fixed skip connection. IEEE J. Biomed. Heal. Inform. **3**(23), 1129–1140 (2019)
4. Du, J., et al.: Super-resolution reconstruction of single anisotropic 3D MR images using residual convolutional neural network. Neurocomputing **392**, 209–220 (2020)
5. Zhao, C., Dewey, B.E., Pham, D.L., Calabresi, P.A., Reich, D.A., Prince, J.L.: SMORE: a self-supervised anti-aliasing and super-resolution algorithm for MRI using deep learning. IEEE Trans. Med. Imaging **340**, 805–817 (2021)
6. Feng, C.M., Wang, K., Lu, S., Xu, Y., Li, X.: Brain MRI super-resolution using coupled-projection residual network. Neurocomputing **456**, 190–199 (2021)
7. Sui, Y., Afacan, O., Gholipour, A., Warfield, S.K.: Isotropic MRI super-resolution reconstruction with multi-scale gradient field prior. In: Shen, D., et al. (eds.) MICCAI 2019. LNCS, vol. 11766, pp. 3–11. Springer, Cham (2019). https://doi.org/10.1007/978-3-030-32248-9_1
8. Sui, Y., Afacan, O., Gholipour, A., Warfield, S.K.: Learning a gradient guidance for spatially isotropic MRI super-resolution reconstruction. In: Martel, A.L., et al. (eds.) MICCAI 2020. LNCS, vol. 12262, pp. 136–146. Springer, Cham (2020). https://doi.org/10.1007/978-3-030-59713-9_14
9. Ma, C., Rao, Y., Cheng, Y., Chen, C., Lu, J., Zhou, J.: Structure-preserving super resolution with gradient guidance. In: Proceedings of IEEE Computer Society Conference on Computer Vision and Pattern Recognition, pp. 7766–7775 (2020)

10. Guo, Y., et al.: Dual Reconstruction Nets for Image Super-Resolution with Gradient Sensitive Loss. arXiv:1809.07099, (2018)

11. Feng, CM., Fu, H., Yuan, S., Xu, Y.: Multi-contrast MRI super-resolution via a multi-stage integration network. In: International Conference on Medical Image Computing and Computer Assisted Intervention (MICCAI 2021), pp. 140–149 (2021)

12. Zeng, K., Zheng, H., Cai, C., Yang, Y., Zhang, K., Chen, Z.: Simultaneous single- and multi-contrast super-resolution for brain MRI images based on a convolutional neural network. Comput. Biol. Med. **99**, 133–141 (2018)

13. Haris, M., Shakhnarovich, G., Ukita, N.: Deep back-projection networks for super-resolution. In: IEEE Conference on Computer Vision and Pattern Recognition (CVPR), pp. 1664–1673 (2018)

14. Wang, Z., Bovik, A.C., Sheikh, H.R., Simoncelli, E.P.: Image quality assessment: from error measurement to structural similarity. IEEE Trans. Image Process. **13**(1), 600–612 (2004)

15. Auricchio, G., Codegoni, A., Gualandi, S., Zambon, L.: The Fourier Loss Function. arXiv:2102.02979 (2021)

16. Paszke, A., et al.: PyTorch: an imperative style, high-performance deep learning library. In: Advances in Neural Information Processing Systems, vol. 32, pp. 8024–8035. Curran Associates, Inc. (2019)

17. Ravishankar, S., Bresler, Y.: MR image reconstruction from highly undersampled k-space data by dictionary learning. IEEE Trans. Med. Imaging **305**, 1028–1041 (2011)

18. Kim, T.H., Haldar, J.P.: The fourier radial error spectrum plot: a more nuanced quantitative evaluation of image reconstruction quality. In: IEEE 15th International Symposium on Biomedical Imaging, pp. 61–64 (2018)

19. Shi, W., et al.: Real-time single image and video super-resolution using an efficient sub-pixel convolutional neural network. In: IEEE Conference on Computer Vision and Pattern Recognition (CVPR 2016), pp. 1874–1883 (2016)

20. Miller, K.L., et al.: Multimodal population brain imaging in the UK Biobank prospective epidemiological study. Nat. Neurosci. **19**(11), 1523–1536 (2016)

21. Commowick, O., et al. Objective evaluation of multiple sclerosis lesion segmentation using a data management and processing infrastructure. Sci. Rep. **8**, 13650 (2018)

22. Avants, B.B., Tustison, N.J., Stauffer, M., Song, G., Wu, B., Gee, J.C.: The insight ToolKit image registration framework. Front. Neuroinform. **8**, 44 (2014)

Brain Lesion Synthesis via Progressive Adversarial Variational Auto-Encoder

Jiayu Huo[1(✉)], Vejay Vakharia[2], Chengyuan Wu[3], Ashwini Sharan[3], Andrew Ko[4], Sébastien Ourselin[1], and Rachel Sparks[1]

[1] School of Biomedical Engineering and Imaging Sciences (BMEIS), King's College London, London, UK
jiayu.huo@kcl.ac.uk
[2] National Hospital for Neurology and Neurosurgery, Queen Square, London, UK
[3] Division of Epilepsy and Neuromodulation Neurosurgery, Vickie and Jack Farber Institute for Neuroscience, Thomas Jefferson University, Philadelphia, PA, USA
[4] Department of Neurosurgery, University of Washington, Seattle, WA, USA

Abstract. Laser interstitial thermal therapy (LITT) is a novel minimally invasive treatment that is used to ablate intracranial structures to treat mesial temporal lobe epilepsy (MTLE). Region of interest (ROI) segmentation before and after LITT would enable automated lesion quantification to objectively assess treatment efficacy. Deep learning techniques, such as convolutional neural networks (CNNs) are state-of-the-art solutions for ROI segmentation, but require large amounts of annotated data during the training. However, collecting large datasets from emerging treatments such as LITT is impractical. In this paper, we propose a progressive brain lesion synthesis framework (PAVAE) to expand both the quantity and diversity of the training dataset. Concretely, our framework consists of two sequential networks: a mask synthesis network and a mask-guided lesion synthesis network. To better employ extrinsic information to provide additional supervision during network training, we design a condition embedding block (CEB) and a mask embedding block (MEB) to encode inherent conditions of masks to the feature space. Finally, a segmentation network is trained using raw and synthetic lesion images to evaluate the effectiveness of the proposed framework. Experimental results show that our method can achieve realistic synthetic results and boost the performance of down-stream segmentation tasks above traditional data augmentation techniques.

Keywords: Laser interstitial thermal therapy · Adversarial variational auto-encoder · Progressive lesion synthesis

1 Introduction

Mesial temporal lobe epilepsy (MTLE) is one of the most common brain diseases and affects millions of people worldwide [11]. First-line treatment for MTLE is anti-seizure medicine but up to 30% of patients do not achieve seizure control,

C. Zhao et al. (Eds.): SASHIMI 2022, LNCS 13570, pp. 101–111, 2022.
https://doi.org/10.1007/978-3-031-16980-9_10

in these patients resective neurosurgery may be curative [15]. As a minimally invasive treatment, laser interstitial thermal therapy (LITT) can accurately locate and ablate target lesion structures within the brain [17]. LITT has been shown as an effective treatment for MTLE, and ablation of specific structures can be predictive of seizure freedom [16]. Region of interest (ROI) segmentation needs to be performed to enable quantitative analyses of LITT [18] (e.g., lesion volume quantification and ablation volume estimation). However, manual delineation is inevitably time-consuming and requires domain knowledge expertise. Automated lesion segmentation could improve the speed and reliability of lesion segmentation for this task.

In the literature, some segmentation methods for the post-ablation area have already been exploited. Ermiş et al. [2] developed Dense-UNet to segment resection cavities in glioblastoma multiforme patients. Pérez-García et al. [14] proposed an algorithm to simulate resections from preoperative MRI and utilized synthetic images to assist the brain resection cavity segmentation. Although the segmentation performance seems to be satisfied, it can be constrained by a small-scale dataset. Also, generated images of the rule-based resection simulation method can be less diverse, and imperfect synthetic results may compromise the performance of the segmentation model.

To mitigate the huge demand of images for training CNNs, methods utilizing generative adversarial network (GAN) [4] have been presented. Han et al. [6] generated 2D brain images with tumours from random noise to create more training samples. Kwon et al. [10] implemented a 3D α-GAN for brain MRI generation, including tumour and stroke lesion simulation. While these methods demonstrate the potential of GANs, there are some limitations. First, not all synthetic brain images have corresponding lesion masks, which means these methods may not be suitable to use for some down-stream tasks such as lesion segmentation. Additionally, these methods need extensive training samples to generate realistic results, which implies that the generalizability and robustness of these networks can not be ensured when the number of training samples is limited. Recently, Zhang et al. [19] designed a lesion-ware data augmentation strategy to improve brain lesion segmentation performance. However, its effectiveness still can be affected due to limited training samples.

To address the aforementioned issues, we develop a novel progressive brain lesion synthesis framework based on an adversarial variational auto-encoder, and refer it as PAVAE. Instead of simulating lesions directly, we decompose this task into two smaller sub-tasks (i.e., mask generation and lesion synthesis) to alleviate the task difficulty. For mask generation, we utilize a 3D variational auto-encoder as the generator to avoid mode collapses. We adopt a WGAN [1] discriminator with the gradient penalty [5] to encourage the generator to give more distinct results. We also design a condition embedding block (CEB) to encode semantic information (i.e., lesion size) to guide mask simulation. For lesion generation, we utilize a similar structure except replacing the CEB with a mask embedding block (MEB), to encode the shape information provided by masks to guide lesion synthesis. In the inference stage, we first sample from a

Gaussian distribution to form the shape latent vector for mask simulation. Next, we combine the generated mask with an intensity latent vector sampled from a Gaussian distribution, and feed them into the lesion synthesis network to create the lesion image. Finally, we create new post-LITT ablation MR images from the generated lesion images. We train a lesion segmentation model using the framework nnUNet [7] to show the effectiveness of our method in synthesizing training images.

2 Methodology

Overall, the brain lesion synthesis task is decomposed into two smaller sub-tasks as described in Sect. 2.1. First, we design an adversarial variational auto-encoder to generate binary masks. To assist mask generation, we present a CEB to help encode mask conditions into the feature space, so that mask simulation can be guided by high-level semantic information. We adopt a similar architecture to generate lesions guided by binary lesion masks. Lesion masks are embedded into the feature space using a MEB. These additional blocks are described in Sect. 2.2. Finally, all models are trained using a four-term loss function as described in Sect. 2.3 to ensure reconstructions are accurate, latent spaces are approximately Gaussian, and the real and simulated distributions are similar.

2.1 Model Architecture

Figure 1 illustrates our progressive adversarial variational auto-encoder for brain lesion synthesis. We design a progressive 3D variational auto-encoder to approximate both shape and intensity information of post-LITT ablation lesions as Gaussian distributions. Besides, a following discriminator can ensure that generated images are more realistic. The kernel size of all convolutional layers is set to $3 \times 3 \times 3$, and Instance Normalization (InstanceNorm) and Leaky Rectified Linear Unit (LeakyReLU) are used after each convolutional layer. For the last convolutional layer, we use a Sigmoid function to scale output values between 0 and 1.

New lesion synthesis is performed as shown in Fig. 1(c). We first randomly sample from a Gaussian distribution to build shape latent vectors which are input into D_S to generate new masks. Next, new masks and intensity latent vectors sampled from a Gaussian distribution are used as input for D_I to generate new lesions. Here new masks are responsible for controlling new shapes and intensity latent vectors are responsible for intensity patterns.

2.2 Condition and Mask Embedding Blocks

To add additional guidance for models in order to generate better results, we propose two separate modules shown in Fig. 2, a CEB and a MEB. For MEB, we follow the approach presented by SPADE [12]. First, masks are resized to the feature map resolution using nearest-neighbor downsampling. Next, learned scale

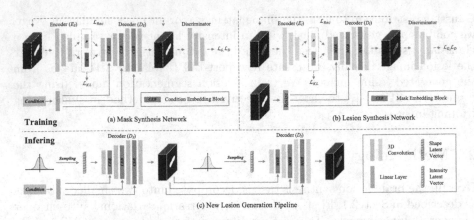

Fig. 1. The pipeline of our proposed framework for progressive brain lesion synthesis. Our method contains two separate networks with similar structures for (a) mask simulation and (b) lesion synthesis, respectively. For the inference (c), we sample shape latent vectors and intensity latent vectors from Gaussian distributions to generate new lesions.

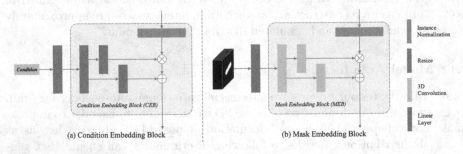

Fig. 2. The structure of (a) condition embedding block (CEB) and (b) mask embedding block (MEB).

and bias parameters are produced by three 3D convolutional layers. Finally, the normalized feature maps are modulated by the learned scale and bias parameters. For CEB, the structure is similar to MEB, but all 3D convolutional layers are replaced with linear layers since all input conditions are vectors.

2.3 Loss Functions

To optimize the encoder, decoder and discriminator so that reasonable masks and realistic lesions are generated, four loss functions are utilized in our work: reconstruction Loss $\mathcal{L}_{Rec}$, KL divergence $\mathcal{L}_{KL}$, and GAN specific losses $\mathcal{L}_G$ and $\mathcal{L}_D$. First, the reconstruction loss $\mathcal{L}_{Rec}$ is used to ensure outputs have high fidelity to the ground truth images. The Kullback-Leibler (KL) loss $\mathcal{L}_{KL}$ is imposed on the model to minimize the KL divergence between the intractable posterior distribution and the prior distribution (*i.e.*, Gaussian distribution in latent space). Furthermore, we add Wasserstein loss functions ($\mathcal{L}_G$ and $\mathcal{L}_D$) to the GAN in order to prevent results generated by the decoder from being fuzzy.

The reconstruction loss implemented in our framework is mean squared error (MSE) defined as:

$$\mathcal{L}_{Rec} = \sum_i \left\| x_g^{(i)} - x_r^{(i)} \right\|^2, \tag{1}$$

where $x_r^{(i)}$ refers to the ith real image within a mini-batch, and $x_g^{(i)}$ denotes the ith generated image obtained from the decoder. MSE guarantees that real images and synthetic images look similar in general. However, synthetic images may lose some detailed information, which will make them appear indistinct.

The KL loss is defined as the KL divergence $\mathcal{D}_{KL}$ between the posterior distribution $q(z|\cdot)$ and the prior distribution $p(z)$, which is formulated as:

$$\mathcal{L}_{KL} = \sum_i \mathcal{D}_{KL} \left[q\left(z|x_r^{(i)} \right) \parallel p(z) \right], \tag{2}$$

where $q\left(z|x_r^{(i)} \right)$ is the posterior latent distribution under the condition of $x_r^{(i)}$, and $p(z)$ is a normal distribution for the latent vector z. By minimizing the KL divergence between the two distributions, the conditional distribution of the latent vector z approximates a Gaussian distribution.

To avoid generating images with blurriness and instability during training, we deploy the loss functions from WGAN [1] instead of the original GAN. The Wasserstein loss can be defined as:

$$\mathcal{L}_D = \mathbb{E}_{x_g \sim \mathbb{P}_g} \left[D\left(x_g \right) \right] - \mathbb{E}_{x_r \sim \mathbb{P}_r} \left[D\left(x_r \right) \right] + \lambda \mathbb{E}_{\hat{x} \sim \mathbb{P}_{\hat{x}}} \left[\left(\| \nabla_{\hat{x}} D(\hat{x}) \|_2 - 1 \right)^2 \right], \tag{3}$$

$$\mathcal{L}_G = -\mathbb{E}_{x_g \sim \mathbb{P}_g} \left[D\left(x_g \right) \right]. \tag{4}$$

Compared with original GAN using a discriminator to differentiate whether images are real or fake, WGAN uses the Wasserstein distance to directly estimate the difference between two distributions $\mathbb{P}_r$ and $\mathbb{P}_g$. This Wasserstein distance can be formulated as $\mathcal{D}_W = \mathbb{E}_{x_r \sim \mathbb{P}_r} \left[D\left(x_r \right) \right] - \mathbb{E}_{x_g \sim \mathbb{P}_g} \left[D\left(x_g \right) \right]$, where $\mathbb{E}$ denotes the maximum likelihood estimation and $D(\cdot)$ denotes the discriminator. In addition, we further include a gradient penalty regularization [5] to constrain $\mathcal{L}_D$ to satisfy the 1-Lipschitz condition, so that $\mathcal{L}_D$ will remain stable during network training. The gradient penalty regularization is formalized as $\lambda \mathbb{E}_{\hat{x} \sim \mathbb{P}_{\hat{x}}} \left[\left(\| \nabla_{\hat{x}} D(\hat{x}) \|_2 - 1 \right)^2 \right]$, where $\hat{x}$ denotes random interpolation between real samples and generated samples, and λ is a weighting factor. In our experiments, we fix the value of λ to 10.

3 Experiments

3.1 Dataset

In this study, 47 T1-weighted MRI scans of 47 patients are collected from a high-volume epilepsy surgery center which has already established expertise in using

LITT for MTLE. Consecutive patients are included if they received LITT for MTLE and had concordant semiology, scalp electroencephalography (EEG) and structural MRI features of mesial temporal sclerosis, or had seizure onset confirmed within the hippocampus following stereo-EEG (SEEG) investigation. Ethical approval for the study was provided by institutional review board approval for the retrospective use of anonymized imaging. All T1-weighted images are first aligned to the MNI152 brain template [3]. A random split of the dataset is performed, keeping 20% (10 cases) of the whole dataset as the test set with the remaining 80% (37 cases) being used as the training set.

3.2   Implementation Details

Our framework is implemented within PyTorch 1.10.0 [13]. For network training, encoder and decoder layers are treated as the generator and optimized together. To optimize the generator and discriminator networks, we use two Adam optimizers [8]. The initial learning rate is set to $5e$-5, and the batch size is set to 13 due to GPU memory limitations. For each model, we train for 1000 epochs individually using only data in the training set. For input images, we extract a $64 \times 64 \times 64$ cube from raw MRI scans corresponding to a ROI containing the mask to ensure the entire lesion area is included within the image.

3.3   Evaluation Metrics

All metrics are evaluated and reported on the test set. First, we evaluate the lesion synthesis performance using three metrics, *i.e.*, peak signal-to-noise ratio (PSNR), structural similarity (SSIM), and normalized mean square error (NMSE). Moreover, to prove that generated brain lesions can further boost the performance of down-stream tasks, we use four metrics to measure brain lesion segmentation performance: Dice coefficient, Jaccard index, the average surface distance (ASD), and the 95% Hausdorff Distance (95HD).

3.4   Experimental Results

Comparison of Lesion Synthesis Performance. We first qualitatively compare the synthetic results of our framework with other existing methods. Specifically, we employ 3D VAE and 3D VAE w/WGAN-GP as baseline models. For 3D VAE, only $\mathcal{L}_{Rec}$ and $\mathcal{L}_{KL}$ is utilized for model training. For 3D VAE w/WGAN-GP, the structure is similar to the lesion synthesis network and all loss functions are utilized for training, but MEB has not been included. Note that all models are implemented with 3D convolution and 3D InstanceNorm layers. Triplanar views of synthetic lesions are shown in Fig. 3. Here, 3D VAE w/WGAN-GP refers to 3D VAE followed by a WGAN-GP discriminator, PAVAE (Syn Mask) indicates lesion synthesis utilizes generated masks derived from the mask synthesis network. PAVAE (Real Mask) indicates that real masks are utilized to guide lesion synthesis. As can be found in Fig. 3, 3D VAE always generates fuzzy lesion

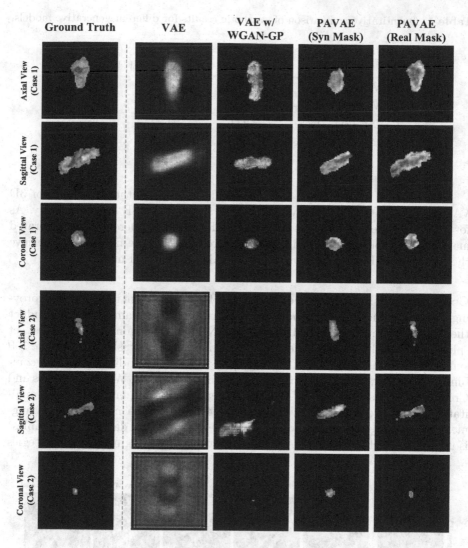

Fig. 3. Qualitative comparison for different generative models.

images. Also, small lesions seem to be diffused, indicating the model has trouble in simulating small lesions. When a WGAN-GP discriminator is added to 3D VAE, results are clearer for big lesions. However, WGAN-GP still can not simulate small lesions. For our model, using synthetic masks to guide lesion generation *i.e.*, PAVAE (Syn Mask), we observe even small lesions are successfully generated. Utilizing real masks for guidance results in synthetic lesions are closest to the ground truth among all compared methods (the rightmost column in Fig. 3). This highlights that the lesion synthesis network can generate realistic image intensity when provided a realistic lesion mask.

Table 1. Quantitative comparison of synthetic results for different generative models.

Method	Metrics		
	PSNR [dB]	SSIM [%]	NMSE
3D VAE [9]	21.40	10.18	76.34
3D VAE w/WGAN-GP [5]	22.05	92.15	152.87
PAVAE (Syn Mask)	23.67	94.90	76.98
PAVAE (Real Mask)	**32.74**	**99.29**	**15.68**

Quantitative results shown in Table 1 indicate that neither 3D VAE nor 3D VAE w/WGAN-GP can achieve high SSIM and low NMSE simultaneously. As for our model, we obtain relatively good synthetic results merely using generated masks. If we replace generated masks with real masks, the final results achieve the highest PSNR and SSIM, and lowest NMSE among all methods.

Comparison of Lesion Segmentation Performance. For the purpose of proving the effectiveness of synthetic results generated by our framework, we conduct the brain segmentation model based on nnUNet. For the training set and test set split, we follow the same manner with the lesion synthesis task. We generate 100 synthetic lesion images using CarveMix [19] and PAVAE individually, and combine them with raw images to create new training datasets. We use Dice loss and Cross-entropy loss to train nnUNet for 200 epochs. Both quantitative and qualitative results are shown in Table 2 and Fig. 4. Here, NoDA means no data augmentation strategy is employed and only the real training dataset (37 samples) is used to train the model. TDA means traditional data augmentation strategies

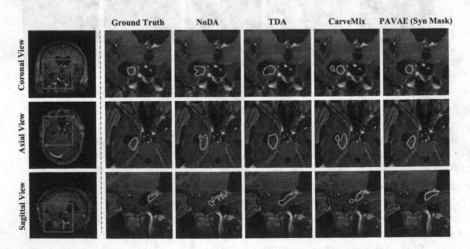

Fig. 4. Segmentation results from different training datasets for nnUNet models.

Table 2. Comparison of segmentation results using different data augmentation techniques during training.

Method	Metrics			
	Dice [%]	Jaccard [%]	ASD [voxel]	95HD [voxel]
NoDA [7]	66.69	51.19	1.17	3.52
TDA [7]	72.25	57.67	1.08	3.15
CarveMix [19]	73.29	58.77	**0.97**	3.24
PAVAE (Syn Mask)	**74.18**	**59.95**	1.00	**2.77**

implemented in nnUNet, including random flip and rotations, and *etc.*. As shown in Table 2, our method has the best performance for three metrics (Dice, Jaccard, 95HD) and for the final metric ASD, only CarveMix has a slightly lower value. Furthermore, in Fig. 4, we can observe that all the results of the competing methods over-segment the LITT ablation volume. Our method yields accurate segmentation results, which most closely resembles the expert annotation.

4 Discussion and Conclusion

Building a 3D generative model may face several problems. The biggest ones can be mode collapses due to limited training samples and increasing computational complexity compared with 2D generative models. To tackle these issues, we have presented a progressive adversarial variational auto-encoder for brain lesion synthesis, which can generate reasonable masks and realistic brain lesions in a step-wise fashion. We further develop two types of blocks (*i.e.*, CEB and MEB) to utilize both semantic and shape information to facilitate this lesion synthesis. Experimental results show that our framework can create high-fidelity brain lesions and boost the down-stream segmentation model training compared with existing methods. However, as can be found in the quantitative results (Fig. 3), ground truth masks are still able to synthesize more realistic lesion images indicating a potential room for improvement when creating masks. Besides, all data used in this study was from a single center, further validation is required to evaluate its effectiveness on multi-center data and especially data acquired on different MRI scanners.

Acknowledgement. This work was supported by Centre for Doctoral Training in Surgical and Interventional Engineering at King's College London. This research was funded in whole, or in part, by the Wellcome Trust [218380/Z/19/Z, WT203148/Z/16/Z]. For the purpose of open access, the author has applied a CC BY public copyright licence to any Author Accepted Manuscript version arising from this submission. This research was supported by the UK Research and Innovation London Medical Imaging & Artificial Intelligence Centre for Value Based Healthcare. The research was funded/supported by the National Institute for Health Research (NIHR) Biomedical Research Centre based at Guy's and St Thomas' NHS Foundation Trust and King's College London and supported by the NIHR Clinical Research Facility (CRF) at Guy's and St Thomas'. The views expressed are those of the author(s) and not necessarily those of the NHS, the NIHR or the Department of Health.

References

1. Arjovsky, M., Chintala, S., Bottou, L.: Wasserstein generative adversarial networks. In: International Conference on Machine Learning, pp. 214–223. PMLR (2017)
2. Ermiş, E., et al.: Fully automated brain resection cavity delineation for radiation target volume definition in glioblastoma patients using deep learning. Radiat. Oncol. **15**(1), 1–10 (2020)
3. Fonov, V., Evans, A., McKinstry, R., Almli, C.R., Collins, D.: Unbiased nonlinear average age-appropriate brain templates from birth to adulthood. NeuroImage **47** (2009)
4. Goodfellow, I., et al.: Generative adversarial nets. In: Advances in Neural Information Processing Systems, vol. 27 (2014)
5. Gulrajani, I., Ahmed, F., Arjovsky, M., Dumoulin, V., Courville, A.C.: Improved training of Wasserstein GANs. In: Advances in neural Information Processing Systems, vol. 30 (2017)
6. Han, C., et al.: GAN-based synthetic brain MR image generation. In: 2018 IEEE 15th International Symposium on Biomedical Imaging (ISBI 2018), pp. 734–738. IEEE (2018)
7. Isensee, F., Jaeger, P.F., Kohl, S.A., Petersen, J., Maier-Hein, K.H.: nnU-Net: a self-configuring method for deep learning-based biomedical image segmentation. Nat. Methods **18**(2), 203–211 (2021)
8. Kingma, D.P., Ba, J.: Adam: a method for stochastic optimization. arXiv preprint arXiv:1412.6980 (2014)
9. Kingma, D.P., Welling, M.: Auto-encoding variational bayes. arXiv preprint arXiv:1312.6114 (2013)
10. Kwon, G., Han, C., Kim, D.: Generation of 3D brain MRI using auto-encoding generative adversarial networks. In: Shen, D., et al. (eds.) MICCAI 2019. LNCS, vol. 11766, pp. 118–126. Springer, Cham (2019). https://doi.org/10.1007/978-3-030-32248-9_14
11. Nevalainen, O., et al.: Epilepsy-related clinical characteristics and mortality: a systematic review and meta-analysis. Neurology **83**(21), 1968–1977 (2014)
12. Park, T., Liu, M.Y., Wang, T.C., Zhu, J.Y.: Semantic image synthesis with spatially-adaptive normalization. In: Proceedings of the IEEE/CVF Conference on Computer Vision and Pattern Recognition, pp. 2337–2346 (2019)
13. Paszke, A., et al.: Pytorch: an imperative style, high-performance deep learning library. In: Advances in Neural Information Processing Systems, vol. 32 (2019)
14. Pérez-García, F., et al.: A self-supervised learning strategy for postoperative brain cavity segmentation simulating resections. Int. J. Comput. Assist. Radiol. Surg. **16**(10), 1653–1661 (2021). https://doi.org/10.1007/s11548-021-02420-2
15. Rosenow, F., Lüders, H.: Presurgical evaluation of epilepsy. Brain **124**(9), 1683–1700 (2001)
16. Satzer, D., Tao, J.X., Warnke, P.C.: Extent of parahippocampal ablation is associated with seizure freedom after laser amygdalohippocampotomy. J. Neurosurg. **135**(6), 1742–1751 (2021)

17. Sun, X.R., Patel, N.V., Danish, S.F.: Tissue ablation dynamics during magnetic resonance-guided, laser-induced thermal therapy. Neurosurgery **77**(1), 51–58 (2015)
18. Vakharia, V.N., et al.: Automated trajectory planning for laser interstitial thermal therapy in mesial temporal lobe epilepsy. Epilepsia **59**(4), 814–824 (2018)
19. Zhang, X., et al.: CarveMix: a simple data augmentation method for brain lesion segmentation. In: de Bruijne, M., et al. (eds.) MICCAI 2021. LNCS, vol. 12901, pp. 196–205. Springer, Cham (2021). https://doi.org/10.1007/978-3-030-87193-2_19

Contrastive Learning for Generating Optical Coherence Tomography Images of the Retina

Sinan Kaplan(✉)⬛ and Lasse Lensu⬛

Department of Computational Engineering, Lappeenranta-Lahti University of Technology LUT, P.O. Box 20, 53850 Lappeenranta, Finland
sinan.kaplan@student.lut.fi, lasse.lensu@lut.fi

Abstract. As a self-supervised learning technique, contrastive learning is an effective way to learn rich and discriminative representations from data. In this study, we propose a variational autoencoder (VAE) based approach to apply contrastive learning for the generation of optical coherence tomography (OCT) images of the retina. The approach first learns embedding representation from data by contrastive learning. Secondly, the learnt embeddings are used to synthesize disease-specific OCT images using VAEs. Our results reveal that the diseases are separated well in the embedding space and the proposed approach is able to generate high-quality images with fine-grained spatial details. The source code of the experiments in this paper can be found on Github (https://github.com/kaplansinan/OCTRetImageGen_CLcVAE).

Keywords: Optical coherence tomography · Contrastive learning · Variational autoencoder · Deep generative model · Deep learning · Artificial intelligence

1 Introduction

An increasing amount of effort has been put to the research and development of deep learning (DL) and its applications [6]. This methodology has shown its effectiveness as the state-of-the-art solution for many tasks [5] including medical image analysis. DL has also leveraged the potential for early detection and recognition of abnormalities, such as diabetic retinopathy and age-related macula degeneration, from retinal images [1]. One of the retinal imaging techniques that has benefited from DL is OCT [9]. This imaging modality sheds light on pathological structures of the retina in 3D, through which it is possible to reliably diagnose diseases such as choroidal neovascularization (CNV) and diabetic macular edema (DME). As a result of progress in both fields, DL based solutions are studied for the detection and recognition of such abnormalities from OCT images.

Supplementary Information The online version contains supplementary material available at https://doi.org/10.1007/978-3-031-16980-9_11.

Despite its potential and successful applications in a variety of tasks, the practical utilisation of deep neural network (DNN) in safety-critical tasks like medical diagnosis systems is limited [11]. One of the underlying reasons of this is the black-box nature of the DL models [6]. The term black-box refers to the inability of understanding how the DL algorithm makes a particular decision [33]. This arises from the inherent structure of DL models, which are complex, non-linear, challenging to interpret, and the amount of data needed to train such models is typically large. To address the issues arising from the nature of DL models, there exists several solutions under the name of an emerging field called explainable artificial intelligence (XAI) [2,24,33]. XAI represents the techniques and methods to understand why artificial intelligence (AI) makes a particular decision. It is considered as key methodology to understand model decisions and build trust between the users and AI solutions [3,26].

In XAI literature, the methods are split into two categories [2]: global and local. The global methods try to explain a particular model and data set used for training the model, whereas the local methods are utilized for understanding post-hoc decisions at instance level [24]. For example, considering a DL model trained to recognize certain diseases in OCT images [29], post-hoc XAI methods help in explaining which features in a target image are relevant to the model while performing inference. Such explanation is achieved by highlighting relevant regions in the target image [36]. Post-hoc explanations are often used for sensitivity analysis [19,25], where the aim is to understand how the behavior of a model changes while manipulating the input image. There are different instance manipulation techniques [24] such as applying specific image transformations and augmentations like cropping, deleting certain part of the image [32], color transformation, and copy-pasting a part of the image.

An ideal solution for sensitivity analysis would be to avoid the limitations of existing data with synthetic data generated from an underlying distribution of real data used for training a DL model. To do so, one may apply deep generative models [16] like generative adversarial networks (GANs) [8] and VAEs [15] for image generation. In this paper, we propose a framework to synthesize OCT images using conditional variational autoencoder (cVAE) and contrastive learning [17]. The goal is to generate high-quality OCT images, which can be further used for the sensitivity analysis of OCT image classification tasks [13,36]. In addition, the framework can be used to synthesize images for augmenting data sets, or constructing a benchmark OCT set.

The rest of the paper is organized as follows: Sect. 2 reviews the studies in OCT imaging, how DL is used for OCT image analysis and OCT image generation tasks. Section 3 introduces the proposed solution and Sect. 4 presents the experimental results. Finally, we present the conclusions that can be made based on the current experiment and give possible future directions in Sect. 5.

2   Related Work

OCT Imaging and Deep Learning. OCT is a technique to acquire high resolution images of cross-sections of the retina [9]. It enables diagnosis of retinal disorders. For instance, CNV, DME, and DRUSEN are such disease, which can be diagnosed through OCT imaging [13,23]. To detect such diseases from OCT images, techniques based on DL have received substantial attention in the medical image analysis field. For instance, classification [13] and segmentation tasks [9] are implemented to support clinicians while diagnosing specific abnormalities using OCT imaging.

OCT Image Generation by Deep Generative Models. The potential of deep generative models for synthesizing high quality images have been proposed for OCT image generation tasks [20]. As part of deep generative models, GANs are studied widely compared to VAEs. For instance, Zha et al. proposed conditional generative adversarial networks (cGANs) to solve the class imbalance problem exhibit in OCT data sets [37]. In addition, by considering the difficulty of finding rare disease examples in OCT data sets, Xiao et al. adapted a GAN based method to generate and create an open OCT data set [34]. Furthermore, in another study [35], the authors aimed to improve the performance of OCT image classification tasks by using cGANs to generate images, thereby increasing the number of data samples.

OCT Image Generation by Variational Autoencoder. Although it has not received that much attention in OCT image generation tasks [7,22], VAEs are an option for deep image generation. Compared to GANs, VAEs are easy to train and do not suffer from mode collapse [18]. In addition, another important advantage of VAEs is that they learn the characteristics of input data samples by mapping them into a latent space [16]. After training, new data samples are generated by sampling from this latent space. This way VAEs introduce a controlled way for the generation.

Our Work. Since VAEs enable us to alter and explore the variations over the data, we choose VAEs to generate OCT images. To do so, generation is conditioned on learnt embeddings via the contrastive learning approach. Thus, our work combines contrastive learning and VAEs to synthesize disease-specific OCT images with appropriate visual details. To best of our knowledge, no other study has proposed this solution for the synthesis of OCT images of the retina.

3   Methods

The proposed solution consists of two stages. In the first stage, we use contrastive learning [17] to have class-wise discrimination in the learned embedding space. The embedding as a discriminative data representation enables class-specific image generation. In the second stage, we train cVAEs to generate the disease-specific OCT images. As the conditioning is done using the embeddings from the first stage, we are able to control the disease-wise data generation. Figure 1 illustrates the model architectures used in the two stages.

Contrastive learning is a self-supervised learning technique widely applied for image retrieval tasks [4,17]. The goal is to learn an embedding space in which the distances between similar samples are minimized while the distances between dissimilar samples are maximized. To learn such an embedding space, contrastive learning models are trained with specific loss functions, such as SimCLR [4], triplet-loss [27], and n-pair loss [30].

In our work, the contrastive learning model is inspired by the work in [14]. As being an effective batch construction method and reducing convergence time of the model, We use n-pair loss [30] to train the contrastive learning part. In addition, instead of using Resnet34 as the encoder part of the contrastive model, we use Resnet50 to increase the learning capacity of the model, thus having more discriminative embeddings for each class.

To generate new samples, we use a variational autoencoder representing one of the deep generative models. VAE maps the input data into a latent space in a probabilistic way by an encoder module. Afterwards, a decoder module is used to synthesize new data samples by sampling a latent vector from the latent space [16]. In a VAE, the goal is to minimize the distance between distribution of the input data and the distribution of the latent space using Kullback–Leibler (KL) divergence loss [15]. In this paper, we apply a cVAE, which conditions the synthesis of new samples on a given extra information, such as labels [16]. This contributes to the generation of the data in a desired way.

Conditional variational autoencoder is optimized with a weighted set of loss functions. VAEs often generate blurry images due to pixel-wise reconstruction loss. To avoid this issue, we replace the reconstruction loss by perceptual loss [10] and deep feature loss [21]. Hence, the objective of our cVAEs is to minimize the following weighted loss function:

$$L_{CVAE} = w_1 * L_{perceptual} + w_2 * L_{feature} + w_3 * L_{KL} \tag{1}$$

where $L_{perceptual}$ is perceptual loss, $L_{feature}$ is feature loss and L_{KL} is KL divergence loss.

It is important to note that whilst designing the architecture of cVAE, in the decoder part we use sub-pixel convolutional layer [28] to increase the quality of generated images. This layer basically learns an array of image upscaling filters described in the original paper.

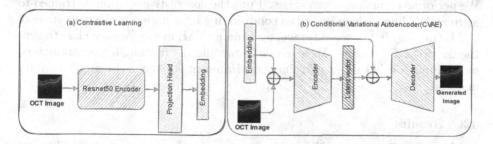

Fig. 1. The architectures of the proposed solution: a) contrastive learning model trained in Stage 1 and b) cVAE model trained in Stage 2. CVAE is conditioned on the embedding learnt by the contrastive learning part.

4   Experiments and Results

In this section, we cover characteristics of the training data, training procedure and results from contrastive learning and cVAE.[1]

4.1   Dataset

We use OCT data from the study in [12]. It consists of 84 495 labeled images split into 4 categories as follows: 37 200 CNV, 8 618 DRUSEN, 11 300 DME and 26 300 NORMAL (healthy) images. The data has the issue of class imbalance. As a remedy, we apply a representative sampling approach given in the supplementary material. After the representative sampling, we reduce the data size to 19 980 samples equally distributed across each category. A few representative samples from the training set are presented in Fig. 2.

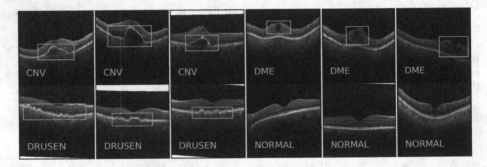

Fig. 2. Representative samples of OCT data for each category in the set. The red rectangle highlights the characteristics of each disease in an image. (Color figure online)

4.2   Model Training

We performed training in two stages. First the contrastive learning is trained to learn embeddings, which is used as conditioning information in the next stage of cVAE training. In the second stage, we train a cVAE model for each class to synthesize new OCT images. More details regarding the training hyperparameters, model input/output size, and training environment is given in the supplementary material.

4.3   Results

Contrastive Learning. The goal of contrastive learning is to learn discriminative embedding from each class. To verify this after the model training,

---

[1] The in-depth details regarding the data set, training hyperparameters, and randomly generated OCT images by the trained model and the supplementary material can be found in the Github repo.

we visualize the embedding space by principal-component analysis (PCA). Based on the visualization in Fig. 3, the contrastive learning provides good discrimination between each class in the embedding space. This is important for accurately mapping the input data into the latent space in the next stage.

It is also important to notice the representation of the NORMAL (healthy) cases in the embedding space. Based on the visualization, they are at the intersection of each disease and this strengthens the idea that the generation of new disease-specific OCT images representing different levels of severity of the condition is possible. While studying the existing images individually, we observed that the further an instance is located from the center of NORMAL cases, the more severe the disease is.

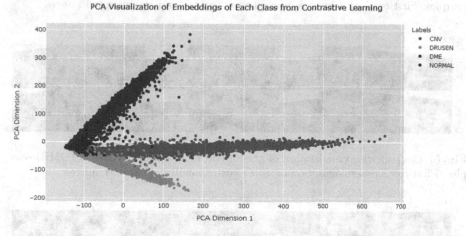

Fig. 3. Principal-component analysis projection of embedding of training set from contrastive learning.

CVAE. In the second stage, by training a cVAE model for each disease, we generate high quality images that capture the characteristics of each disease successfully. We demonstrate pairwise visual comparison of generated images for each disease in Fig. 4, Fig. 5 and Fig. 6, respectively[2].

Pathological structures in the OCT images are captured well with disease specific details. However, we observe that the quality of generated images are better if there is less variation within a class. For instance, not all the fine-grained details are captured in the CNV class. The underlying reason behind this is that the class contains far more variability of images compared to DME and DRUSEN classes. The variation in CNV also exhibits in the embedding space of contrastive learning model (see Fig. 3).

---

[2] Randomly generated samples from each class are presented in the supplementary material, which can be found in the Github repo.

In some of the generated images (see the supplementary material), we encounter checkerboard artefacts, which is due to the upsampling layers used in the decoder module of cVAE [31].

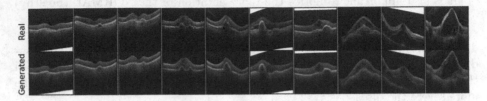

Fig. 4. The pair-wise visualization of generated choroidal neovascularization (CNV) samples: First row - real images; Second row - corresponding generated images.

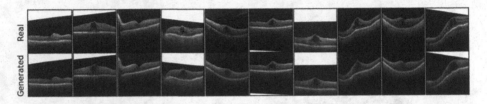

Fig. 5. The pair-wise visualization of generated diabetic macular edema (DME) samples: First row - real images; Second row - corresponding generated images.

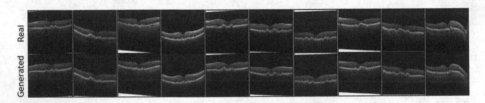

Fig. 6. The pair-wise visualization of generated DRUSEN samples: First row - real images; Second row - corresponding generated images.

5   Conclusions

In this paper, we study a contrastive learning based approach for synthesizing OCT images using cVAE. The contrastive learning is applied to extract rich representations from the data, which is further used by cVAE. to generate new samples. Based on the presented results, the proposed method enables successful synthesis of visually quality OCT images representing CNV, DME, DRUSEN in fine-grained details. Among the aforementioned diseases, DME, DRUSEN cases are synthesized better than CNV.

Although, our main motivation is to generate images to be used in sensitivity analysis tasks, the image generation can be used variety of other tasks such as augmenting existing sets, counterfactual image generation and disease progression simulation. In the future work, we plan to combine OCT image classification done on the same set and use the proposed cVAE model to conduct sensitivity analysis and simulate disease progression. Also, in the extended study of this work, we plan to incorporate expert opinions to validate our observation about the different levels of severity of the diseases revealed in the contrastive learning part. We believe this can be helpful for both automated grading of the diseases from OCT images and simulating the progression of a certain disease.

References

1. Badar, M., Haris, M., Fatima, A.: Application of deep learning for retinal image analysis: a review. Comput. Sci. Rev. **35** (2020)
2. Bai, X., et al.: Explainable deep learning for efficient and robust pattern recognition: a survey of recent developments. Pattern Recogn. **120** (2021)
3. Bruckert, S., Finzel, B., Schmid, U.: The next generation of medical decision support: a roadmap toward transparent expert companions. Front. Artif. Intell. **3**, 75 (2020)
4. Chen, T., Kornblith, S., Norouzi, M., Hinton, G.: A simple framework for contrastive learning of visual representations. In: International Conference on Machine Learning, pp. 1597–1607. PMLR (2020)
5. Dargan, S., Kumar, M., Ayyagari, M.R., Kumar, G.: A survey of deep learning and its applications: a new paradigm to machine learning. Arch. Comput. Methods Eng. **27**(4), 1071–1092 (2020)
6. Dong, S., Wang, P., Abbas, K.: A survey on deep learning and its applications. Comput. Sci. Rev. **40** (2021)
7. Gan, M., Wang, C.: Esophageal optical coherence tomography image synthesis using an adversarially learned variational autoencoder. Biomed. Opt. Express **13**(3), 1188–1201 (2022)
8. Goodfellow, I., et al.: Generative adversarial nets. In: Advances in Neural Information Processing Systems, vol. 27 (2014)
9. Islam, M.S., et al.: A deep-learning approach for automated OCT En-face retinal vessel segmentation in cases of optic disc swelling using multiple En-face images as input. Transl. Vis. Sci. Technol. **9**, 1–15 (2020). https://doi.org/10.1167/TVST.9.2.17
10. Johnson, J., Alahi, A., Fei-Fei, L.: Perceptual losses for real-time style transfer and super-resolution. In: Leibe, B., Matas, J., Sebe, N., Welling, M. (eds.) ECCV 2016. LNCS, vol. 9906, pp. 694–711. Springer, Cham (2016). https://doi.org/10.1007/978-3-319-46475-6_43
11. Kelly, C.J., Karthikesalingam, A., Suleyman, M., Corrado, G., King, D.: Key challenges for delivering clinical impact with artificial intelligence. BMC Med. **17**(1), 1–9, (2019)
12. Kermany, D., Zhang, K., Goldbaum, M., et al.: Labeled optical coherence tomography (OCT) and chest X-ray images for classification. Mendeley Data **2**(2) (2018)
13. Kerman, D.S., et al.: Identifying medical diagnoses and treatable diseases by image-based deep learning. Cell **172**(5), 1122–1131 (2018)

14. Khosla, P., et al.: Supervised contrastive learning. Adv. Neural. Inf. Process. Syst. **33**, 18661–18673 (2020)
15. Kingma, D.P., Welling, M.: Auto-encoding variational bayes. arXiv preprint arXiv:1312.6114 (2013)
16. Kingma, D.P., Welling, M.: An introduction to variational autoencoders. arXiv preprint arXiv:1906.02691 (2019)
17. Le-Khac, P.H., Healy, G., Smeaton, A.F.: Contrastive representation learning: a framework and review. IEEE Access **8**, 193907–193934 (2020)
18. Liu, Z.S., Siu, W.C., Chan, Y.L.: Photo-realistic image super-resolution via variational autoencoders. IEEE Trans. Circ. Syst. Video Technol. **31**, 1351–1365 (2021). https://doi.org/10.1109/TCSVT.2020.3003832
19. Markus, A.F., Kors, J.A., Rijnbeek, P.R.: The role of explainability in creating trustworthy artificial intelligence for health care: a comprehensive survey of the terminology, design choices, and evaluation strategies. J. Biomed. Inform. **113** (2021)
20. Pan, H., Yang, D.I., Yuan, Z., Liang, Y.: More realistic low-resolution OCT image generation approach for training deep neural networks. OSA Continuum **3**(11), 3197–3205 (2020). https://doi.org/10.1364/OSAC.408712
21. Park, T., Liu, M.Y., Wang, T.C., Zhu, J.Y.: Semantic image synthesis with spatially-adaptive normalization. In: Proceedings of the IEEE/CVF Conference on Computer Vision and Pattern Recognition, pp. 2337–2346 (2019)
22. Pesteie, M., Abolmaesumi, P., Rohling, R.N.: Adaptive augmentation of medical data using independently conditional variational auto-encoders. IEEE Trans. Med. Imaging **38**, 2807–2820 (2019). https://doi.org/10.1109/TMI.2019.2914656
23. Ran, A., Cheung, C.Y.: Deep learning-based optical coherence tomography and optical coherence tomography angiography image analysis: An updated summary. Asia-Pacif. J. Ophthal. **10**, 253–260 (2021). https://doi.org/10.1097/APO.0000000000000405
24. Samek, W., Montavon, G., Vedaldi, A., Hansen, L.K., Müller, K.-R. (eds.): Explainable AI: Interpreting, Explaining and Visualizing Deep Learning. LNCS (LNAI), vol. 11700. Springer, Cham (2019). https://doi.org/10.1007/978-3-030-28954-6
25. Samek, W., Wiegand, T., Müller, K.R.: Explainable artificial intelligence: understanding, visualizing and interpreting deep learning models. arXiv preprint arXiv:1708.08296 (2017)
26. Schoonderwoerd, T.A., Jorritsma, W., Neerincx, M.A., Van Den Bosch, K.: Human-centered XAI: developing design patterns for explanations of clinical decision support systems. Int. J. Hum Comput Stud. **154** (2021)
27. Schroff, F., Kalenichenko, D., Philbin, J.: Facenet: A unified embedding for face recognition and clustering. In: Proceedings of the IEEE Conference on Computer Vision and Pattern Recognition, pp. 815–823 (2015)
28. Shi, W., et al.: Real-time single image and video super-resolution using an efficient sub-pixel convolutional neural network. In: Proceedings of the IEEE Conference on Computer Vision and Pattern Recognition, pp. 1874–1883 (2016)
29. Singh, A., Mohammed, A.R., Zelek, J., Lakshminarayanan, V.: Interpretation of deep learning using attributions: application to ophthalmic diagnosis. doi: In: Conference: Applications of Machine Learning, pp. 39-49 (2020). https://doi.org/10.1117/12.2568631
30. Sohn, K.: Improved deep metric learning with multi-class n-pair loss objective. In: Advances in Neural Information Processing Systems, vil. 29 (2016)

31. Sugawara, Y., Shiota, S., Kiya, H.: Super-resolution using convolutional neural networks without any checkerboard artifacts. In: 2018 25th IEEE International Conference on Image Processing (ICIP), pp. 66–70. IEEE (2018)
32. Uzunova, H., Ehrhardt, J., Kepp, T., Handels, H.: Interpretable explanations of black box classifiers applied on medical images by meaningful perturbations using variational autoencoders. In: Conference: Image Processing (2019). https://doi.org/10.1117/12.2511964
33. van der Velden, B.H., Kuijf, H.J., Gilhuijs, K.G., Viergever, M.A.: Explainable artificial intelligence (XAI) in deep learning-based medical image analysis. Med. Image Anal. **79**, 102470 (2022)
34. Xiao, Y., et al.: Open-set OCT image recognition with synthetic learning. In: 2020 IEEE 17th International Symposium on Biomedical Imaging (ISBI), pp. 1788–1792. IEEE (2020)
35. Yoo, T.K., Choi, J.Y., Kim, H.K.: Feasibility study to improve deep learning in OCT diagnosis of rare retinal diseases with few-shot classification. Med. Biol. Eng. Comput. **59**, 401–415 (2 2021). https://doi.org/10.1007/S11517-021-02321-1/FIGURES/12, https://link.springer.com/article/10.1007/s11517-021-02321-1
36. Yoon, J., et al.: Optical coherence tomography-based deep-learning model for detecting central serous chorioretinopathy. Sci. Rep. **10**(1), 1–9, (2020)
37. Zha, X., Shi, F., Ma, Y., Zhu, W., Chen, X.: Generation of retinal OCT images with diseases based on CGAN. Med. Imaging 544–549 (2019). https://doi.org/10.1117/12.2510967

A Novel Method Combining Global and Local Assessments to Evaluate CBCT-Based Synthetic CTs

Chelsea Sargeant[1](✉)[iD], Andrew Green[1][iD], Jane Shortall[1][iD],
Robert Chuter[1,2][iD], Jiaofeng Xu[3], Daniel Thill[3], Nicolette O'Connell[3],
and Alan McWilliam[1,2][iD]

[1] The University of Manchester, Manchester, UK
chelsea.sargeant@postgrad.manchester.ac.uk
[2] The Christie NHS Foundation Trust, Manchester, UK
[3] Elekta AB, Stockholm, Sweden

Abstract. Deep learning models are increasingly used to generate synthetic images. Synthetic CTs (sCTs) generated from on-treatment cone-beam CTs (CBCTs) hold potential for adaptive radiotherapy, promising a high-quality representation of daily anatomy without requiring additional imaging or dose to the patient. However, validating sCT is very challenging as an accurate and appropriate ground truth is hard to come by in medical imaging. Current global metrics in the literature fail to provide a complete picture of how accurate synthetic images are. We introduce a novel method to evaluate sCTs utilising global error assessment and a local, voxel-wise statistical assessment of the sCT and the current ground truth, a deformably registered CT (dCT). Our methodology allows for the identification of individual cases where the sCT might offer an improved representation of the daily anatomy due to changes that occur over time, as well as showing regions where either the model or image registration under-performs. Our methodology can be used to guide future model development to improve the mapping between modalities, and also assist in deciphering when it is most appropriate to choose a sCT for image guided radiotherapy over the existing standard, the dCT.

Keywords: Synthetic CT evaluation method · Adaptive radiotherapy · Image synthesis validation

1 Introduction

Cycle-generative adversarial networks (cycleGANs) are an established deep learning tool for the translation between two image modalities. cycleGANs focus on the extraction of features from each modality and discovering the relationship between them to generate synthetic images. cycleGANs use two generative adversarial networks (GANS), each consisting of a generator and discriminator;

C. Zhao et al. (Eds.): SASHIMI 2022, LNCS 13570, pp. 122–131, 2022.
https://doi.org/10.1007/978-3-031-16980-9_12

the first to generate a synthetic target image from the source image, and a second to perform the opposite translation. The two GANs learn simultaneously, essentially trying to fool each other, and a cyclic loss function constrains the model to enable unpaired image-to-image translation [11].

However, unpaired image-to-image translation means that there is no ground truth for network validation. Ideally, simultaneous imaging would be required. Such paired data would provide the ground truth for voxel-wise correspondence to the synthetic image, but paired imaging is infeasible in practice. cycleGANs are gaining much attention in our exemplar application in radiotherapy. Radiotherapy is the treatment of cancer with targeted high energy x-rays, delivered in a number of fractions over 1–6 weeks. Cone-beam computed tomography (CBCT) images are used to provide an on-the-day representation of the patient; monitoring anatomical changes and ensuring x-rays are targeted correctly [3]. However, the physical imaging characteristics lead to scattering and noise artefacts, reducing the quality of the image and limiting the use of CBCT for positional and anatomical verification. Therefore, considerable interest has been directed toward the conversion of CBCTs into synthetic-CT (sCT) images using cycle-GANs. In doing so, the Hounsfield units (HUs) of the CBCT can be recovered, artefacts mitigated and image quality improved. cycleGANs have now been successfully applied to numerous treatment sites [2,4–6,8].

In this context, validation is generally performed by aligning the planning CT (pCT), used to plan the radiotherapy, with the daily CBCT by deformable image registration (DIR). The resulting deformed CT (dCT) is considered the best approximation to the ground truth since it keeps the same HU accuracy as the real pCT [6]. However, the dCT suffers from uncertainties within the registration algorithm, leading to anatomical inaccuracies and registration artefacts. The pelvic area is particularly complex for deformable registration as abdominal organs show large daily changes in the soft tissue, for example bladder filling or bowel/rectal gas [1].

Existing studies attempt to increase the suitability of the accepted ground truth with dCT correction. Szmul et al. [9] manually edit the dCT, replacing gas regions originating from the pCT as water and gas regions from the CBCT as air. This approach is limited as registration errors do not solely impact gas regions. Similarly, Liu et al. [7] copy gas pockets from the pCT to CBCT and vice versa to assist DIR and AI models in their study. In a recent study, Yang et al. [10] perform a comparison between sCT and dCT using a combination of conventional metrics and a geometrical investigation based on bladder volume to recommend when it is more appropriate to use either image.

Current validation approaches used for the evaluation of cycleGANs are unable to separate the uncertainty in the generated ground truth (the dCT) from the model performance. In addition, global image metrics are used in the evaluation, where investigating local image accuracy will highlight regions of the generated image where performance is sub-optimal. In this work, we propose a novel method to fully evaluate sCT quality by 1) separating uncertainties in the dCT from the sCT to quantify global differences; 2) performing a local (voxel-wise) image comparison to highlight regions where model accuracy can be further improved.

2   Methods

2.1   Data Acquisition and Processing

The pCT and CBCT data was acquired during radiotherapy for 10 prostate cancer patients from a single centre. The pCT was acquired approximately 14 days prior to the first treatment fraction CBCT and 7 CBCTs were available for each patient, including the first and last CBCT.

ADMIRE (v3.35.1, ELEKTA, Stockholm, Sweden), was used to generate both the sCT and dCT for each CBCT. ADMIRE uses a 2D cycleGAN, based upon the original network described in Zhu *et al.* [11], with an additional loss term (threshold SSIM-weighted L1-norm) introduced to constrain the model further and improve pixel-wise accuracy. The model was trained using 205 paired pCT-CBCT patient volumes from seven clinical centres. Once trained, only the CBCT-sCT generator model is required to generate sCTs. As the model was trained using CBCT from the same manufacturer (but independent of the test images in this experiment), CBCT images did not require pre-processing to generate sCTs.

The dCTs were obtained by applying a DIR in ADMIRE on the pCT. The ADMIRE DIR algorithm comprises a rigid registration to correct for global differences in position and orientation between two images of the same patient, a coarse block-matching DIR to obtain a robust initial alignment, and a dense non-linear image transformation to further refine results and align image details. All registrations were visually checked for large errors.

A total of 220 images were included in the study (10 pCTs, 70 CBCTs, 70 dCTs, 70 sCTs). To ensure the data was accurately paired, all images were resampled and rigidly registered to the pCT frame of reference. Rigid registration was used to minimise deformation error in the analysis. A binary mask was created per patient based on the pCT external contour to separate the subject from non-anatomical information, for example, the treatment couch. As the CBCT has a smaller field of view (FOV), and has end-of-FOV artefacts from the beam shape, the mask was next eroded and cropped to 25 slices.

2.2   Validation Methodology

Global Analysis. The global methodology consisted of several image subtractions to isolate uncertainty in either the DIR and sCT generation. Essentially, the methodology assumes that:

- pCTs differ from CBCTs in terms of anatomical changes and image quality
- pCTs differ from sCTs in terms of anatomical changes and model error
- pCTs differ from dCTs in terms of anatomical changes and DIR error
- CBCTs differ from sCTs in terms of image quality and model error

– CBCTs differ from dCTs in terms of image quality and DIR error

By visualising these comparisons as a cyclic diagram, as shown in Fig. 1, paths can be defined where image subtractions can isolate anatomical changes (red arrows and boxes) and image quality (green arrows and boxes). The remaining differences in signal after the defined subtractions capture the accuracy of the deformable registration and model performance.

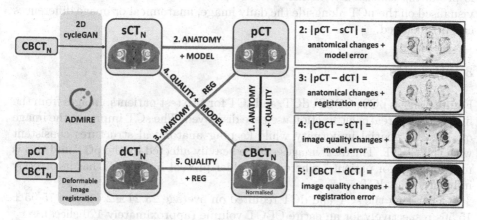

Fig. 1. Diagram of differences obtainable from the four core patient scans; the planning CT (pCT), on-treatment CBCT, synthetic-CT (sCT) and deformed CT (dCT). Attributed to each difference is an assumed cause; model or registration error, as well as anatomical or image quality changes (red and green respectively). For completeness, we assume the difference between the pCT and CBCT is due to only anatomy and quality, however this comparison is not required for the methodology. (Color figure online)

To remove any impact of daily fluctuations in CBCT calibration, the CBCTs were normalised based upon grey levels within the prostate contour prior to subtractions. The mean absolute pixel value of the difference for each time point per patient was calculated. Difference 2 was compared to difference 3 and difference 4 was compared to difference 5 using a paired intra-patient Mann-Whitney U test. We tested for the alternative hypothesis to determine if the median difference in one arm of the comparison is significantly greater than in the other. A greater value corresponds to worse performance and a value of $p<0.05$ considered significant. Statistical analysis was performed in RStudio Version 1.3.959.

Local Analysis. To investigate local differences, a voxel-wise, paired Student T-test was implemented. For this, the dCT was labelled as 0 and the sCT labelled as 1, and the test statistic (t-value) was calculated in each voxel to provide a 3D distribution of the t-value magnitude – a t map. Permutation testing was used to test for statistical significance: the image labels were permuted, and the t-value recalculated to approximate the distribution of the statistic under the null hypothesis that there is no difference between the dCT and sCT. For each permutation (1000 in this study), a new t-map is generated, allowing for the calculation of the most extreme (positive and negative) values of t. The ranking of the extreme t-values for all permutations enables the identification of regions in which there is a significant difference between images for varying levels of significance. For this work, we chose the 90th percentile of extreme t. This allows a visualisation of where the two approaches perform equally well, or one is producing consistently higher or lower pixel values. When these t-maps are visualised on the pCT alongside the daily image, anatomical or image differences can be allocated.

3   Results

Figure 2 shows pCT, CBCT, dCT, and sCT for two test patients. Images from the first and last treatment fraction used are displayed. The sCT improves the image quality and spatial uniformity while keeping anatomical structures consistent with the CBCT. The dCT images can be heavily affected by the pCT and this is most obvious for patient 7 where the bladder present in the pCT has incorrectly influenced the dCT.

Generating the sCT and dCT required on average 23.24 ± 2.43s and 75.05 ± 15.56s respectively for an entire CBCT volume (approximately 120 slices).

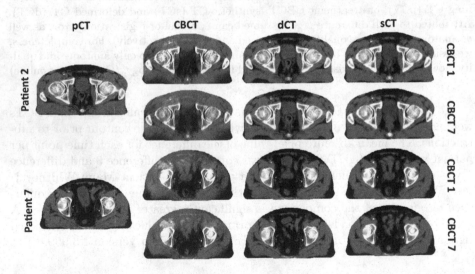

Fig. 2. pCT, CBCT, dCT and sCTs generated by the cycleGAN model for two test patients. Images from the first and last available treatment fraction are displayed.

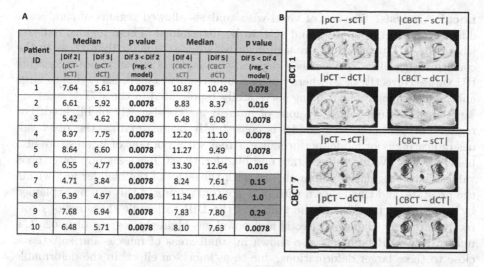

A

Patient ID	Median		p value	Median		p value
	|Dif 2| (pCT-sCT)	|Dif 3| (pCT-dCT)	Dif 3 < Dif 2 (reg. < model)	|Dif 4| (CBCT-sCT)	|Dif 5| (CBCT dCT)	Dif 5 < Dif 4 (reg. < model)
1	7.64	5.61	0.0078	10.87	10.49	0.078
2	6.61	5.92	0.0078	8.83	8.37	0.016
3	5.42	4.62	0.0078	6.48	6.08	0.0078
4	8.97	7.75	0.0078	12.20	11.10	0.0078
5	8.64	6.60	0.0078	11.27	9.49	0.0078
6	6.55	4.77	0.0078	13.30	12.64	0.016
7	4.71	3.84	0.0078	8.24	7.61	0.15
8	6.39	4.97	0.0078	11.34	11.46	1.0
9	7.68	6.94	0.0078	7.83	7.80	0.29
10	6.48	5.71	0.0078	8.10	7.63	0.0078

Fig. 3. A) Intra-patient Mann-Whitney U test results. Highlighted boxes indicate sCT error < dCT error. B) Absolute difference maps for the first and last available on-treatment image for Patient 2. Difference maps are compared within columns to determine superiority of model or DIR. Darker pixels indicated areas of disagreement between the pCT or CBCT and dCT or sCT.

3.1 Validation Methodology

Global Analysis. In Fig. 3A, the results of the intra-patient Mann-Whitney U test are included alongside the median signal from each subtraction arm, calculated from the mean absolute difference across all timepoints. Figure 3B shows difference maps for the first and last available on-treatment image for an example patient, generated as a result of calculating the differences. Darker pixels indicate areas of disagreement between the scans being compared.

Considering the comparisons in the anatomy arm of the analysis: pCT-sCT and pCT-dCT, the registration error (Dif 3) is significantly smaller across treatment than the model error (Dif 2) in 100% of cases. This is visualised in Fig. 3B where sCT maps appear darker than dCT maps and anatomical differences are more frequent. This may highlight that the images used in training the network are not directly comparable to the images available in our centre, resulting in a incorrect translation of the HU in the sCT.

For the image quality comparisons: CBCT-sCT and CBCT-dCT, the registration error (Dif 5) is significantly smaller than the model error (Dif 4) across treatment in 60% of cases. In Fig. 3, bony anatomy is highlighted as an area of discrepancy; the sCT models assign incorrect values to these regions. When looking at cases where the model error is less than the registration error, it is clear that in these cases the DIR fails to produce the correct daily anatomy. An example of this is shown in Fig. 2.

Local Analysis. The use of voxel-wise analysis allowed regions of significant difference between the dCT and sCT to be determined. These regions indicate where the sCT pixel values are significantly larger or smaller than those in the corresponding dCT. In identified regions, the model is either 1) not allocating HU values correctly; or 2) where the dCT uncertainty is high, likely due to large anatomical change that is being successfully represented in the sCT.

Across the test cohort, regions of interest are consistently highlighted. For regions on bone, the sCT model is consistently overestimating the pixel values indicating poor model performance. Areas within organs of interest are also being flagged. Within the prostate and bladder, the sCT is assigning lower pixel values. These regions are often aligned with the edges of the bladder and within the prostate, and when shown with pCT contours in Fig. 4 this can be explained by anatomical changes and the failure of the DIR to handle these regions correctly. Similarly, changes in rectal and bowel gas highlight regions of poor dCT uncertainty. DIR failure is also shown in small areas of muscle and soft tissue close to these larger deformations, due to a 'knock-on effect' in the deformable registration.

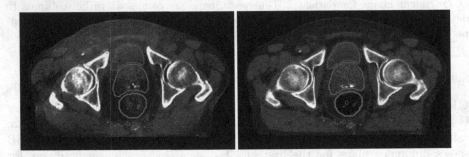

Fig. 4. Highlighted regions of difference between the sCT and dCT across all time points overlayed on both the CBCT (left) and pCT (right). The planning contours for the bladder (red), prostate (green) and rectum (blue) are included for context. Regions outlined in green and purple indicate where the sCT grey values are consistently lower and higher than the corresponding dCT values respectively. (Color figure online)

Interestingly, in cases where artefacts are present on the CBCT, our methodology did not flag the artefact as a region of significant difference. This implies that the sCT model is adequately suppressing CBCT artefacts, like the ring artefact shown in Fig. 5.

4   Discussion

In this work, we propose a novel method to evaluate sCTs generated from routine CBCTs. For this, sCTs and dCTs were used with the pCT and CBCT to investigate the accuracy of sCT generation. Visually, the poor image quality of

 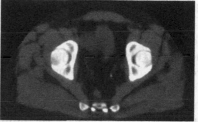

Fig. 5. CBCT images are susceptible to artefacts such as ring artefacts (indicated by the red arrow). Overlayed on the CBCT are the regions of difference highlighted by the proposed methodology. The lack of differences highlighted surrounding the artefact suggests that the cycleGAN model suppresses artefacts when generating sCTs. The corresponding sCT on the right shows the model's correction of the ring artefact. (Color figure online)

CBCT is improved in the sCT and daily patient anatomy is well preserved. sCT appears to handle internal changes, such as gas and organ filling, better than the current ground truth dCT; structures appear better defined.

The proposed framework to evaluate sCT comprises both global and local investigations, with the aim of isolating areas of model and registration failure, across all available images from an individual. The methodology utilises images from multiple time points for each patient, introducing an additional dimension of data, something that is seldom seen within the literature. Existing studies often evaluate the first fraction CBCT to determine validate the 'most perfect' sCT. However, in the context of radiotherapy it is important to consider how accurate the sCT will be in the case of the largest changes or worst artefacts as that is when they will become most useful. This work provides an overall picture of how the model is performing across treatment.

The global analysis is based on assumed differences between patient images. When considering the anatomical arm of the comparisons; an intra-patient Mann-Whitney U test indicated that the mean absolute difference between the pCT and dCT is significantly smaller than that between pCT and sCT. It is expected that the registration error is lower than the model error as DIR typically does not handle large internal changes well. dCT will be closer to pCT anatomy, while sCT, if accurate, will be closer to CBCT anatomy. Further, the dCT will maintain the pCT pixel values so the impact of differences in image quality will be negligible. The anatomy arm of the global framework highlights challenges that arise as a result of using the dCT as a ground truth for evaluating sCTs. In the image quality arm, CBCT − sCT was significantly smaller than CBCT − dCT in 40% of cases. In these cases, the patients experience obvious anatomical changes. This suggests that the overall image quality differences, the disparity between sCT and pCT pixel values, is the driving factor in model error but this is only outweighed when there are large anatomical changes present.

The local analysis was introduced in order to quantify the significance of differences between the dCT and sCT. Our methodology highlights regions where the dCT or sCT pixel values are significantly larger than those in the other image, and so regions where the model or registration is under-performing. Within the test cohort, we are seeing stable regions of interest highlighted. The allocation of model and registration performance to the areas of significance difference will enhance model development in future as it highlights where the model needs improving. The proposed evaluation framework should be validated on an increased cohort, including additional anatomical sites. Further, it would be of interest to investigate how the proposed methodology can be used in combination with traditional image similarity metrics (e.g. the mean absolute error) to evaluate additional synthesis models.

A further reason for large regions of local difference between the dCT and sCT and impacting the global analysis will be due to machine calibration. CBCT machines are not calibrated to the same standard as pCT as their purpose is evaluating patient set-up. Also, scatter conditions will be patient dependent. Differences between CBCT machines can result in large differences in signal intensities and if the training data does not cover this variation then the model performance will suffer. Additionally, it is not uncommon for a patient to be treated on several different machines. We believe that is a potential issue in this study, where we see the sCT maps HU higher in the CBCTs, particularly for bony anatomy. This is useful information for improving model training by indicating how training should be optimised.

For improved visualisation in image guided radiotherapy, the improvement of sCT will enable more accurate position verification and aid clinicians in making a more informed decision on whether to adapt treatment. For applications such as recalculation of dose, our method tells us areas where the mapping between the two image domains needs to be improved, if this is incorrect in the sCT the re-planned treatment dose will also be incorrect. Before clinical implementation, sCT should also be validated with respect to segmentation and dosimetric accuracy. Further investigation into whether dCT error; incorrect anatomy, is more detrimental to treatment than incorrect pixel values on the sCT is required.

5   Conclusion

We have developed a novel method to evaluate synthetic medical images. Our method combines both the strengths of global and local evaluation techniques to provide a detailed understanding of cycleGAN model performance. We have utilised images acquired during radiotherapy as an exemplar application, but the techniques are generalisable to any domain where longitudinal images are available. The combination of global and local methods isolate the uncertainty in a generated ground truth (dCT) and the model performance. Regions are identified where model performance can be further optimised, improving generalisability and resulting in increased patient benefit.

Acknowledgements. This research was supported by NIHR Manchester Biomedical Research Centre, Elekta AB, and CRUK Manchester Centre.

References

1. Boulanger, N., et al.: Deep learning methods to generate synthetic CT from MRI in radiotherapy: A literature review. Physica Med. **89**, 265–281 (2021). https://doi.org/10.1016/j.ejmp.2021.07.027
2. Eckl, M., et al.: Evaluation of a cycle-generative adversarial network-based cone-beam CT to synthetic CT conversion algorithm for adaptive radiation therapy. Physica Med. **80**, 308–316 (2020). https://doi.org/10.1016/j.ejmp.2020.11.007
3. Jaffray, D.A., Siewerdsen, J.H., Wong, J.W., Martinez, A.A.: Flat-panel cone-beam computed tomography for image-guided radiation therapy. Int. J. Radiat. Oncol. Biol. Phys. **53**, 1337–1349 (2002). https://doi.org/10.1016/S0360-3016(02)02884-5
4. Kida, S., et al.: Visual enhancement of Cone-beam CT by use of CycleGAN. Med. Phys. **47**, 998–1010 (2020). https://doi.org/10.1002/mp.13963
5. Kurz, C., et al.: CBCT correction using a cycle-consistent generative adversarial network and unpaired training to enable photon and proton dose calculation. Phys. Med. Biol. **64** (2019). https://doi.org/10.1088/1361-6560/ab4d8c
6. Liang, X., et al.: Generating synthesized computed tomography (CT) from cone-beam computed tomography (CBCT) using cyclegan for adaptive radiation therapy. Phys. Med. Biol. **64** (2019). https://doi.org/10.1088/1361-6560/ab22f9
7. Liu, Y., et al.: CBCT-based synthetic CT generation using deep-attention cycle-GAN for pancreatic adaptive radiotherapy. Med. Phys. **47**, 2472–2483 (2020). https://doi.org/10.1002/mp.14121
8. Maspero, M., et al.: A single neural network for cone-beam computed tomography-based radiotherapy of head-and-neck, lung and breast cancer. Phys. Imaging Radiat. Oncol. **14**, 24–31 (2020). https://doi.org/10.1016/J.PHRO.2020.04.002
9. Szmul, A., et al.: Developing a framework for CBCT-to-CT synthesis in paediatric abdominal radiotherapy. In: Conference on Medical Image Understanding and Analysis (2021)
10. Yang, B., et al.: A comparison study between CNN-based deformed planning CT and CycleGAN-based synthetic CT methods for improving iCBCT image quality. Front. Oncol. **12**, 2339 (2022). https://doi.org/10.3389/FONC.2022.896795
11. Zhu, J.Y., Park, T., Isola, P., Efros, A.A.: Unpaired image-to-image translation using cycle-consistent adversarial networks. In: Proceedings of the IEEE International Conference on Computer Vision 2017, pp. 2242–2251 (2017). https://doi.org/10.1109/ICCV.2017.244

SuperFormer: Volumetric Transformer Architectures for MRI Super-Resolution

Cristhian Forigua[✉][ID], Maria Escobar[ID], and Pablo Arbelaez[ID]

Center for Research and Formation in Artificial Intelligence,
Universidad de los Andes, Bogotá, Colombia
{cd.forigua,mc.escobar11,pa.arbelaez}@uniandes.edu.co

Abstract. This paper presents a novel framework for processing volumetric medical information using Visual Transformers (ViTs). First, We extend the state-of-the-art Swin Transformer model to the 3D medical domain. Second, we propose a new approach for processing volumetric information and encoding position in ViTs for 3D applications. We instantiate the proposed framework and present SuperFormer, a volumetric transformer-based approach for Magnetic Resonance Imaging (MRI) Super-Resolution. Our method leverages the 3D information of the MRI domain and uses a local self-attention mechanism with a 3D relative positional encoding to recover anatomical details. In addition, our approach takes advantage of multi-domain information from volume and feature domains and fuses them to reconstruct the High-Resolution MRI. We perform an extensive validation on the Human Connectome Project dataset and demonstrate the superiority of volumetric transformers over 3D CNN-based methods. Our code and pretrained models are available at https://github.com/BCV-Uniandes/SuperFormer.

Keywords: MRI reconstruction · Super-resolution · Visual transformers

1 Introduction

High Resolution (HR) Magnetic Resonance Imaging (MRI) contains detailed anatomical structures that are crucial for accurate analysis and diagnosis of several diseases. This modality is commonly used in specialized medical centers. Still, its broader adoption is hindered by costly equipment and long scan times, resulting in small spatial coverage and low Signal-to-Noise Ratio (SNR) [3]. In contrast, Low Resolution (LR) imaging requires lower acquisition time, less storage space, and less sophisticated scanners [17]. Nevertheless, LR medical images suffer from artifacts of patient's motion and lack detailed anatomical structures. Therefore, volumetric image Super-Resolution (SR) is a promising framework for generating HR MRIs by mapping them from a LR input while keeping the advantages of the LR acquisition.

The human Connectome Project (HCP) dataset [20] has been widely used to study the medical imaging SR framework since it provides HR volumetric MRI

C. Zhao et al. (Eds.): SASHIMI 2022, LNCS 13570, pp. 132–141, 2022.
https://doi.org/10.1007/978-3-031-16980-9_13

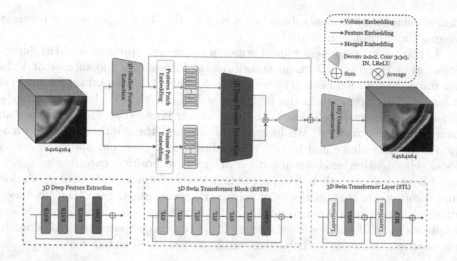

Fig. 1. Overview of our method. SuperFormer encodes features and volume embeddings for deep feature extraction through volumetric transformers and combines the multi-domain representations to reconstruct the super-resolved volume.

from 1,113 subjects [2,3,22]. There are two different approaches that tackle the problem of medical imaging SR. On one hand, 2D oriented methods interpret the 3D information as a set of slices without any volumetric interaction [16,18]. On the other hand, 3D-based approaches exploit the inherent connections of the volumetric information [6,7,9,15]. For instance, the seminal works mDCSRN [2] and MRDG48 [22] propose 3D Generative Adversarial Networks (GANs) to super-resolve MRI volumes with high perceptual quality on the HCP dataset. However, there is a lack of a standardized evaluation framework for 3D medical image SR, and the proposed methods are not publicly available, limiting the progress in this area.

Recently, the computer vision community has experienced the revolution of Vision Transformers (ViT)s [5] for several computer vision tasks [1,4,14]. Unlike CNNs, which have restricted receptive fields, ViTs encode visual representations from a sequence of 2D patches and leverage self-attention mechanisms for capturing long-range global information [10]. Since ViTs learn stronger feature representations, they are commonly used as feature encoders for further downstream tasks. Liu *et al.* proposed Shifted windows (Swin) Transformer, a 2D transformer backbone that uses non-overlapping windows to compute self-attention at multi-scale modeling. Since its introduction, Swin Transformers have achieved state-of-the-art results in several computer vision tasks [14]. Although transformers are being adopted in the medical imaging domain for problems such as 3D medical segmentation [10,11,19,25,26], their potential remains unexplored on the 3D medical SR framework. Feng *et al.* [8] proposed Task Transformer Network, a transformer-based method for MRI reconstruction and SR. However, this 2D-oriented approach does not fully leverage the continuous information in the 3D domain since they process volumes on a slice by slice basis, ignoring the inherent volumetric information of MRIs.

In this paper, we present SuperFormer, a volumetric approach for MRI Super-Resolution based on 3D visual transformers. Inspired by the success of ViTs for image restoration tasks [12], we create a volumetric adaptation for medical imaging. This approach is the first to use ViTs in the 3D domain for medical imaging Super-Resolution to the best of our knowledge. Figure 1 shows an overview of our method. We leverage the 3D and the multi-domain information from the volume and feature embeddings. Moreover, our approach uses a local self-attention mechanism with a 3D relative position encoding to generate SR volumes by volumetric processing. We perform an extensive validation and demonstrate the superiority of volumetric transformers over 3D CNN-based methods. Additionally, our results indicate that using multi-domain embeddings improves the performance of volumetric transformers compared to single-domain approaches. Our main contributions can be summarized as follows:

1. We propose a 3D generalization of the Swin Transformer framework to serve as a general-purpose backbone for medical tasks on volumetric data.
2. We introduce a new approach for processing volumetric information and encoding position in ViTs for 3D frameworks, increasing the transformer's receptive field and ensuring a volumetric understanding.
3. We present SuperFormer, a novel volumetric visual transformer for MRI Super-Resolution. Our method leverages the 3D and multi-domain information from volume and feature embeddings to reconstruct HR MRIs using a local self-attention mechanism.

Furthermore, we provide a medical SR toolbox to promote further research in 3D MRI Super-Resolution. Our toolbox includes the extension of one transformer-based and two CNN methods into the 3D framework. Our toolbox, source code, dataset division, and pre-trained models are publicly available.

2   Method

We propose SuperFormer, a transformer-based network that generates HR MRI volumes by mapping them from a LR volume to the high-resolution space. SuperFormer leverages the 3D information of medical images and multi-domain information by using volumetric transformers that analyze the image and feature domains of the input volume. Then, SuperFormer processes both domains together to reconstruct the HR output. Figure 1 shows an overview of the proposed method.

Volumetric Transformer Processing. Transformer architectures for natural images operate on a sequence of 1D input embeddings extracted from the 2D domain. In the 3D domain, we need to compute these embeddings from volumetric information. Given an input volume $X \in \mathbb{R}^{H \times W \times D \times C}$, we first extract

3D tokens as non-overlapping patches with a resolution of (H', W', D') from X. Each token has a dimension of $H' \times W' \times D' \times C$. Subsequently, we project the 3D tokens into a C_{emb}-dimensional space, which remains constant throughout the transformer layers via an embedding layer. Then, we flatten the embedded representations to obtain the one-dimensional embeddings that the transformers process. Under this configuration, the transformers can operate on 1D embeddings that encode the 3D information and provide a volumetric perception of the input volume, have a larger receptive field depending on the patch resolution, and have fewer computational costs and hardware constraints.

2.1   Feature Embedding

To compute the feature representation of the input volume, SuperFormer first extracts 3D shallow features directly from the input. Then, the feature patch embedding layer extracts 3D tokens from these features and projects them for further volumetric transformer processing. Since the shallow features encode low-frequency information of the input volume, the Feature Embedding ensures the transformers consider the low frequencies for recovering the lost anatomical details.

3D Shallow Feature Extraction. Given a LR volume $V_{LQ} \in \mathbb{R}^{H \times W \times D \times C_{in}}$, where H, W, D and C_{in} are the image height, width, depth and input channel number, respectively, we use a $3 \times 3 \times 3$ convolutional layer to extract the shallow features $F_0 \in \mathbb{R}^{H \times W \times D \times C_{emb}}$, where C_{emb} is the embedding dimension. By putting this layer at an early stage of processing, we achieve better results and more stable optimization [24], while mapping the input channel dimension to a higher dimensional space for volumetric processing.

2.2   Volume Embedding

The intensity information in the 3D domain contains relevant information about patterns and anatomical structures that are volumetrically organized in the MRI. Thus, encoding the volume domain provides a clear idea of the structures we want to recover. SuperFormer encodes volume representations by processing the input directly in the volume domain. We use a volumetric patch embedding layer that computes the 3D tokens directly from the input and projects them into the C_{emb}-dimensional space.

2.3   3D Deep Feature Extraction

SuperFormer processes the feature and volume embedding representations by extracting 3D deep features for each domain. To compute these deep representations, SuperFormer employs K 3D Residual Swin Transformer blocks (RSTB) and a final $3 \times 3 \times 3$ convolutional layer. Each RSTB is a residual block that consists of L 3D Swin transformer layers (STL), a $3 \times 3 \times 3$ convolution layer, and a residual connection.

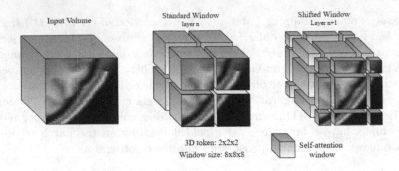

Fig. 2. 3D Shifted window for computing self-attention in the Deep Feature Extraction for $2 \times 2 \times 2$ 3D token and $8 \times 8 \times 8$ window size.

3D Swin Transformer Layer. In contrast to the standard multi-head self-attention of the original visual transformer [21], we model volumetric interactions between tokens as three-dimensional local self-attention with a 3D shifted window mechanism [14]. Then, we partition the input volume into non-overlapping windows to compute the local self-attention, as shown in Fig. 2. Precisely, at STL n, we compute windows of size $M \times M \times M$ to split the input 3D token into $[\frac{H'}{M}] \times [\frac{W'}{M}] \times [\frac{D'}{M}]$ regions. Then, at STL $n + 1$, we shift the previous windows by $\frac{M}{2}$ voxels along each dimension. Inspired by [14,19], we adopt a 3D cyclic-shifting for the continuous computation of the shifted partitions.

Moreover, for a feature in a local window we compute the *query (Q)*, *key (K)* and *value (V)* matrices as

$$Q = XP_Q, \qquad K = XP_K, \qquad V = XP_V \qquad (1)$$

where X is the local window feature, P_Q, P_K and P_V are the shared projection matrices between all windows. We then compute the self-attention as

$$Attention(Q, K, V) = Softmax(\frac{QK^T}{\sqrt{d + B}})V. \qquad (2)$$

where B is a relative position encoding for learning the locations of the 3D tokens regarding the input volume. Unlike most ViTs-based models for 3D image processing [10,19], which use absolute position embeddings [21], we adapt the 2D absolute position bias to the 3D framework. This positional encoding has been proved to lead to better results in the natural image domain [12,14]. The whole STL configuration, as shown in Fig. 1, consists of the standard or shifted local attention mechanism, normalization layers, and a Multi-Layer Perceptron (MLP).

2.4 HQ Volume Reconstruction

SuperFormer learns a deep representation from the shallow features and volume domains to reconstruct the SR volume. First, we combine the information of the two domains by averaging the deep features and aggregating the shallow features with a residual connection. Since deep features differ in size because of the volumetric processing, we employ an up-sampling layer to match the dimensions. Intuitively, the shallow features convey low-frequency information, while the deep features concentrate on recovering the high frequencies. The residual connection transfers the low frequencies directly into the reconstruction stage to recover high frequencies. Specifically, we reconstruct the HR volume by a $3 \times 3 \times 3$ and $1 \times 1 \times 1$ convolutional layers with a LeakyReLU activation function.

3   Experimental Setup

Dataset. We use the Human Connectome Project (HCP) dataset [20] to train and test our method, a large publicly accessible brain structural MRI dataset containing high spatial resolution 3D T1W images from 1,113 healthy subjects. All the images were acquired via Siemens 3T platform using a 32-channel head coil on multiple centers and come in high spatial resolution as 0.7 mm isotropic with a matrix size of $320 \times 320 \times 256$. Ground truth annotations come from these high-quality images, which provide detailed anatomical structures. We used the same data distribution as in [2,22]; 780 for training, 111 for validation, 111 for evaluation, and 111 for testing. We calculate three evaluation metrics for quantitatively measuring the similarity between HR and SR volumes: Peak Signal to Noise Ratio (PSNR), Normalized Root Mean Squared Error (NRMSE), and subject-wise average Structural Similarity Index (SSIM).

Low-Resolution Volumes Generation. Since we need a paired dataset of LR and HR images to train and test SR models, we generate the LR images from the HR ones by following the approach used in [3]. First, we convert the HR volumes into k-space by applying the Fast Fourier Transform (FFT). Then, we degrade the resolution by truncating the outer part of the 3D k-space by a factor of 2×2. Finally, we convert back to the image domain by applying the inverse FFT and linear interpolation to the original HR volume size. This approach mimics the actual acquisition process of LR and HR MRIs since it does not perform any dimensional change but undersamples the frequency k-space [2].

3.1   Implementation Details

We implement SuperFormer in PyTorch and train the model on a workstation with 4 Nvidia RTX 8000 GPUs during 55k iterations during four days. We use an ADAM optimizer with a learning rate of 2e−4 to minimize the L1 loss function with a batch size of 4. For the ablation studies, we use 252 as embedding dimension, six RSTBs, each with six STLs and six attention heads to compute the local self-attention. In SuperFormer's configuration, we use three RSTBs instead of six because of hardware constraints. In addition, we use a patch resolution of $2 \times 2 \times 2$ for volumetric processing.

Table 1. Comparison of our method against the state-of-the-art methods on the test split. SuperFormer outperforms 3D CNN and transformer-based approaches.

	#Params	PSNR ↑	SSIM ↑	NRMSE ↓
2D SwinIR [12]	22.5 M	31,4285 ± 3,5496	0,8297 ± 0,0303	0,2002 ± 0,0761
3D EDSR	41.2 M	31,0217 ± 3,1195	0,9147 ± 0,0314	0,2050 ± 0,0636
3D RRDBNet	115 M	31,3059 ± 3,3876	**0,9355 ± 0,0207**	0,2006 ± 0,0692
SuperFormer	**20 M**	**32,4742 ± 2,9847**	0,9059 ± 0,0271	**0,1747 ± 0,0635**

3.2   Results

Comparison with the State-of-the-Art. We evaluate SuperFormer against two CNN-based methods: EDSR [13], and RRDBNet [23]. Since these methods are originally designed for 2D SR, we extend them for the 3D domain. In addition, we compare our method against the 2D transformer-based SwinIR [12] to demonstrate the advantages of leveraging volumetric information. We can not directly compare our approach against mDCSRN [2] nor MRDG48 [22] because there is no publicly available code for these methods and their experimental framework is different.

Table 1 shows the results in our test split of the HCP dataset. First, by comparing SuperFormer and SwinIR against 3D EDSR and 3D RRDBNet, we find that using a transformer-based approach is greatly beneficial for the task of SR. In fact, SuperFormer outperforms both 3D CNN methods in the PSNR and NRMSE metrics. Moreover, using a 2D transformer like SwinIR still produces higher results than the 3D CNN counterparts. These findings validate the superiority of transformers for deep feature extraction in SR. Second, the comparison between SuperFormer and SwinIR empirically demonstrates that leveraging 3D information through volumetric transformers improves the performance of MRI SR. This finding is consistent with our intuition since the volumetric transformer interprets a three-dimensional vision of the anatomical structures and acquires a broader context for generating a more coherent SR output. Furthermore, Superformer performs significantly better (p-value < 0.05) and has fewer parameters.

Figure 3 shows qualitative results that support the findings of Table 1. In particular, the improvement in perceptual quality is noticeable when comparing the 2D SwinIR baseline against our implementation of volumetric transformers. The images super-resolved with volumetric transformers have sharper structures in comparison with their 2D SwinIR counterpart.

Ablation Study. Our ablation studies include a thorough analysis of Super-Former's embedding configuration. We compare our method against three different configurations: *SR-Features* when we compute the deep features only from the shallow features embedding, *SR-Volume* when we extract them just from the volume embedding, and *SR-Avg* when we take the average between the volume and feature embeddings to compute the deep representations.

Input 3D EDSR 3D RRDBNet 2D SwinIR SuperFormer GT

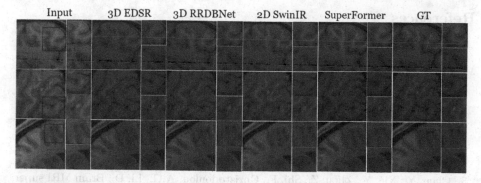

Fig. 3. Qualitative comparison of our method against CNN and 2D transformer-based methods on the axial, coronal and sagittal anatomical axes.

Table 2 shows the results of our final model and the ablation experiments for the validation set of the HCP dataset. These results empirically validate the relevance of using multi-domain embeddings in our final method. If we use the embedding representation of only one domain, regardless of which one, the PSNR decreases by 1 decibel. Additionally, we explore how our approach merges the two embedding representations. The results demonstrate that averaging the extracted deep features brings an improvement across all metrics compared to averaging the embedding representations. These ablation experiments show that SuperFormer's embedding configuration is beneficial for 3D MRI SR.

Table 2. Ablation experiments for SuperFormer's branch configuration on the HCP validation set. We report the results of our final method and ablation experiments.

	PSNR ↑	SSIM ↑	NRMSE ↓
SR-Volume	$31,5354 \pm 2,145$	$0,8644 \pm 0,015$	$0,1829 \pm 0,035$
SR-Features	$31,5195 \pm 3,5209$	$\mathbf{0,9085 \pm 0,344}$	$0,1906 \pm 0,0659$
SR-Avg	$32,0557 \pm 3,1081$	$0,8950 \pm 0,0294$	$0,1777 \pm 0,0570$
SuperFormer	$\mathbf{32,5164 \pm 3.028}$	$0,9059 \pm 0.027$	$\mathbf{0,1668 \pm 0.046}$

4 Conclusion

In this work, we present SuperFormer, a method for SR that leverages the 3D information of MRIs by using volumetric transformers. To the best of our knowledge, SuperFormer is the first method for this task that implements 3D visual transformers and uses a volumetric local self-attention mechanism. We experimentally demonstrate that leveraging the 3D information through volumetric transformers and multi-domain embeddings leads to better results compared to state-of-the-art approaches. Furthermore, our generalizable framework will push the envelope further in the development of volumetric Visual transformers for medical imaging.

References

1. Carion, N., Massa, F., Synnaeve, G., Usunier, N., Kirillov, A., Zagoruyko, S.: End-to-end object detection with transformers. In: Vedaldi, A., Bischof, H., Brox, T., Frahm, J.-M. (eds.) ECCV 2020. LNCS, vol. 12346, pp. 213–229. Springer, Cham (2020). https://doi.org/10.1007/978-3-030-58452-8_13
2. Chen, Y., Shi, F., Christodoulou, A.G., Xie, Y., Zhou, Z., Li, D.: Efficient and accurate MRI super-resolution using a generative adversarial network and 3D multi-level densely connected network. In: Frangi, A.F., Schnabel, J.A., Davatzikos, C., Alberola-López, C., Fichtinger, G. (eds.) MICCAI 2018. LNCS, vol. 11070, pp. 91–99. Springer, Cham (2018). https://doi.org/10.1007/978-3-030-00928-1_11
3. Chen, Y., Xie, Y., Zhou, Z., Shi, F., Christodoulou, A.G., Li, D.: Brain MRI super resolution using 3D deep densely connected neural networks. In: 2018 IEEE 15th International Symposium on Biomedical Imaging (ISBI 2018), April 2018. https://doi.org/10.1109/isbi.2018.8363679
4. Cheng, B., Choudhuri, A., Misra, I., Kirillov, A., Girdhar, R., Schwing, A.G.: Mask2former for video instance segmentation. arXiv preprint arXiv:2112.10764 (2021)
5. Dosovitskiy, A., et al.: An image is worth 16x16 words: transformers for image recognition at scale. arXiv preprint arXiv:2010.11929 (2020)
6. Du, J., Wang, L., Gholipour, A., He, Z., Jia, Y.: Accelerated super-resolution MR image reconstruction via a 3D densely connected deep convolutional neural network. In: 2018 IEEE International Conference on Bioinformatics and Biomedicine (BIBM), pp. 349–355 (2018). https://doi.org/10.1109/BIBM.2018.8621073
7. Du, J., Wang, L., Liu, Y., Zhou, Z., He, Z., Jia, Y.: Brain MRI super-resolution using 3D dilated convolutional encoder-decoder network. IEEE Access 8, 18938–18950 (2020). https://doi.org/10.1109/ACCESS.2020.2968395
8. Feng, C.-M., Yan, Y., Fu, H., Chen, L., Xu, Y.: Task transformer network for joint MRI reconstruction and super-resolution. In: de Bruijne, M., et al. (eds.) MICCAI 2021. LNCS, vol. 12906, pp. 307–317. Springer, Cham (2021). https://doi.org/10.1007/978-3-030-87231-1_30
9. Georgescu, M.I., Ionescu, R.T., Verga, N.: Convolutional neural networks with intermediate loss for 3D super-resolution of CT and MRI scans. IEEE Access 8, 49112–49124 (2020). https://doi.org/10.1109/access.2020.2980266
10. Hatamizadeh, A., et al.: Unetr: transformers for 3D medical image segmentation. In: Proceedings of the IEEE/CVF Winter Conference on Applications of Computer Vision, pp. 574–584 (2022)
11. Karimi, D., Vasylechko, S.D., Gholipour, A.: Convolution-free medical image segmentation using transformers. In: de Bruijne, M., et al. (eds.) MICCAI 2021. LNCS, vol. 12901, pp. 78–88. Springer, Cham (2021). https://doi.org/10.1007/978-3-030-87193-2_8
12. Liang, J., Cao, J., Sun, G., Zhang, K., Van Gool, L., Timofte, R.: Swinir: image restoration using swin transformer. In: Proceedings of the IEEE/CVF International Conference on Computer Vision, pp. 1833–1844 (2021)
13. Lim, B., Son, S., Kim, H., Nah, S., Mu Lee, K.: Enhanced deep residual networks for single image super-resolution. In: Proceedings of the IEEE Conference on Computer Vision and Pattern Recognition Workshops, pp. 136–144 (2017)
14. Liu, Z., et al.: Swin transformer: hierarchical vision transformer using shifted windows. In: Proceedings of the IEEE/CVF International Conference on Computer Vision, pp. 10012–10022 (2021)

15. Pham, C.H., et al.: Multiscale brain MRI super-resolution using deep 3D convolutional networks. Comput. Med. Imaging Graph. **77**, 101647 (2019). https://doi.org/10.1016/j.compmedimag.2019.101647. https://www.sciencedirect.com/science/article/pii/S0895611118304105

16. Qiu, D., Zheng, L., Zhu, J., Huang, D.: Multiple improved residual networks for medical image super-resolution. Future Gener. Comput. Syst. **116**, 200–208 (2021). https://doi.org/10.1016/j.future.2020.11.001. https://www.sciencedirect.com/science/article/pii/S0167739X20330259

17. Sarracanie, M., LaPierre, C.D., Salameh, N., Waddington, D.E., Witzel, T., Rosen, M.S.: Low-cost high-performance MRI. Sci. Rep. **5**(1), 1–9 (2015). https://doi.org/10.1038/srep15177

18. Shi, J., et al.: MR image super-resolution via wide residual networks with fixed skip connection. IEEE J. Biomed. Health Inform. **23**(3), 1129–1140 (2019). https://doi.org/10.1109/JBHI.2018.2843819

19. Tang, Y., et al.: Self-supervised pre-training of swin transformers for 3D medical image analysis. In: Proceedings of the IEEE/CVF Conference on Computer Vision and Pattern Recognition, pp. 20730–20740 (2022)

20. Van Essen, D.C., Smith, S.M., Barch, D.M., Behrens, T.E., Yacoub, E., Ugurbil, K.: The WU-Minn human connectome project: an overview. Neuroimage **80**, 62–79 (2013). https://doi.org/10.1016/j.neuroimage.2013.05.041

21. Vaswani, A., et al.: Attention is all you need. In: Advances in Neural Information Processing Systems, vol. 30 (2017)

22. Wang, J., Chen, Y., Wu, Y., Shi, J., Gee, J.: Enhanced generative adversarial network for 3D brain MRI super-resolution. In: Proceedings of the IEEE/CVF Winter Conference on Applications of Computer Vision, pp. 3627–3636 (2020)

23. Wang, X., et al.: Esrgan: enhanced super-resolution generative adversarial networks. In: Proceedings of the European Conference on Computer Vision (ECCV) Workshops (2018)

24. Xiao, T., Singh, M., Mintun, E., Darrell, T., Dollár, P., Girshick, R.: Early convolutions help transformers see better. Adv. Neural. Inf. Process. Syst. **34**, 30392–30400 (2021)

25. Xie, Y., Zhang, J., Shen, C., Xia, Y.: CoTr: efficiently bridging CNN and transformer for 3D medical image segmentation. In: de Bruijne, M., et al. (eds.) MICCAI 2021. LNCS, vol. 12903, pp. 171–180. Springer, Cham (2021). https://doi.org/10.1007/978-3-030-87199-4_16

26. Zhang, Y., et al.: A multi-branch hybrid transformer network for corneal endothelial cell segmentation. In: de Bruijne, M., et al. (eds.) MICCAI 2021. LNCS, vol. 12901, pp. 99–108. Springer, Cham (2021). https://doi.org/10.1007/978-3-030-87193-2_10

Evaluating the Performance of StyleGAN2-ADA on Medical Images

McKell Woodland[1,2(✉)] ⓘ, John Wood[1], Brian M. Anderson[1,4] ⓘ,
Suprateek Kundu[1], Ethan Lin[1], Eugene Koay[1], Bruno Odisio[1],
Caroline Chung[1], Hyunseon Christine Kang[1] ⓘ, Aradhana M. Venkatesan[1],
Sireesha Yedururi[1], Brian De[1] ⓘ, Yuan-Mao Lin[1] ⓘ, Ankit B. Patel[2,3],
and Kristy K. Brock[1] ⓘ

[1] The University of Texas MD Anderson Cancer Center, Houston, TX 77030, USA
MEWoodland@mdanderson.org
[2] Rice University, Houston, TX 77005, USA
[3] Baylor College of Medicine, Houston, TX 77030, USA
[4] University of California San Diego, La Jolla, CA 92093, USA

Abstract. Although generative adversarial networks (GANs) have shown promise in medical imaging, they have four main limitations that impede their utility: computational cost, data requirements, reliable evaluation measures, and training complexity. Our work investigates each of these obstacles in a novel application of StyleGAN2-ADA to high-resolution medical imaging datasets. Our dataset is comprised of liver-containing axial slices from non-contrast and contrast-enhanced computed tomography (CT) scans. Additionally, we utilized four public datasets composed of various imaging modalities. We trained a StyleGAN2 network with transfer learning (from the Flickr-Faces-HQ dataset) and data augmentation (horizontal flipping and adaptive discriminator augmentation). The network's generative quality was measured quantitatively with the Fréchet Inception Distance (FID) and qualitatively with a visual Turing test given to seven radiologists and radiation oncologists.

The StyleGAN2-ADA network achieved a FID of 5.22 (±0.17) on our liver CT dataset. It also set new record FIDs of 10.78, 3.52, 21.17, and 5.39 on the publicly available SLIVER07, ChestX-ray14, ACDC, and Medical Segmentation Decathlon (brain tumors) datasets. In the visual Turing test, the clinicians rated generated images as real 42% of the time, approaching random guessing. Our computational ablation study revealed that transfer learning and data augmentation stabilize training and improve the perceptual quality of the generated images. We observed the FID to be consistent with human perceptual evaluation of medical images. Finally, our work found that StyleGAN2-ADA consistently produces high-quality results without hyperparameter searches or retraining.

Keywords: StyleGAN2-ADA · Fréchet Inception Distance · Visual turing test · Data augmentation · Transfer learning

C. Zhao et al. (Eds.): SASHIMI 2022, LNCS 13570, pp. 142–153, 2022.
https://doi.org/10.1007/978-3-031-16980-9_14

1   Introduction

Recently, generative adversarial networks (GANs) have shown promise in many medical imaging tasks, including data augmentation in computer-aided diagnosis [21], image segmentation [29], image reconstruction [18], treatment planning [1], image translation [10], and anomaly detection [23]. Despite their potential in medical imaging, GANs have several drawbacks that impede both their capabilities and utilization in the medical field. These obstacles include computational cost, data requirements, flawed measures of assessment, and training complexity.

GANs are computationally expensive. The original StyleGAN2 project took 51.06 GPU years to create, 0.23 of which were used for training the Flickr-Faces-HQ (FFHQ) weights used in our paper [15]. Despite being the state-of-the-art generative model for high-resolution images, StyleGAN2 is often not used in medical imaging literature due to its expense [24]. If it is used, images are brought to lower resolutions to offset the cost [20,22]. While StyleGAN [14] (the predecessor to StyleGAN2) has been applied to high-resolution medical images [7], we believe our paper is the first rigorous evaluation of StyleGAN2 on multiple high-resolution medical imaging datasets.

At high-resolutions, GANs require hundreds of thousands of images to effectively train, a requirement that is extremely challenging to satisfy in the medical field. With limited data, the GAN's discriminator overfits on the training examples, obstructing the GAN's ability to converge. Adaptive discriminator augmentation (ADA) was designed to reduce discriminator overfitting through a wide range of data augmentations that do not "leak" to the generated distribution. When applied to a histopathology dataset, ADA improved the FID by 84% [12]. In our paper, we perform a computational ablation study that examines how ADA and transfer learning affects performance on medical images.

One of the greatest challenges in GANs is constructing robust quantitative evaluation measures [17]. The Fréchet Inception Distance (FID) [9] is the standard for state of the art evaluation for generative modeling in natural imaging. It relies on an Inception network that was trained on ImageNet, which does not contain medical images [6], for its calculation. As such, a common assumption in related literature is that the FID is not applicable to medical images. We revisit this assumption by testing the correlation between the FID and human perceptual evaluation on medical images.

GANs are notoriously challenging to train. They have numerous hyperparameters and suffer from training instability. In a large empirical evaluation of various GANs, Lučić et al. [17] found that GAN training is extremely sensitive to hyperparameter settings. A separate study illustrated this sensitivity by performing 1,500 hyperparameter searches on three unique medical imaging datasets with various GAN architectures. The authors found that few models produced meaningful images; even fewer models achieved reasonable metric evaluations [26]. Neither of these studies examined StyleGAN2. Our work is unique in that we test the stability of StyleGAN2, along with its ability to generate quality images without a hyperparameter search.

The main contributions of our research are as follows:

– We apply StyleGAN2 to a variety of high-resolution medical imaging datasets.
– We perform a computational ablation study on the effect of transfer learning and data augmentation on a limited-data medical imaging dataset.
– We provide empirical evidence that the FID is consistent with human perceptual evaluation of medical images.
– We evaluate StyleGAN2's stability and ability to produce quality results without a hyperparameter search.
– We achieve state-of-the-art FIDs on four public datasets.

2   Methods

2.1   Data

We used the 97 non-contrast and 108 contrast enhanced abdominal computed tomography (CT) scans presented in [2]. To accentuate the liver, the data was windowed to a level 50 and a width 350, consistent with the preset values for viewing the liver in a commercial treatment planning system (RayStation v10, RaySearch Laboratories, Stockholm, Sweden). All axial slices that contained no liver information were discarded. Voxel values were mapped to the range [0, 255] and converted each axial slice to a PNG image. In all, our training dataset contained 10,600 512 × 512 images. Three randomly sampled images from our training dataset are shown in the first row of Fig. 1. We used an additional 143,345 512 × 512 images for one experiment in our ablation study. These images were obtained by applying the above mentioned preprocessing steps to 3,029 abdominal CT scans (301 patients) that were retrospectively acquired under an IRB approved protocol.

Separately, our methods were applied to several publicly available datasets. For the "Segmentation of the Liver Competition 2007" (SLIVER07) dataset[1] [8], we used the 20 scans available in the training dataset and converted each slice to a PNG image without any further preprocessing. In total, this dataset consisted of 4,159 512 × 512 images. To our knowledge, the previous best FID (29.06) on this dataset was achieved by Skandarani et al. using the StyleGAN network.

The ChestX-ray14 dataset[2] [28] consists of 112,120 1024 × 1024 Chest X-ray images in PNG format. The previous best FID on the ChestX-ray14 dataset of 8.02 was achieved using a Progressive Growing GAN [24]. No preprocessing on this dataset was performed. The Automated Cardiac Diagnosis Challenge (ACDC) dataset[3] [3] consists of 150 cardiac cine-magnetic resonance imaging (MRI) exams. We used the training dataset, which consists of 100 exams. The images were rescaled to the range [0, 255] using SimpleITK [16] and padded with zeros. Each slice was then converted to a 2D PNG image. In total, this dataset consisted of 1,902 512 × 512 images. The previous best FID on the ACDC training dataset (24.74) was achieved with StyleGAN [26].

---

[1] https://sliver07.grand-challenge.org/.
[2] https://nihcc.app.box.com/v/ChestXray-NIHCC.
[3] https://acdc.creatis.insa-lyon.fr/.

Additionally, we applied StyleGAN2-ADA to a dataset whose FID had not been previously evaluated: the brain tumor data from the Medical Segmentation Decathlon[4] [25], which contains 750 4D MRI volumes. The gadolinium-enhanced T1-weighted 3D images were extracted and windowed to the range [0, 255] using SimpleITK. Slices were converted to 2D PNG images. This dataset consists of 103,030 256×256 PNG images.

2.2 Generative Modeling

Due to its state-of-the-art performance on high-resolution images, we used a StyleGAN2 network as our generative model [15]. For our experiments, we utilized the StyleGAN2 configuration of the official StyleGAN3 repository[5] [13]. We used the default parameters provided by the implementation, with the exception of changing β_0 to 0.9 in the Adam optimizer and disabling mixed precision. We did not perform a hyperparameter search. We explored the effects of transfer learning and data augmentation in an ablation study with the following experimental designs:

1. **Baseline** Disable all StyleGAN2 augmentations and train from scratch.
2. **Pretrained** Disable all augmentations and begin training with pretrained weights from StyleGAN2 trained on the FFHQ dataset.
3. **Augmented** Enable mirroring (horizontal flipping) and ADA and train from scratch.
4. **Pretrained and Augmented** Enable mirroring and ADA and begin training with the official FFHQ StyleGAN2 weights.

Each of these experiments was performed on our liver CT training dataset. A variation of Experiment 1 was also performed where 143,345 liver images were added to the training dataset. Furthermore, Experiment 4 was performed on the four public datasets. Each experiment was performed on a DGX with eight 40GB A100 GPUs. DGXs were accessed using the XNAT platform [19]. Experiments ran for 6,250 ticks with metrics calculated and weights saved every 50 ticks. Each experiment took approximately 1.5, 4, and 7 days to complete for 256×256, 512×512, and 1024×1024 sized datasets, respectively. We repeated each experiment five times to test algorithm stability.

2.3 Evaluation Measures

Fréchet Inception Distance. The FID is the standard for state of the art GAN evaluation in natural imaging. It is the Fréchet distance between two multivariate Gaussians constructed from representations extracted from the coding layer of an Inception network that was pretrained on ImageNet [9]. Several advantages of the FID include its ability to distinguish generated from real samples, agreement with human perceptual judgements, sensitivity to distortions, and computational

---

[4] http://medicaldecathlon.com/.
[5] https://github.com/NVlabs/stylegan3.

and sample efficiency [4,9]. As such, we used the FID as our quantitative metric. For each run, we reported the best FID achieved during training. We used the model weights associated with each best FID for further qualitative analysis. For statistical testing, we used permutation tests with $\alpha = 0.05$.

Because ImageNet does not contain medical images, prior publications have argued that the FID is not applicable to medical imaging [5,11,27]. As such, they substitute the Inception network with their own encoding networks. This trend has several limitations. First, the FID is only consistent as a metric inasmuch as the same encoding model is used. By using a new model, the reported distance can no longer be considered in the context of prior work that utilizes the FID. Second, the algorithm designer is formulating their own evaluation metric, which will likely introduce unquantified bias into the presented results. Due to these limitations, we use the original definition of the FID for our calculations.

Visual Turing Tests. Because the applicability of the FID to medical imaging is not well understood, our first visual Turing test evaluated the correlation between the FID and human perception on medical images. The test was administered in a Google Form with four sections (created in random order), one per experiment. Each section contained 40 randomly shuffled images, 20 real and 20 generated. All images were randomly selected and only appeared once in the test. The test was given to five participants with a medical physics background who were not familiar with the images. We evaluated the test with the false positive rate (FPR) and false negative rate (FNR).

The purpose of the second visual Turing test was to rigorously validate the perceptual quality of the images generated by the pretrained StyleGAN2-ADA model on our dataset. This test consisted of 50 real and 50 generated images randomly sampled and shuffled. Each section contained one image, a question asking the participant if the image was real or fake, and a Likert scale assessing how realistic the image was. The Likert scale was between 1 (fake) and 5 (real). The test was given to seven radiologists or radiation oncologists with an average of 10 years of radiological experience. The results of the Turing test were evaluated with precision, recall, accuracy, FPR, and FNR metrics. Additionally, we computed the average Likert values for both real and generated images. For statistical testing, we used permutation tests with $\alpha = 0.10$.

3   Results

On our dataset, the average ($\pm$SD) FIDs, n = 5, achieved were 10.70 ($\pm$0.72), 7.62 ($\pm$0.35), 7.51 ($\pm$0.89), and 5.22 ($\pm$0.17), for Experiments 1–4, respectively. Both transfer learning and data augmentation were effective tools in mitigating overfitting on limited medical data. Individually, they improved upon the baseline FID by about 30% (95% confidence). Even greater improvements were achieved (50% decrease) in the FID when transfer learning and augmentations were used in tandem (95% confidence). Data augmentation significantly decreased the generator's loss and stabilized training, as shown in Fig. 3 in the Appendix (95%

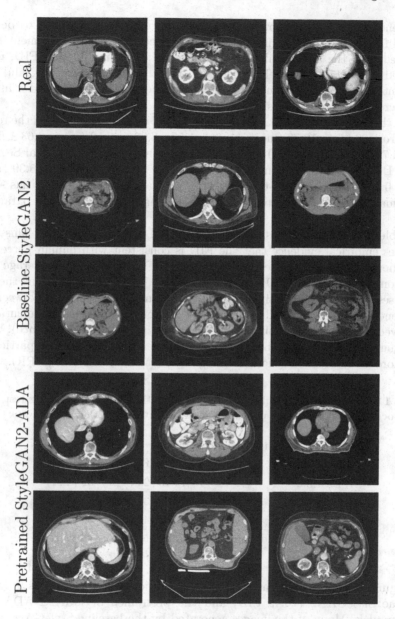

Fig. 1. The first row contains images from our training dataset. The second and third rows contain images generated by the baseline StyleGAN2 model. The fourth and fifth rows contain images generated by the pretrained StyleGAN2-ADA model with augmentations. All images were randomly selected. The images generated by the pretrained StyleGAN2-ADA model demonstrate reduced noise artifacts, enhanced detail, and superior anatomical accuracy

confidence). Our results show that transfer learning does not need to be performed from a medical imaging dataset to be effective. When Experiment 1 was repeated with the additional 143,345 images, the average (± SD) FID, n = 5, attained was 8.45 (±0.20). This demonstrates that transfer learning and data augmentation, both in conjunction and independently, outperformed a fifteen-fold increase in the dataset size.

On the SLIVER07, ChestX-ray14, and ACDC datasets, we lowered the record FIDs from 29.06 to 10.78 (mean 11.99 ± 1.57), 8.02 to 3.52 (mean 3.63 ± 0.07), and 24.74 to 21.17 (mean 21.43 ± 0.32), respectively. For the Medical Segmentation Decathlon (brain tumors) data, we set a new record FID of 5.39 (mean 5.53 ± 0.01). These state-of-the-art results indicate that StyleGAN2 has stable performance and can generate quality medical images without a hyperparameter search.

Table 1 shows the results of the multi-model visual Turing test. This table provides empirical evidence that the FID is consistent with human perceptual judgement on medical images: the lower the FID, the higher the average FPR (Pearson correlation of −0.91, 90% confidence). This suggests that as the FID decreases, it becomes increasingly difficult for humans to distinguish between real and generated images. In addition, the FPRs demonstrate that augmentations improved the perceptual quality of the generated images (90% confidence). When data augmentation was combined with transfer learning, the average participant was more likely to say a generated image was real than fake (55% FPR).

Table 1. Average (±SD) results, n = 5, of the multi-model visual Turing test. FIDs are associated with the model used to generate the images in the Turing tests.

Multi-model visual turing test results			
Experiment	FID	FPR [%]	FNR [%]
1. Baseline	10.43	29 (±27)	32 (±21)
2. Pretrained	7.78	34 (±19)	32 (±18)
3. Augmented	7.15	49 (±11)	34 (±18)
4. Pretrained and Augmented	**5.06**	**55** (±9)	**41** (±11)

Figure 1 displays randomly selected real and generated images from the baseline StyleGAN2 (10.43 FID) and the pretrained StyleGAN2-ADA (5.06 FID) models. Many of the images generated by the baseline StyleGAN2 model contain noise artifacts, especially in the liver. Images generated by the pretrained StyleGAN2-ADA model show reduced noise, enhanced detail, and superior anatomical accuracy. This perceptual improvement substantiates the claim that the FID is applicable to medical images. The Appendix contains auxiliary pretrained StyleGAN2-ADA generated images (Fig. 4) and a larger image demonstrating noise artifacts in the baseline StyleGAN2 model (Fig. 2).

The results of the Turing test given to clinicians, shown in Table 2, further confirm the high-quality nature of the generated images. Overall, the clinicians

Table 2. Results of the visual Turing test given to clinicians.

Clinician visual turing test results					
Clinician	Precision [%]	Recall [%]	Accuracy [%]	FPR [%]	FNR [%]
1	80	86	82	22	14
2	76	44	65	14	56
3	56	80	58	64	20
4	79	62	73	16	38
5	58	98	64	70	2
6	54	88	56	76	12
7	59	48	57	34	52
Average (±SD)	66 (±12)	72 (±21)	65 (±10)	42 (±27)	28 (±21)

classified generated images as real 42% of the time, approaching the equivalent of random guessing. Those that had low FPRs typically had higher FNRs and vice versa (Pearson correlation of -0.71, 90% confidence), indicating a tendency of clinicians to favor either "real" or "fake" when they were unsure. This tendency was likely a factor in the high interobserver variability among the FPRs. Another likely factor was the experience of the clinicians. For the Likert scale, we found that real images achieved an average score of 3.99 (±1.00) and generated images a score of 3.23 (±1.21). The overlapping 95% confidence intervals further demonstrate both the challenging nature of the task and the high-quality nature of the generated images.

4   Conclusion

We applied StyleGAN2 to multiple high-resolution medical image datasets. Combined with transfer learning and data augmentation, the architecture achieved state-of-the-art results consistently, without any hyperparameter searches or retraining. The generated images were of sufficient quality that an expert's ability to tell whether or not an image was generated approached random guessing. Additionally, we found that the "realness" score, based on a 5-point Likert scale, differed between the generated and real images by less than the standard deviation between clinicians. Across a variety of medical imaging modalities, we were able to set new record FID scores on four publicly-available datasets.

Furthermore, our research provided empirical evidence that the FID is consistent with human perceptual judgement on medical images. A multi-model visual Turing test revealed that as the FID improved, the participants perceived artificially generated images as real more frequently. Qualitatively, we saw an appreciable improvement in the fidelity of the generated images as the FID improved from 10.43 to 5.06. From these results, we concluded that the FID is indeed an appropriate metric for medical images.

Acknowledgements. This work was supported by the Tumor Measurement Initiative through the MD Anderson Strategic Initiative Development Program (STRIDE). We thank the NIH Clinical Center for the ChestX-ray14 dataset.

Appendix

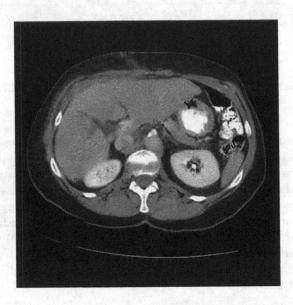

Fig. 2. This image was generated by the baseline StyleGAN2 model (10.43 FID). It was chosen to demonstrate the noise artifacts contained in many of the images generated by the model.

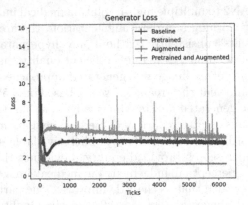

Fig. 3. The average generator loss (with standard deviation bars) across training. We see that augmentation not only significantly decreases the loss, but also leads to more stable convergence.

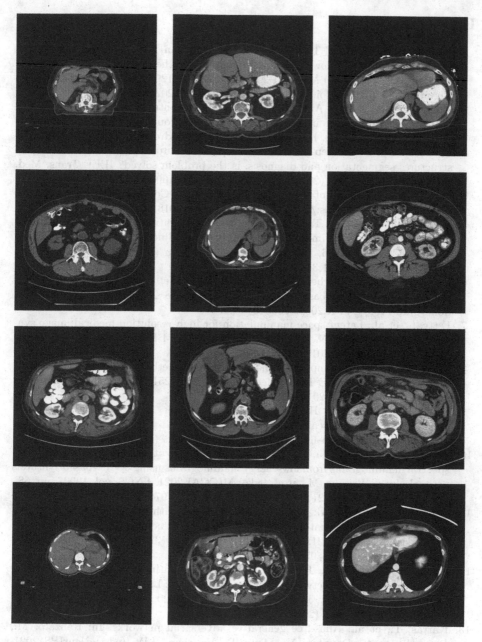

Fig. 4. Randomly selected images generated by the pretrained StyleGAN2-ADA model (5.06 FID).

References

1. Aleef, T.A., Spadinger, I.T., Peacock, M.D., Salcudean, S.E., Mahdavi, S.S.: Rapid treatment planning for low-dose-rate prostate brachytherapy with TP-GAN. In: de Bruijne, M., et al. (eds.) MICCAI 2021. LNCS, vol. 12904, pp. 581–590. Springer, Cham (2021). https://doi.org/10.1007/978-3-030-87202-1_56
2. Anderson, B.M., et al.: Automated contouring of contrast and noncontrast computed tomography liver images with fully convolutional networks. Adv. Radiat. Oncol. **6**, 100464 (2021). https://doi.org/10.1016/j.adro.2020.04.023
3. Bernard, O., et al.: Deep learning techniques for automatic MRI cardiac multi-structures segmentation and diagnosis: is the problem solved? IEEE Trans. Med. Imaging **37**, 2514–2525 (2018). https://doi.org/10.1109/TMI.2018.2837502
4. Borji, A.: Pros and cons of GAN evaluation measures. Comput. Vis. Image Underst. **179**, 41–65 (2019). https://doi.org/10.1016/j.cviu.2018.10.009
5. Chen, J., Wei, J., Li, R.: TarGAN: target-aware generative adversarial networks for multi-modality medical image translation. In: de Bruijne, M., et al. (eds.) MICCAI 2021. LNCS, vol. 12906, pp. 24–33. Springer, Cham (2021). https://doi.org/10.1007/978-3-030-87231-1_3
6. Deng, J., Dong, W., Socher, R., Li, L.J., Li, K., Fei-Fei, L.: Imagenet: a large-scale hierarchical image database. In: CVPR 2009, pp. 248–255. IEEE (2009). https://doi.org/10.1109/CVPR.2009.5206848
7. Fetty, L., et al.: Latent space manipulation for high-resolution medical image synthesis via the StyleGAN. Z. Med. Phys. **30**, 305–314 (2020). https://doi.org/10.1016/j.zemedi.2020.05.001
8. Heimann, T., et al.: Comparison and evaluation of methods for liver segmentation from CT datasets. IEEE Trans. Med. Imaging **28**, 1251–1265 (2009). https://doi.org/10.1109/TMI.2009.2013851
9. Heusel, M., Ramsauer, H., Unterthiner, T., Nessler, B., Hochreiter, S.: GANs trained by a two time-scale update rule converge to a local nash equilibrium. In: NeurIPS 2017, pp. 6629–6640. Curran Associates Inc. (2017)
10. Jiang, Y., Zheng, Y., Jia, W., Song, S., Ding, Y.: Synthesis of contrast-enhanced spectral mammograms from low-energy mammograms using cGAN-based synthesis network. In: de Bruijne, M., et al. (eds.) MICCAI 2021. LNCS, vol. 12907, pp. 68–77. Springer, Cham (2021). https://doi.org/10.1007/978-3-030-87234-2_7
11. Jung, E., Luna, M., Park, S.H.: Conditional GAN with an attention-based generator and a 3D discriminator for 3D medical image generation. In: de Bruijne, M., et al. (eds.) MICCAI 2021. LNCS, vol. 12906, pp. 318–328. Springer, Cham (2021). https://doi.org/10.1007/978-3-030-87231-1_31
12. Karras, T., Aittala, M., Hellsten, J., Laine, S., Lehtinen, J., Aila, T.: Training generative adversarial networks with limited data. In: Larochelle, H., Ranzato, M., Hadsell, R., Balcan, M., Lin, H. (eds.) NeurIPS 2020, vol. 33, pp. 12104–12114. Curran Associates, Inc. (2020)
13. Karras, T., et al.: Alias-free generative adversarial networks. In: Ranzato, M., Beygelzimer, A., Dauphin, Y., Liang, P., Vaughan, J.W. (eds.) NeurIPS 2021, vol. 34, pp. 852–863. Curran Associates, Inc. (2021)
14. Karras, T., Laine, S., Aila, T.: A style-based generator architecture for generative adversarial networks. In: CVPR 2019, pp. 4396–4405. IEEE (2019). https://doi.org/10.1109/CVPR.2019.00453
15. Karras, T., Laine, S., Aittala, M., Hellsten, J., Lehtinen, J., Aila, T.: Analyzing and improving the image quality of StyleGAN. In: CVPR 2020, pp. 8107–8116. IEEE (2020). https://doi.org/10.1109/CVPR42600.2020.00813

16. Lowekamp, B., Chen, D., Ibanez, L., Blezek, D.: The design of simpleitk. Front. Neuroinform. **7**, 45 (2013). https://doi.org/10.3389/fninf.2013.00045

17. Lučić, M., Kurach, K., Michalski, M., Gelly, S., Bousquet, O.: Are GANs created equal? A large-scale study. In: Bengio, S., et al. (eds.) NeurIPS 2018, vol. 31. Curran Associates, Inc. (2018)

18. Luo, Y., et al.: 3D transformer-GAN for high-quality PET reconstruction. In: de Bruijne, M., et al. (eds.) MICCAI 2021. LNCS, vol. 12906, pp. 276–285. Springer, Cham (2021). https://doi.org/10.1007/978-3-030-87231-1_27

19. Marcus, D.S., Olsen, T.R., Ramaratnam, M., Buckner, R.L.: The extensible neuroimaging archive toolkit: an informatic platform for managing, exploring, and sharing neuroimaging data. Neuroinformatics **5**, 11–33 (2007). https://doi.org/10.1385/ni:5:1:11

20. Montero, A., Bonet-Carne, E., Burgos-Artizzu, X.P.: Generative adversarial networks to improve fetal brain fine-grained plane classification. Sensors **21**, 7975 (2021). https://doi.org/10.3390/s21237975

21. Pang, T., Wong, J.H.D., Ng, W.L., Chan, C.S.: Semi-supervised GAN-based radiomics model for data augmentation in breast ultrasound mass classification. Comput. Methods Programs Biomed. **203**, 106018 (2021). https://doi.org/10.1016/j.cmpb.2021.106018

22. Pocevičiūtė, M., Eilertsen, G., Lundström, C.: Unsupervised anomaly detection in digital pathology using GANs. In: ISBI 2021, pp. 1878–1882 (2021). https://doi.org/10.1109/ISBI48211.2021.9434141

23. Schlegl, T., Seeböck, P., Waldstein, S.M., Schmidt-Erfurth, U., Langs, G.: Unsupervised anomaly detection with generative adversarial networks to guide marker discovery. In: Niethammer, M., et al. (eds.) IPMI 2017. LNCS, vol. 10265, pp. 146–157. Springer, Cham (2017). https://doi.org/10.1007/978-3-319-59050-9_12

24. Segal, B., Rubin, D.M., Rubin, G., Pantanowitz, A.: Evaluating the clinical realism of synthetic chest X-rays generated using progressively growing GANs. SN Comput. Sci. **2**(4), 1–17 (2021). https://doi.org/10.1007/s42979-021-00720-7

25. Simpson, A.L., et al.: A large annotated medical image dataset for the development and evaluation of segmentation algorithms. CoRR abs/1902.09063 (2019). https://doi.org/10.48550/arXiv.1902.09063

26. Skandarani, Y., Jodoin, P.M., Lalande, A.: GANs for medical image synthesis: an empirical study. CoRR abs/2105.05318 (2021). https://doi.org/10.48550/arXiv.2105.05318

27. Tronchin, L., Sicilia, R., Cordelli, E., Ramella, S., Soda, P.: Evaluating GANs in medical imaging. In: Engelhardt, S., et al. (eds.) DGM4MICCAI/DALI -2021. LNCS, vol. 13003, pp. 112–121. Springer, Cham (2021). https://doi.org/10.1007/978-3-030-88210-5_10

28. Wang, X., Peng, Y., Lu, L., Lu, Z., Bagheri, M., Summers, R.: Chestx-ray8: hospital-scale chest x-ray database and benchmarks on weakly-supervised classification and localization of common thorax diseases. In: CVPR 2017, pp. 3462–3471. IEEE (2017). https://doi.org/10.1109/CVPR.2017.369

29. Xun, S., et al.: Generative adversarial networks in medical image segmentation: a review. Comput. Biol. Med. **140**, 105063 (2022). https://doi.org/10.1016/j.compbiomed.2021.105063

Backdoor Attack is a Devil in Federated GAN-Based Medical Image Synthesis

Ruinan Jin[✉] and Xiaoxiao Li[✉]

The University of British Columbia, Vancouver, Canada
ruinanjin@alumni.ubc.ca, xiaoxiao.li@ece.ubc.ca

Abstract. Deep Learning-based image synthesis techniques have been applied in healthcare research for generating medical images to support open research. Training generative adversarial neural networks (GAN) usually requires large amounts of training data. Federated learning (FL) provides a way of training a central model using distributed data from different medical institutions while keeping raw data locally. However, FL is vulnerable to backdoor attack, an adversarial by poisoning training data, given the central server cannot access the original data directly. Most backdoor attack strategies focus on classification models and centralized domains. In this study, we propose a way of attacking federated GAN (FedGAN) by treating the discriminator with a commonly used data poisoning strategy in backdoor attack classification models. We demonstrate that adding a small trigger with size less than 0.5% of the original image size can corrupt the FedGAN model. Based on the proposed attack, we provide two effective defense strategies: global malicious detection and local training regularization. We show that combining the two defense strategies yields a robust medical image generation.

Keywords: GAN · Federated learning · Backdoor attack

1 Introduction

While deep learning (DL) has significantly impacted healthcare research, its impact has been undeniably slower and more limited in healthcare than in other application domains. A significant reason for this is the scarcity of patient data available to the broader machine learning research community, largely owing to patient privacy concerns. Furthermore, even if a researcher is able to obtain such data, ensuring proper data usage and protection is a lengthy process governed by stringent legal requirements. Therefore, synthetic datasets of high quality and realism can be used to accelerate methodological advancements in medicine [4,7].

Like most DL-based tasks, limited data resources is always a challenge for the generative adversarial network (GAN)-based medical synthesis, and data collaboration between different medical institutions makes effects to build a robust

Code is available at https://github.com/Nanboy-Ronan/Backdoor-FedGAN.

© The Author(s), under exclusive license to Springer Nature Switzerland AG 2022
C. Zhao et al. (Eds.): SASHIMI 2022, LNCS 13570, pp. 154–165, 2022.
https://doi.org/10.1007/978-3-031-16980-9_15

model. But this operation will cause data privacy problems which could be a risk of exposing patient information. Federated learning (FL) [15], a privacy-preserving tool, which keeps data on each client locally and exchanges model weights by the server during learning a global model collaboratively. Due to its property of privacy, it is a popular research option in healthcare [24].

However, FL is vulnerable to malicious participants and there are already studies deep dive into different kinds of attacks for classification models in federated scenarios, like gradient inversion attacks and backdoor attacks [2,13]. In a backdoor attack for classification, the attacker adds a trigger signal, such as a small patch with random noise, to its training data and changes the correct label to a wrong one [25]. In FL training, malicious clients can poison training data using a backdoor attack and mislead the global to make incorrect predictions. It is possible for medical imaging backdoor triggers to be induced by (un)intentional artifacts occurring during the sensor acquisition and preparation processes. Recent work [2] observed that backdoor attack takes advantage of the classification model's tendency to overfit the trigger rather than the actual image. This notion inspires us to think about how we can integrate it into generative models in FL.

Exiting backdoor attacks are specifically designed for the classification task or model training in centralized domain. In this work, we focus on backdoor attack on federated GAN (FedGAN) via data poisoning, which under-explored in existing literature. The success of this attack is subsequently determined to be the result of some local discriminators overfitting on the poisoned data and corrupting the local GAN equilibrium, which then further contaminates other clients when averaging the generator's parameters during federated training and yields high generator loss. Based on the attack, we suggest two potential ways of defending it from global- and local-level of FL: detecting the client's adversarial behavior on the server-side and blocking it from dispersing to further, and applying a robust training procedure locally for each client. In our experiment, we apply our adversarial and defense mechanisms to a widely used skin cancer dataset. We show that the adversarial strategy is able to corrupt FedGAN only by adding a trigger with 0.39% size of the original image in the malicious training set.

2 Methods

2.1 Federated Generative Adversarial Network

Figure 1 depicts the framework of the FedGAN in our study. As discriminators in GAN have direct access to clients' private data, exposing the risk of data leakage by inverting their gradients in FL training [13], our FedGAN framework only exchanges generator's parameters with the server while keeping the whole discriminator locally. To this end, our FedGAN locally trains both discriminator and generator pairs and globally shares generators' parameters, which is modified from [22].

Formally, we assume that a trusted central generator G_{server} synthesizes images from a set of N federated clients. Each client C_i, for $i \in [N]$ consists a locally trained discriminator D_i, and a generator G_i. G_i takes random Gaussian

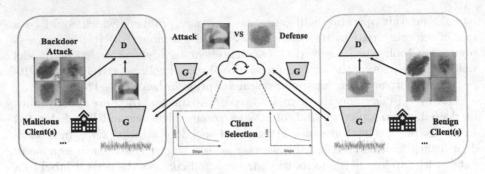

Fig. 1. The overview of our proposed framework.

noise z as input to generate synthetic images, and D_i distinguish the synthetic image $\tilde{x} = G(z)$ v.s. private image x. We adopt FedAvg [18] to aggregate G_i to G_{server}, while keeping D_i locally. At the end, our federated GAN generate synthetic medical data $G_{\text{server}}(z) \sim p_{\text{data}}$ on the server side.

Also, we assume every client, including those malicious ones, follows the given training protocol. For example, they compute gradient correctly as the way instructed by the server and update the exact parameters when they are required to. This is possible by enforcing local FL computations taking place on trusted hardware [20].

2.2 Backdoor Attack Strategies

Backdoor attack is a training time attack that embeds a backdoor into a model by poisoning training data (e.g., adding triggers on the images). State-of-the-art backdoor attack focus on image classification model [5,17] and has been recently studied on FL [2]. Current studies of backdoor attacks in Deep Generative Models train the GAN on a poisoned dataset and input a backdoored noise vector into the generator so that GAN failed to produce images with similar distribution as the data [23,26]. We suggest a way of attacking federated GAN only through the poisoned data with more details below.

Adversarial Goals: Our goal is to perform a backdoor attack, where the objective of the attacker is to corrupt the server generator using poisoned images so that the generator can no longer generate fake medical images with high fidelity. That is, $p_{\tilde{x}} \neq p_{data}$.

Adversarial Capabilities: As mentioned in Sect. 2.1 that the trusted server has control over the local training process. The only room for attack is through providing poisoned data to the local discriminator as shown in Fig. 1.

Adversarial Motivation: A vanilla GAN optimizes loss function in the manner outlined in [9], where the discriminator seeks to maximize the accuracy of the real and fake image classification while the generator seeks to minimize the likelihood that its generated image will be classified as fake. Specifically, the objective is written as follows:

$$\min_{G} \max_{D} \mathbb{E}_{x \sim p_{\text{data}}(x)}[\log D(x)] + \mathbb{E}_{z \sim p_z(z)}[1 - \log D(G(z))] \qquad (1)$$

The optimization of GAN is recognized to be difficult, nevertheless, because the generator is subpar upon learning that $log(D(G(z)))$ is probably saturating [9]. Given the unbalanced nature of GAN, we implement the overfitting on trigger principle into the discriminator of FedGAN's training. The following part gives a detailed explanation of our adversarial model.

Adversarial Model: Our threat model contains a set of M adversarial clients, where $|M| = \alpha|N|$ and $0 < \alpha < 0.5$. For every adversarial client, C_i', the attacker is able to add a trigger δ to every sample $x \in T_i$. The goal of the attacker is to fool the central server generator to produce corrupted images which do not have medical research value.

2.3 Defense Strategies

Existing defense strategies for backdoor attack range from model level to data level. As data are not accessible in FL, model level defense is desired, where a model level detector is built to find the adversarial behavior and refrain it from training with others [11], known as *malicious detection*. Apart from detection, *robust training* is another approach that refines training protocol [19]. To the best of our knowledge, defense for FedGAN is under-explored.

Defender's Capabilities: Let's recall from our setting that a trusted server and more than half of the benign clients are part of our trusted FL pipeline. The benign server have access to the *model parameters* and *training loss*. Note that sharing training loss barely impacts data privacy. Our defense strategies are motivated by the observation that model with backdoor attacks tend to overfit the trigger rather than the actual image [2]. Specifically, in GAN's training, the discriminator overfits on the trigger and perfectly classifies fake and real images, while the generator does not receive effective feedback from the discriminator and then yields high loss and even diverges. To this end, we propose to defend against backdoor attack from both global- and local-level by leveraging malicious detection and robust training strategies in FL.

Global Malicious Detection: Given that malicious clients with poisoning images can easily overfit discriminating the triggers, resulting in worse generator training performance, we ask clients to upload their loss along with the model parameters of the generator and perform an outlier detection on the server-side. At the beginning of training on the server-side, we assign every client with an initial weight $w_i = \frac{1}{|N|}$. Starting from epoch m as a warmup, we activate the Isolation Forest [16] on clients' losses of generator to red flag suspicious clients. Recall that there are less than half malicious clients in our adversarial model. Thus, the valid detection algorithm should produce a set of potential malicious clients O, where $|O| < \frac{1}{2}|N|$ following literature studying adversaries in FL [8]. We perform malicious detection per global iteration and keep track of the number of 'malicious' red flags assigned to each client C_i over the training process, denoting as c_i.

In each global iteration, the aggregation weight of clients detected as an outlier will decay according to a decay constant d and the total time it has been detected c_i. Namely, if a client is more frequently detected as malicious, it receives a smaller aggregation weight. The detailed algorithm is described in Algorithm 1.

Algorithm 1. Global Malicious Detection

Notations: Clients C indexed by i; local discriminator D_i, and generator G_i, local generator loss l_{G_i}, global generator G_{server}, aggregation weight $w_i \in [0,1]$; times of being detected as malicious i-th client c_i, local updating iteration K; global communication round T, total number of clients N, decay rate d, warmup iteration m.

1: $c_i \leftarrow 0$, $w_i \leftarrow \frac{1}{N}$ ▷ Initializataion
2: For $t = 0 \rightarrow T$, we iteratively run **Procedure A** then **Procedure B**
3: **procedure A.** CLIENTUPDATE(t, i)
4:      $G_i(t, 0) \leftarrow G_{\text{server}}(t)$ ▷ Receive global generator weights update
5:      **for** $k = 0 \rightarrow K - 1$ **do**
6:          $D_i(t, k+1) \leftarrow$ Optimize $l_D(D_i(t,k), G_i(t,k))$ ▷ Update D using Eq. (1)
7:          $G_i(t, k+1) \leftarrow$ Optimize $l_G(D_i(t,k+1), G_i(t,k))$ ▷ Update G using Eq. (1)
8: **procedure B.** SERVEREXECUTION(t):
9:      **for** each client C_i **in parallel do**
10:         $G_i, l_{G_i} \leftarrow$ CLIENTUPDATE(t, i) ▷ Receive local model weights and loss.
11:         **if** $t > m$ **then**   ▷ Start detection after warmup
12:             $O \leftarrow$ ISOLATIONFOREST$(l_{G_1}...l_{G_N})$
13:             **if** $0 < |O| < \frac{1}{2}|N|$ **then**   ▷ Detect valid number of outliers
14:                 **for** each detected client C_i **in** O **do**
15:                     $c_i \leftarrow c_i + 1$ ▷ Increment total count C_i been detected as outlier
16:                     $w_i \leftarrow w_i \times d^{c_i}$ ▷ Decay weights for outliers
17:     $G_{\text{server}}(t+1) \leftarrow \sum_{i \in [N]} \frac{w_i}{\sum_{i \in |N|} w_i} G_i(t)$ ▷ Aggregation on server

---

Local Training Regularization: In order to prevent the malicious discriminator from overfitting on the trigger and ultimately dominating training, we suggest regularizing discriminator training of GAN with proper loss regularization. One practical solutions is to replace the minmax loss (Eq. (1)) of vanilla GAN' [9] with Wasserstein distance to regularize GAN training due to its uniform gradient throughout [1]. To further confine the loss function within 1-Lipschitz, we propose to use WGAN with gradient penalty (WGAN-DP) [10] as the local image generation model.

3   Experiments

In this section, we first apply backdoor to the FedGAN pipeline and show its efficacy on a medical dataset with trigger sizes even less than 0.5% of the true image size. Then, we experiment with the two defensing strategies.

3.1   Experimental Settings

Datasets: We train our federated generative adversarial network on the International Skin Imaging Collaboration (ISIC) dataset [6], which is widely used for medical image analysis for skin cancer. Images are resized to 256×256. We present sample ISIC images in Fig. 2(a).

Generated Adversarial Networks: We apply the generator of StyleGAN2-ADA [14], given its generator produces images with high qualities in the majority of datasets and may have the capability to generate high-resolution medical images for clinical research. For the discriminator, we adopt that of the DCGAN's architecture [21], one of the most widely used GAN frameworks, as our basic network. It is worth noting that our attack strategy has the potential to apply to other state-of-the-art generative models. In the training for attack, we use Adam optimizer with learning rate of 2×10^{-4} for both generator and discriminator. The batch size is set to be 32 as per limit of a 32 GB Tesla V100 GPU.

FL: Considering the total available sample size, we establish FedGAN on four clients where each client is trained on 1000 randomly sampled images from the ISIC dataset. We update the local generator parameters to the global server every local epoch and train the FedGAN with 200 global epochs using FedAvg [18]. The synthetic medical images with vanilla FedGAN (no attack and defense induced) are presented in Fig. 2(b).

Metrics: In order to quantitatively evaluate the synthetic images, we apply the three classic GAN evaluation measures: Inception score (IS), Fréchet Inception Distance (FID), and Kernel Inception Distance (KID). Inception Score (IS) calculates the KL divergence over the generated data [27]. FID calculates the Wassertstein-2 distance over real and generated images [12]. Both IS and FID are limited in small datasets scenarios. Thus, we also include KID, which measures the dissimilarity between real and generated images [3].

3.2 Implementation of Attack

Among four clients in the simulated FedGAN system, one is randomly selected as the malicious client. The three benign clients are trained with normal ISIC images, while the malicious client is trained with poisoned images. We apply the trigger strategy proposed by [25], which has shown to be effective for backdoor attacks in classification tasks. Specifically, we adopt a 16×16 random matrix of colors that has a different pattern from the actual image and is only about 0.39% of the size of the original image. The same trigger is pasted onto the bottom right of all the training images in the malicious client before launching FedGAN training. The examples of poisoned images are shown in Fig. 1, which are fed into the discriminator D of malicious clients.

3.3 Implementation of Defense

In the attack described in Sect. 3.2, the malicious clients train on poisoned data, the discriminator quickly overfits on the trigger and leads the whole FL model suffers from training instability. In order to defend against this attack, we attempt global malicious detection and local training regularization.

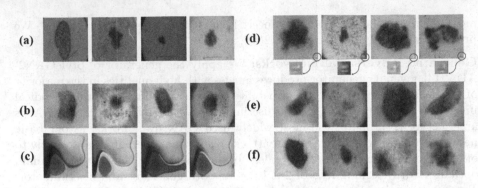

Fig. 2. Visualization on: (a) Original ISIC images; and generated images of (b) Vanilla GAN; (c) Attack on vanilla GAN; (d) Local defence using WGAN-DP; (e) Global defence on vanilla GAN and (f) Full (global + local) defense. Note that backdoor attack is applied to (c–f).

Table 1. Quantitative Comparison for Attack and Defense. ↑ indicates the lager the better and ↓ indicates the smaller the better.

Settings	Vanilla GAN	Attack	Global defence	Local defense*	Full defense*,⋆
IC ↑	2.58	1.48	2.90	2.85	2.88
FID ↓	121.76	393.86	131.72	110.40	102.53
KID $\times 10^3$ ↓	70.22	454.52	78.04	62.09	54.67

* Use WGAN-DP loss for local GAN training.

⋆ Full defense means combining both global and local defense strategies.

As we can see in Fig. 2(d), locally apply WGAN-GP indeed enhances the federated GAN's performance under the same level of attack. The server generator can produce a diversity of quality data that will be valuable for further clinical studies. This also corresponds to the quantitative analysis in Table 1 that the FID improves from 393 to 110 and KID imrpves from 454 to 62. However, the trigger is still discernible in some generated images as shown in Fig. 2(d). We present the attack results with larger trigger sizes (range from 16^2 to 64^2) in Appendix B, which shows more obvious attack patterns. In general, we observe that locally applying WGAN-GP helps alleviate the attack, but it does not fully resolve the adversarial in terms of GAN's fidelity.

Implementation of Global Malicious Detection: Global malicious detection is applied to the global aggregation step on the server-side. To ensure robust detection, recall our global malicious detection method described in Algorithm 1 requires a warmup process to allow enough time to for the malicious clients to overfit the backdoor and behave differently from those benign ones. In our experiments, we set the warmup epoch $m = 10$. After $m > 10$, generators' losses are required to share with the server to perform malicious detection. A decay constant $d = 0.9$ is used to penalize weights for the clients detected as an anomaly in every epoch using Isolation Forests [16]. We accumulatively count the times of being detected as malicious for each client $c_i(t)$ upon global iteration t, at which the calibrated client weights are decayed by timing $d^{c_i}(t)$. Note in the global aggregation, we normalize w_i so that clients' aggregation weights are sum to 1.

Implementation of Local Training Regularization: Local training regularization is applied to each local clients. In this defence setting, we apply the same FL framework and GAN architecture as the attack's part. We only replace the local training process with WAN-GP and replace Batch Normalization with Instance Normalization in order to calculate gradient penalty [10]. At the same time, RMSprop has taken the position of the Adam optimizer to provide superior gradient control in non-stationary scenarios as suggested in [28]. Everything else is controlled to be the same as the Vanilla GAN and WGAN-GP.

3.4 Results and Discussion

Attack: As we can see in Fig. 2(c) that the generated images are fully corrupted in comparison to the original images in Fig. 2(a). In addition, comparing all the three similarity metrics in Table 1, our proposed backdoor attack ('Attack' column) substantially worsen the quality of the generated images. During the training, we observe that the loss of the malicious discriminator quickly approaches zero even at the very beginning of the training, while the losses of those benign clients are fluctuating as normal. With training, the malicious discriminator assigns the generated images a big loss, which we leverage in defense later.

Defense: By combining our proposed global- and local-level defense strategies (denoted as 'full defense' in Fig. 2(f) and Table 1), we achieves superior image generation results. Qualitatively, Fig. 2(f) presents sample synthetic images with high-fidelity and variability. Quantitatively, the FID and KID scores of using 'full defense' are better than training vanilla GAN [9] in FedGAN, as shown in Table 1. The indicated better synthetic data quality even under bookdoor attack is probably facilitate by the more stable loss used.

Ablation Study: Furthermore, we present the synthetic impact of combining both global- and local-level defense strategies via ablation studies. First, we experiment with performing local training regularization defense with WGAN-DP, which is shown in Fig. 2(d). The server generator produces quality images compared to before. However, the shape of the trigger is still visible. Specifically, we can see that the three quantitative metrics of using full defense have improved compared to applying local defense alone, where the KID decreases by 13.57%. Furthermore, the trigger observed in Fig. 2(d) has completely vanished when using full defense. Next, we experiment with applying global malicious client detection on vanilla GAN in FL, shown in Fig. 2(e). It indeed blocks the adversarial behavior. However, quantitatively, its generated images are still worse than what's produced in our full defense setting.

4 Conclusion

Motivated by the idea of backdoor attacks in classification models, we investigate the pitfalls of backdoor attacks in training FedGAN models. We show that by adding triggers to the images fed into local discriminators, the FedGAN model could be fooled. Such an attack is strong enough to corrupt the generated images with trigger size less than 0.5% of the image size. Based on the attack, we establish two potential defense ways with global malicious detection and local training stabilization. The combination of both defense strategies significantly improves the security of FedGAN. As the first step towards understanding backdoor attacks in FedGAN for medical image synthesis, our work brings insight into building a robust and trustworthy model to advance medical research with synthetic data. Our future work includes widely investigating the hyper-parameters, scaling up the FL system with more clients, and testing on various medical datasets.

Acknowledgement. This work is supported in part by the Natural Sciences and Engineering Research Council of Canada (NSERC) and NVIDIA Hardware Award. We thank Chun-Yin Huang and Nan Wang for their kind instruction to Ruinan Jin and assistance with implementation.

A   More Experiment Results

See Fig. 3.

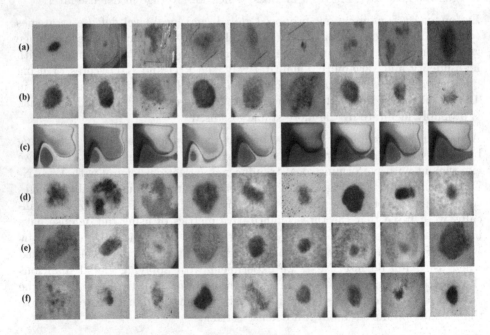

Fig. 3. More Visualization on: (a) Original ISIC images; and generated images of (b) Vanilla GAN; (c) Attack on vanilla GAN; (d) Local defence using WGAN-GP; (e) Global defence on vanilla GAN and (f) Full (global + local) defense. Note that backdoor attack is applied to (c–f).

B   WGAN-GP with Large Trigger Size

See Fig. 4 and Table 2.

Table 2. Quantitative comparison of local and full defense

Settings	16		32		64	
	Local	Full	Local	Full	Local	Full
IC ↑	2.85	2.88	2.67	3.02	2.83	2.93
FID ↓	110.40	102.53	117.07	113.26	114.21	109.85
KID $\times 10^3$ ↓	62.09	54.67	69.68	63.49	63.01	60.53

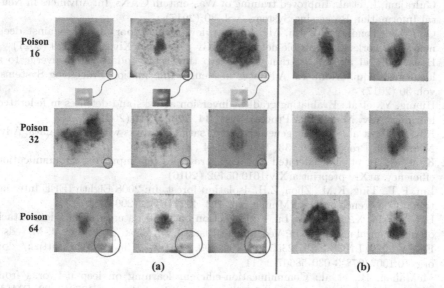

(a)   (b)

Fig. 4. Visualization of WGAN with larger trigger size: (a) Local defense. (b) Full (global + local) defense. The trigger is still visible while only applying local defense.

References

1. Arjovsky, M., Chintala, S., Bottou, L.: Wasserstein generative adversarial networks. In: International Conference on Machine Learning, pp. 214–223. PMLR (2017)
2. Bagdasaryan, E., et al.: How to backdoor federated learning. In: International Conference on Artificial Intelligence and Statistics, pp. 2938–2948. PMLR (2020)
3. Bińkowski, M., et al.: Demystifying mmd gans. arXiv preprint arXiv:1801.01401 (2018)
4. Buczak, A.L., Babin, S., Moniz, L.: Data-driven approach for creating synthetic electronic medical records. BMC Med. Inform. Decis. Mak. **10**(1), 1–28 (2010)

5. Chen, X., et al.: Targeted backdoor attacks on deep learning systems using data poisoning. arXiv preprint arXiv:1712.05526 (2017)
6. Codella, N.C., et al.: Skin lesion analysis toward melanoma detection: a challenge at the 2017 international symposium on biomedical imaging (ISBI), hosted by the international skin imaging collaboration (ISIC). In: 2018 IEEE 15th International Symposium on Biomedical Imaging (ISBI 2018), pp. 168–172. IEEE (2018)
7. Dube, K., Gallagher, T.: Approach and method for generating realistic synthetic electronic healthcare records for secondary use. In: Gibbons, J., MacCaull, W. (eds.) FHIES 2013. LNCS, vol. 8315, pp. 69–86. Springer, Heidelberg (2014). https://doi.org/10.1007/978-3-642-53956-5_6
8. Fang, M., Cao, X., Jia, J., Gong, N.: Local model poisoning attacks to {Byzantine-Robust} federated learning. In: 29th USENIX Security Symposium (USENIX Security 2020), pp. 1605–1622 (2020)
9. Goodfellow, I., et al.: Generative adversarial nets. In: Advances in Neural Information Processing Systems, vol. 27 (2014)
10. Gulrajani, I., et al.: Improved training of Wasserstein GANs. In: Advances in Neural Information Processing Systems, vol. 30 (2017)
11. Guo, W., Tondi, B., Barni, M.: An overview of backdoor attacks against deep neural networks and possible defences. arXiv preprint arXiv:2111.08429 (2021)
12. Heusel, M., et al.: GANs trained by a two time-scale update rule converge to a local nash equilibrium. In: Advances in Neural Information Processing Systems, vol. 30 (2017)
13. Huang, Y., et al.: Evaluating gradient inversion attacks and defenses in federated learning. Adv. Neural. Inf. Process. Syst. **34**, 7232–7241 (2021)
14. Karras, T., et al.: Training generative adversarial networks with limited data. Adv. Neural. Inf. Process. Syst. **33**, 12104–12114 (2020)
15. Konečný, J., et al.: Federated learning: strategies for improving communication efficiency. arXiv preprint arXiv:1610.05492 (2016)
16. Liu, F.T., Ting, K.M., Zhou, Z.H.: Isolation forest. In: 2008 Eighth IEEE International Conference on Data Mining, pp. 413–422. IEEE (2008)
17. Liu, Y., Ma, X., Bailey, J., Lu, F.: Reflection backdoor: a natural backdoor attack on deep neural networks. In: Vedaldi, A., Bischof, H., Brox, T., Frahm, J.-M. (eds.) ECCV 2020. LNCS, vol. 12355, pp. 182–199. Springer, Cham (2020). https://doi.org/10.1007/978-3-030-58607-2_11
18. McMahan, B., et al.: Communication-efficient learning of deep networks from decentralized data. In: Artificial Intelligence and Statistics, pp. 1273–1282. PMLR (2017)
19. Ozdayi, M.S., Kantarcioglu, M., Gel, Y.R.: Defending against backdoors in federated learning with robust learning rate. In: Proceedings of the AAAI Conference on Artificial Intelligence, vol. 35, pp. 9268–9276 (2021)
20. Pillutla, K., Kakade, S.M., Harchaoui, Z.: Robust aggregation for federated learning. arXiv preprint arXiv:1912.13445 (2019)
21. Radford, A., Metz, L., Chintala, S.: Unsupervised representation learning with deep convolutional generative adversarial networks. arXiv preprint arXiv:1511.06434 (2015)
22. Rasouli, M., Sun, T., Rajagopal, R.: FedGAN: federated generative adversarial networks for distributed data. arXiv preprint arXiv:2006.07228 (2020)
23. Rawat, A., Levacher, K., Sinn, M.: The devil is in the GAN: defending deep generative models against backdoor attacks. arXiv preprint arXiv:2108.01644 (2021)
24. Rieke, N., et al.: The future of digital health with federated learning. NPJ Digit. Med. **3**(1), 1–7 (2020)

25. Saha, A., Subramanya, A., Pirsiavash, H.: Hidden trigger backdoor attacks. In: Proceedings of the AAAI Conference on Artificial Intelligence, vol. 34, pp. 11957–11965 (2020)
26. Salem, A., et al.: BAAAN: backdoor attacks against autoencoder and GAN-based machine learning models. arXiv preprint arXiv:2010.03007 (2020)
27. Salimans, T., et al.: Improved techniques for training GANs. In: Advances in Neural Information Processing Systems, vol. 29 (2016)
28. Tieleman, T., Hinton, G.: Lecture 6.5-RMSprop, COURSERA: neural networks for machine learning. University of Toronto, Technical Report 6 (2012)

Author Index

Printed in the United States
by Baker & Taylor Publisher Services